No.	Name	Year	Place
1.	Zajc, Beniamin	1930	Lodz
2.	Blatyda, Abram	1929	Warszawa
3.	Weinszetin, Hanna	1932	Pultusk
4.	Wejsztein, Ufer	1928	"
5.	Wizenfeld, Dawid	1928	Tarnob
6.	Wizenfeld, Jozef	1931	Tarnob
7.	Szwajberg, Pinkus	1931	Jarosla
8.	Szwajberg, Hersz	1940	Lubacz
9.	Szteinberg, Rachela	1933	Tel-Av
10.	Wajsztein, Szmul	1931	Dubien
11.	Gerzewska, Helena	1936	Lodz
12.	Anzibel, Berek	1927	Lezajsk
13.	Bursztyn, Samuel	1928	Tarnobrzeg
14.	Bursztyn, Jakub	1932	Tarnobrzeg
15.	Bursztyn, Leja	1935	Tarnobrzeg
16.	Erlich, Leon	1932	Taratyn
17.	Erlich, Maria	1935	"
18.	Labin, Samuel	1927	Tarnobrzeg
19.	Labin, Manka	1929	Tarnobrzeg
20.	Labin, Zisek	1931	Tarnobrzeg
21.	Labin, Sara	1933	Tarnobrzeg
22.	Lerner, Josef	1929	Huzek
23.	Lerner, Leib	1931	Huzek
24.	Gesundheit, Beniamin	1934	Katowicz
25.	Hering, Juda	1929	Zamona
26.	Hering, Motel	1930	Zamona
27.	Goldman, Abraham	1928	Warszawa
28.	Brylman, Jankiel	1929	Ostrow-Maze Wiscki
29.	Kranz, Kozef	1929	Lerzansk
30.	Kranz, Leja	1930	"
31.	Rubinsztein, Aron	1928	Sokotow
32.	Jaroslawicz, Loner	1929	Lerzansk
33.	Brylman, Szejna	1933	Oztrow-Mazcwiecki
34.	Kornblit, Henryk	1929	Lublin
35.	Lerner, Bejla	1934	Hunsk
36.	Wajsztein, Sara	1933	Pultusk
37.	Orbach, Chaja	1934	Majdan Kolbuszowski
38.	Orbach, Ryuka	1936	"
39.	Ptakiswicz, Bela	1932	Warszawa
40.	Ptakiswicz, Mendel	1933	Warszawa
41.	Bursztyn, Fajga	1930	Tarnobrzeg
42.	Zunsztern, Ryfka	1930	Krzeszow
43.	Zursztern, Rushla	1934	"
44.	Miller, Fiszal	1930	Warszawa
55.	Miller, Jozef	1933	Warszawa
46.	Miller, Izak	1935	Warszawa
47.	Nejblum, Hana	1935	Warszawa
48.	Klein, Klara	1931	Belz
49.	Szarp, Ryszard	1933	Bielsko
50.	Szarp, Malgorzata	1936	Bielsko
51.	Sznejder, Ruta	1935	Warszawa
52.	Kornblit, Mojzesz	1928	Lublin
53.	Sznajder, Moszak	1935	Warszawa
54.	Kawer, Ditla	1938	Soknlow
55.	Lerman, Roza	1928	Belz
56.	Miller, Ita	1928	Warszawa
57.	Margiel, Szlama	1929	Przasmysz
58.	Haber, Igak	1928	Dynow
59.	Gorzewska, Regina	1930	Lodz
60.	Sznajdler, Perla	1928	Warszawa

D0907073

Escape via Siberia

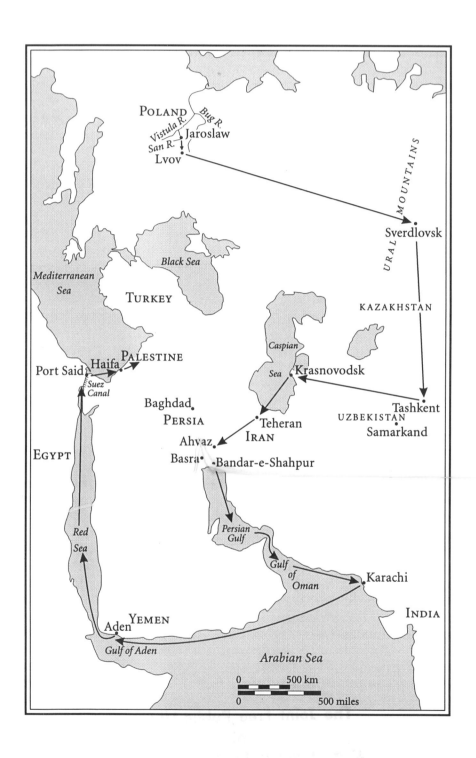

Escape via Siberia

A Jewish Child's Odyssey of Survival

Dorit Bader Whiteman

HM

Holmes & Meier
New York / London

Published in the United States of America 1999 by
Holmes & Meier Publishers, Inc.
160 Broadway   New York, NY 10038

Copyright © 1999 by Holmes & Meier Publishers, Inc.

This book has been printed on acid-free paper.

Library of Congress Cataloging-in-Publication Data

Whiteman, Dorit Bader.
      Escape via Siberia : a Jewish child's odyssey of survival / by Dorit Whiteman.
           p.   cm.
      Includes bibliographical references.
      ISBN 0-8419-1403-6 (alk. paper)
      1. Yaron, Eliott, b. 1929. 2. Jews—Poland—Jarosław Biography. 3. Refugees,
Jewish—Soviet Union Biography. 4. Jews, Polish—Israel Biography. 5. Jews,
Polish—United States Biography. 6. Holocaust, Jewish (1939–1945) 7. Jarosław
(Poland) Biography. 8. Soviet Union Biography.   I. Title.
DS135.P63Y649   1999
943.8'6—dc21
      [B]   99-33705
                                                                             CIP

Manufactured in the United States of America

To My Mother

Whose shared love of history and biography
laid the groundwork for this book

and

To My Husband

Whose extensive knowledge and deep caring
make all my tasks easier.

CONTENTS

FOREWORD

by Yaffa Eliach[1]

We, the Jewish children who survived WWII are now the last link and the remaining eyewitnesses to the greatest tragedy in history—the Holocaust. Our survival was a heartbeat-by-heartbeat existence, on the threshold between life and death. We lived at the mercy of the adults around us, friends and foes, and at the mercy of fate and chance. Our early childhood education was forged in the crucible of the abyss.

Unlike the adult survivors, we were not involved in national, local, and community affairs, nor were we members of political parties. Our values and ideas, like the imagery in which we would later express them, would be shaped in the crucible of war. Having been both insiders and outsiders in the Kingdom of Death, we bring special sensitivity and understanding to the present and the future of the universal family of humankind. Our post-Holocaust education is different from the majority of adult survivors; we continued our education on various levels. We mastered new languages, assimilated ourselves into new cultures and new lands, and many among us devoted their lives to professions that help people. For years adult survivors bypassed us in the major texts of Holocaust and WWII documentation, but now we, the children, are the major link with the past and the center of Holocaust presentations in books, museum exhibits, and on stage and screen.

The "Teheran Children" are a model of child survival in most difficult times due to their fascinating survival wisdom, their dedication to life, their parents and siblings, and their practical understanding of the human spirit, both its shortcomings and grandeur. Outside of Israel, the "Teheran Children" and their stories are rarely known, even among Holocaust experts and survivors. In Israel, in the past and present, they were and are very prominent and active participants in many professions. They are

---

[1] Professor Yaffa Eliach, Brooklyn College, author of *There Once Was A World: A 900-Year Chronicle of the Shtetl of Eishyshek*, a monumental book about Eastern Europe and the universal classic, *Hasidic Tales of the Holocaust*. She is a pioneer scholar in Holocaust Studies and the creator of the *Tower of Life* at the United States Holocaust Memorial Museum in Washington, D.C. The *Tower of Life* has been seen by millions of visitors and is considered by many the most moving exhibit at the Museum.

doctors, lawyers, high commanding officers in the army, business people, farmers, and educators devoted to children.

This book, *Escape via Siberia: A Jewish Child's Odyssey of Survival* by Dorit Bader Whiteman, is a very important contribution to the subject of child survival, and hopefully through it the public will become acquainted with the "Teheran Children." It is the story of Eliott (Lonek), one Teheran Child, as well as history of the "Teheran Children," the story of more than 900 Jewish children from Poland who reached Palestine in February 1943.

Eliott escaped from Poland with his parents in 1939. He and his parents were among three hundred thousand Jews who fled from Poland into the Soviet Union. Eliott and his family, like many others, fled from Siberia to Tashkent. Eliott, with the 1,000 children, all Polish citizens, went from Tashkent to Iran in the summer of 1942. In January 1943, immigration permits were obtained from the Mandatory British authorities. After a six month stay in Teheran, the children sailed to India; by way of the Suez Canal they arrived in Egypt; and from Egypt they traveled by train to Eretz-Israel.

Their ability to leave Russia was part of the agreement signed in 1942 between the Polish Government-In-Exile and the Soviet Government. The Polish Government-In-Exile, with the help of Anders' Army (Polish Army), saved the "Teheran Children" and took them out of the Soviet Union. Thus, they were saved from starvation and epidemics which had killed many of their parents, siblings, and friends.

The children faced another major hurdle in their lives—anti-Semitism. This is a subject which is usually omitted from the Teheran Children's history, yet is accurately presented by Dorit B. Whiteman. The children were torn between two types of Poles: the Poles who saved them from the Soviet Union, and the anti-Semitic Poles who tried to prevent them from boarding the trains, and later on the road attempted to convert them to Catholicism. And, in fact, some children did convert. But the majority of the children, who were consummate survivors, did not succumb to the anti-Semites. A woman who was a Teheran Child comments, "we tolerated it because a little soup and a piece of bread was for us more important" (p. 96).

Upon arriving in Palestine, the children were welcomed with great enthusiasm by the Yishuv, the Jewish community of Eretz-Israel. While staying in Atlit, they were subject to the conflict between the secular and religious groups regarding their residence and education in Eretz-Israel. Henrietta Szold, Hadassah's Palestine leader of Youth Aliyah, who was extremely dedicated to the children, originally planned to place them in non-religious institutions (p. 152). This did not happen. Each child was interviewed about his or her religious observance in the past. As a result of these interviews, significant numbers of children were placed in religious institutions. Eliott was placed in a religious children's village called Kfar Hanoar Hadati.

My husband, Rabbi Dr. David Eliach, at the time a young man who planned to be a lawyer, was asked by Bessie Gotsfeld, founder of the American Mizrachi Women (today Amit), to assist in the religious education of the "Teheran Children." he responded instantly. First he was their counselor and soon became their director at Meshek Yeladim Motzah. It took him and his colleagues months to convince the children not to hide food under their mattresses, not to sleep in their clothes, and not to hold on physically to their younger siblings.

The children lived in constant fear that they would again be taken away and forced out on the road to survive under difficult conditions. Only after months of love, devotion, and great educational commitment, did they begin to trust the people around them and begin to experience a more normal childhood. They slowly began to share their painful experiences. Some of the children described how they had to bury a mother or father who died on the road, placing the body in deep snow and covering the top with branches, crossing frozen rivers, or having to eat dung in the desert to stop their hunger.

David Eliach was greatly impressed with the power of education, its impact on the lives of the "Teheran Children," and how it seemed to transform many of them into normal, happy children. He decided to remain in education and eventually became a world-renowned Jewish educator.

The "Teheran Children" were also a part of my life. We lived together and attended the same elementary and high schools. We shared our prewar memories, our war experiences, our normal lives, and our hope that no other children will ever suffer the way we did.

The story of the "Teheran Children" is a part of the larger puzzle of the fate of Jewish children during WWII. The story will help readers to understand us—the children that stood on the threshold between life and death and had the ability to cross the threshold to life. The source of this strength is partly our own inner ability to survive, and partly the excellent education we received.

We, the Jewish children who survived WWII, are the last link between the Holocaust and the future. Thus we are responsible to educate the next generation of children about peace, love, survival, and humanity.

I hope that this book, *Escape via Siberia: A Jewish Child's Odyssey of Survival*, will contribute to a better future for children and the universal family of humankind.

ACKNOWLEDGMENTS

Writing *Escape via Siberia* took over three years, and along the way many people lent support. Before I even put pen to paper or hands to word processor I met with Miriam Holmes of Holmes & Meier Publishers, Inc. Miriam echoed my feeling of the importance of the story of Eliott—or Lonek—the little Jewish boy whose life mirrored that of hundreds of Jewish children, who were referred to as the Teheran Children. These youngsters fled from Poland to Russia and reached Palestine by a most arduous and circuitous route. I am grateful to Miriam for having faith in my ability to do justice to such an important story.

Fleshing out Eliott's story and describing the times and circumstances of the Teheran Children required much research. Among those who provided important support was Naomi Niv, an Israeli researcher recommended by the Central Zionist Archives for her broad knowledge of Jewish and Israeli history. Scouring Israeli facilities, including libraries and the archives of organizations that had helped rescue the Teheran Children, she unearthed and translated into English vital documents, cablegrams, and personal letters, and she checked appropriate parts of my manuscript for factual accuracy. These materials helped validate Eliott's story, and contributed details and descriptions essential for making its historical context more vivid.

I contacted Professor Jan T. Gross after reading his excellent book *Revolution from Abroad: The Soviet Conquest of Poland's Western Ukraine and Western Belorussia,* which described the brutal part played by Russia after its 1939 invasion of Poland. Jan read the parts of the book that deal with Russia and reviewed them for accuracy. I am most indebted to him for his interest and useful suggestions.

I am also grateful to E. Thomas Wood for his friendly response to my telephone call. He provided a list of the children who arrived in Teheran from Russia in January 1943 from the American Jewish Archives in Cincinnati, Ohio. He guided me to documents in the archives of the Hoover Institution on War, Revolution, and Peace, which contain the oral histories of Polish children who escaped from Russia in the early 1940s. In addition, his revealing book titled *Karski: How One Man Tried to Stop the Holocaust,* written with Stanislaw M. Jankowski, provided a graphic picture of Poland just after the 1939 German invasion. His gracious help is deeply appreciated.

I owe a debt of gratitude to Susan Woodland, Archive Manager of Hadassah, the Women's Zionist Organization of America. Her exhaustive search of the Tourover Collection enabled me to access correspondence dating back to 1941. Among these exchanges were memos between Hadassah leaders, correspondence with English and American government officials, and letters addressed to other persons in high places who could potentially help the Teheran Children. These documents highlight the dramatic and desperate circumstances of the Jewish children in flight.

Additional information was supplied to me from a number of other sources. Michelle Ment of the Association of Teheran Children and their Instructors kindly contributed helpful background information. William Connelly, Technical Information Specialist, of the U.S. Holocaust Memorial Museum Library, provided me with excellent maps of Poland illustrating the political changes since 1939. Alfred Lipson, senior researcher of the Queensborough College Holocaust Library, willingly interrupted his own research to aid me in my search for relevant material. Dorot Yarot and Chaim Jaroslawitz, wife and brother of Eliott, whose story is told in *Escape via Siberia* were kind enough to supply me with some specific items of information. Harriet Bleshman put me in touch with Adrian Kulpa, who ably translated Polish oral histories for me.

Valerie Ben Or of the Yad Vashem Films and Photo Department and Reuven Koffler of the Photo Collection Department of the Central Zionist Archives in Jerusalem located some very moving photographs of the Teheran Children, which lent an immediacy to the children's journey, that it might not otherwise have had.

I am most appreciative of the help of Iwona Drag-Korga of the Pilsudski Institute. She responded with great speed to my requests, searched her files, and supplied me with difficult-to-find and valuable pictures of General Anders and his army.

Early drafts of *Escape via Siberia* were read by the Drs. Marian Anderson, Rhoda Kornrich, and Milton Kornrich, whose encouragement at the beginning stages of writing helped fortify my determination to persist. Dr. Dennis B. Klein also reviewed my manuscript and offered many helpful suggestions.

Ms. Blanche Glaser volunteered for the very painstaking and tedious task of transcribing taped interviews. To ensure that each word was recorded correctly, she patiently played passages over and over again. She also deciphered handwriting on old documents; her persistence left few puzzling scribbles unsolved. She gave most helpful assistance in selecting and organizing the photographs and affixing the appropriate captions. Her cheerful presence and intense interest in the work made her a most valuable and welcome companion.

I could not have finished the manuscript on time except for the help of Maryann Cilia, my secretary, who wrestled with the innumerable bureaucratic and insurance forms encountered in a psychologist's practice, and of my housekeeper, Inez Mangar, who divested me of many domestic chores and tackled daily household questions intrepidly on her own.

The two people most involved in my work were my husband, Martin, and my daughter Lily. Martin participated in every phase of the writing of *Escape via Siberia* from the conception of the idea to the dotting of the last *i*. He discussed ideas with me, which influenced the direction of the book; he scoured libraries for relevant sources; and he made editorial suggestions once the writing was done. Of equal importance was the gracious way in which he uncomplainingly accepted the inconveniences encountered by my having to dedicate most of my time, aside from my regular professional work, to laboring on the manuscript, thus forgoing much of our recreational life.

A writer in her own right, Lily, in spite of being encumbered by time constraints, contributed a most thorough editing job. Going over my writing with a fine-tooth comb, she made innumerable suggestions regarding the conception of the book, as well as its organization, style, and choice of wording. And when she had finished a careful review, she began again, and edited the manuscript a second time just as carefully.

When writing, it is not only editorial comments and practical advice that are helpful. Encouragement and emotional support are essential and were given to me in generous portions by my husband and my daughters Nadine and Lily.

My deepest appreciation goes to Eliott Yaron whose life experiences inspired this book. I learned a great deal by listening to him, and I highly value the friendship we formed.

THIS BOOK: HOW AND WHY

The phone call that inspired this book came about a year after I had finished writing *The Uprooted—A Hitler Legacy: Voices of Those Who Escaped before the "Final Solution."*[1] The following months had been consumed by work related to its publication and with the book's translation into German. During those months, I had been contacted by a number of people who suggested that their escape from a Nazi-occupied country and the subsequent rebuilding of their lives might provide the basis for another book. The stories of the callers were indeed compelling. There is hardly a life story of a Jewish survivor that does not contribute in some measure to the total picture of Jewish survival in the face of Nazi persecution. But I was reluctant to accept these offers because I had just spent over five years on *The Uprooted*. I was now looking forward to devoting more time to my regular work as a psychologist and to my husband.

Then one day I received a telephone call that threw me off my mark. A woman named Dorot called to tell me that her husband, Eliott, had an extraordinary story to tell. Again I explained that for the time being I did not want to become involved in any long-term commitments. "But," she entreated, "he was in Siberia and went on a *Kindertransport* from Russia to Israel." Having just researched *Kindertransports*, I commented that to my knowledge all *Kindertransports* had emanated from various Central European countries. "No," she countered with conviction," my husband's *Kindertransport* was organized in Tashkent, Russia, supported by the British, covered six countries, and took almost a year to arrive at its destination, Israel." I was intrigued by her remarks and went to a Holocaust library to find out about this astonishing transport. I was able to locate only a very brief paragraph in an encyclopedia and another in a reference book. So, I discovered, there had been such a transport. But it had apparently barely been researched in the United States.

A few days later, I drove through snowbanks and icy streets to Dorot and Eliott's house, a two-story home in a comfortable Jewish neighborhood in New York City. Eliott received me, well prepared with documents, photographs, and maps, and related an extraordinary odyssey. It was a story of a ceaseless struggle for survival—first to evade annihilation by the Nazis and then to avoid permanent disappearance in the depths of Russia from which the enslaved rarely returned. It told of a voyage of thousands of miles through many lands which, at that time, had seemed distant as the moon and which covered three continents. It was a journey undertaken by horse carts, railroads, trucks, and ships threatened by floating mines. It included the search for shelter and food, and the constant threat of death.

It was a gripping story, the kind of cliff-hanging, suspenseful drama that is more the subject of fiction than of real life, where an innocent victim is pursued by overpowering, sometimes nameless forces, into an endless void.

Such excruciating circumstances alone might have made Eliott's saga worth telling, although the years between 1935-45 produced myriad tales of torment and calamity. But Eliott's chronicle offered another dimension of great import. His ordeal was typical of those encountered by the thousands of Jews who, with the SS at their heels, managed to flee the German-occupied part of Poland and make their way into Russian-occupied Poland.

This group of Polish Jews was relatively small when compared both to the total number of Jews living in Poland and to the number of Jews who escaped from Germany, Austria, and Czechoslovakia. Why did relatively few Jews from German-occupied Poland survive? The German Jews—though faced with enormous obstacles—could from 1933 to 1939 search for ways to escape the Nazis; the Austrian Jews had approximately one year; the Czech Jews had less than that. By contrast, the Polish Jews had almost no time to flee. After all, the German invasion of Poland in September 1939 marked the start of World War II. Almost immediately, most borders throughout Europe were hermetically sealed. Therefore, most Jews trapped in Poland succumbed to the German troops who marked their invasion by shooting and burning men, women, and children, destroying enclaves, villages, and towns, and rounding up the Jewish population for extermination.

Fortunately, much effort has been made to record the dreadful fate of the Polish Jews who were murdered by the Germans. Less well known is the fate of those Polish Jews who fled to the Russian-occupied part of Poland. Once there, they did not find a refuge. On the contrary, they faced excruciating obstacles and unspeakable disasters. The ill-starred refugees were confronted by a regime steeped in bloodthirstiness, xenophobia, brutality, and anti-Semitism, which had all laid the groundwork for the enslavement of the hapless Jews. When all seemed lost, however, fortune did take an unexpected turn and allowed a number of them to escape.

As a representative of a group of escapees whose experiences had been largely overlooked, Eliott related his saga. I was immediately struck by its urgency. As Elie Wiesel wrote in a note to me: "Those who escaped are also witnesses; their voices, too, must be heard." I wanted to help make the voices of these escapees heard more broadly and more clearly.

But Eliott's story is highly significant for possibly an even more profound reason: Eliott represents the average man, perhaps the "Everyman," who is tossed about by the clashing of colossal powers. A victim of historical forces, he is rendered assailable and defenseless. But no matter how vulnerable, within the very limited opportunities offered him, he discovers ways to fight back valiantly and does so against overpowering odds. The ways in which Eliott struggles may be limited, perhaps even imperceptible to an outsider. But within the consciousness of the victim the effort is gargantuan—that of David against a cruel, unfeeling, despotic Goliath.

It must be remembered that those who were fortunate enough to prevail never knew during their struggles that fate would ultimately offer them a reprieve. No one said to them: "You will suffer for six years, and then you will be freed." No, they could not anticipate that the hunt to annihilate them would ever cease. When the Polish Jews commenced their battle for survival in 1939 by escaping to Russian-occupied Poland, they did not know that Hitler would be defeated in 1945. And when they were banished to the icy forests of Siberia, they could not anticipate that Stalin would ever release them from his monstrous grasp. And yet they labored on from day to day with blind, heroic hope.

To understand the enormity of these endeavors one must place them in their historical and political context. As a result, although I am not a historian, I have chronicled the world-shaking events that almost completely controlled Eliott's fate and those of the other escaping Polish Jews. It is within the framework of these occurrences that the individual struggles must be viewed and evaluated.

Once I made the story of the escaping Polish Jews my next project, I quickly realized that I had found the right person to convey the story to me. Eliott had an uncanny memory for events, people, and places, but initially I feared he might be mistaken about places or dates. When I then compared them with other people's reports and historians' descriptions, invariably I found Eliott's facts to be correct. In addition, Thomas Wood, author of *Karski: How One Man Tried to Stop the Holocaust*, directed me to the American Jewish Archives for a list of children who arrived in Teheran on July 31, 1944. As Eliott had said, his name was on the list. Eliott's saga was still intensely alive for him. Our meetings provided Eliott with the opportunity to tell his tale and to convey to me in his distinctive Polish accent both his experiences and his philosophy of life.

I interviewed Eliott at my house over many hours spread over several weeks. He always arrived punctually, carefully turned out in matching shirt and slacks and various natty sport jackets. He carried a leather briefcase, which, when unlocked by a combination number, yielded relevant supporting information. Yet, Eliott's outwardly pleasant and even jocular demeanor only partially disguised his deep preoccupation with his past and a passionate desire to have it recorded. There were moments when Eliott's bearing was reminiscent of Samuel Taylor Coleridge's ancient mariner who proclaimed his need to retell the past:

> *Since then, at an uncertain hour,*
> *That agony returns:*
> *And till my ghastly tale is told,*
> *This heart within me burns.*

I found my sessions with Eliott informative and at times spellbinding. The sessions had a kind of Scheherezade quality. I could barely wait for the next session to hear more about the many astonishing and unpredictable events of Eliott's life. Eliott did not necessarily tell the events in sequence. He would reminisce about one event, which would bring recollections about other events. It became my task to put Eliott's recollections in their proper sequence and context. The occurrences were fascinating and some anecdotes very amusing. While Eliott conveyed events with a dramatic flair, his grammar was frequently idiosyncratic. The speed of Eliott's speech and the emotional pressure that he felt recounting his life sometimes interfered with clear expression. In order to allow his personality to come through, I altered the syntax only when his grammar distorted his intentions. My occasional corrections included replacing the pronoun *he* with a *she* when he mistakenly confused genders, or omitting words and phrases that he repeated excessively. I also dropped parts of sentences that might confuse the reader. However, I believe that I have not altered his meaning.

One of the most striking aspects of interviewing Eliott was the emotional intensity with which he related events. He seemed to be reliving his childhood, his youth, and young adulthood. His voice reflected it all. Recalling a happy event would make him break into smiles and his voice would sound jubilant. Sad or frightening moments could bring tears to his eyes or prompt him to say "Terrible, terrible" so dramatically that it was impossible not to share his distress and misery. As a result, I found our interviews particularly affecting and I have tried to record his emotions accurately.

I agreed to write about Eliott's harrowing years as a refugee, prisoner, and survivor because his story is not only mesmerizing but significant. The events themselves are dramatic, memorable, and extremely moving. They disclose the emotional and physical strength necessary for survival under the most harrowing of circumstances and the long-term emotional consequences of such vicissitudes.

Before meeting Eliott I had never heard of the Teheran Children. I am grateful to him for teaching me more about this historical period. The record of Eliott's experiences adds another stone to the mosaic of Jewish history.

CHAPTER I

The Whip Descends

Until the Nazi storm trooper's whip descended on his father's head, Lonek's life had consisted of an odd combination of security and threats. With the snapping of the SS man's leather lash on a sunny day in September 1939, anxiety and apprehension irrevocably gave way to fear and terror, and slowly, the loving protectiveness of his parents melted away, leaving him abandoned and destitute.

In his hometown of Jaroslaw, Poland, ten-year-old Eliezer Jaroslawicz, affectionately called Lonek, had always experienced a life full of contrasts. On the one hand, he was enveloped by a sense of security which radiated from his devoted parents and the well-established, financially comfortable, and well-run home they provided. On the other hand, life outside the intimate family setting for a Jewish boy like Lonek was less reassuring. At a fairly early age, he became aware of a sense of animosity, the basis of which he later recognized as anti-Semitism.

Lonek and his family lived in a handsome house enhanced by a balcony. The spacious and well-furnished quarters were ample enough to contain a living room, a dining room, a separate bedroom for Lonek, and even a spare room for the country girl Sosa, who watched Lonek and his little brother Chaim, affectionately known as Heimek. Sosa picked up Lonek from school, and helped his mother cook and clean. Lonek's sense of security was further bolstered by observing his father almost daily in his position as a well-to-do owner of a broom and brush factory located on the ground floor of the family home, where he employed five men—three Jewish and two Catholic. His factory was so well respected for producing high-level merchandise that even the Polish army patronized his store. Lonek's father also set aside time to train and employ some blind people who needed additional training and supervision to work.

Lonek (or was it Eliott?) seated across from me in my study, spoke of his father with an almost tangible sense of pride. In our interviews, when I was taping Eliott, there seemed to be three people in the room: Eliott, Lonek, and myself. Actually, Eliott and Lonek are one and the same person. In his youth he was called Lonek. When he arrived in New York after the war, he assumed the name Eliott. But at this point, it seemed as if Lonek and Eliott were two different people. Eliott, American in mode of dress and manner-isms—though not quite in language—was sitting across from me recollect-ing his youth with intensity, laughter, and tears. Yet also present was Lonek, the struggling little Polish boy. As a result, I was dealing with two people: Eliott, the man who reminisced, and Lonek, whose story we were reliving.

With great pride, Eliott recalled: "My father was a very clever man. He spoke Polish, Yiddish, Russian, and Ukrainian. Many times people used to come to our house just to hear stories from him; just to get advice on many, many things, like how to get papers they need from the government. He used to write letters for them. He was all the time standing in court giving advice without a degree in law."

The immediate neighborhood was a friendly place. Lonek delighted in the big playground located right outside the factory. Whenever his father could spare time, he relished watching Lonek play soccer. Lonek always felt safe in these surroundings. A warm and affectionate feeling connected the Jewish neighbors who were comfortably situated in agreeable apart-ments. Eliott recalls that there "were about four or five families—Jewish families. I remember this because in the holy days we used to decorate a long table and eat together. So I remember they were Jewish families." However, in contrast to the large majority of the Jewish population, Lonek's family was not Orthodox, although they kept kosher, lit candles on Friday nights, occasionally went to temple, and celebrated the High Holy days. They did not wear traditional garb, did not attend synagogue regularly, or adhere to strict religious laws.

Memories of the closeness of Lonek's family remain strong. His pater-nal grandfather, the owner of a liquor store, was considered a man of means. He was always neatly turned out and sported a white beard. The little boy tended not so much to look at his grandfather's face but to gaze with fasci-nation at his boots, always shined to perfection. Planting himself in front of them, Lonek enjoyed studying his own face in their polished surface. Lonek's mother was a strong, determined woman who sometimes remi-nisced about the hard times of her own youth. Her father had been a He-brew teacher and money was very scarce. When her own mother had died young, Lonek's mother had to leave school at a very early age. "Her father did not let her go to school, so that she could take care of the other sisters and brothers. But whenever she had time during the day, she would run to school for an hour or two. The principal and teachers made her an example saying to the other children: 'You don't want to learn but look at this girl whose father won't let her go to school and she comes in the middle of the day just to learn a few words.' I remember she always used to tell us this." Lonek enjoyed family stories, particularly the one about his brother Heimek, who was born in 1938 when Lonek was nine years old. The doctor had come to deliver the baby: "My father picked up the baby with one hand and me with the other and he said: 'You have a baby brother. If you don't like him, we will sell him.'" Lonek, displaying the practical bent of his mind that lasted a lifetime, replied: "If he is here, then let him stay." Eliott was still amused at this family reminiscence.

Lonek's hometown of Jaroslaw, located in southeast Poland near the San River, was a medium–size town, appealing in appearance. Its Middle European–type houses, arcaded buildings, a park that boasted peacocks, wide squares, and even a theater suggested some sophistication. One of the more impressive buildings contained a large arcade divided into a number of stores: One of these belonged to Lonek's parents and was managed by his mother, where goods produced in the brush factory were sold. The large, fenced piazza in front of the stately city hall provided enough space for the Gypsies to gather during their seasonal visits in their covered wagons loaded with goods and children. The Gypsies earned a living by trading horses, selling chickens, mending pots, and—justified or not—they had a reputation for stealing and trading pilfered goods. Although not esteemed by the local population, they were neither much noticed nor harmed and were treated with indifference.

The town's attitude toward the Jews had historically been less benign than that toward the Gypsies. During the hundreds of years that Jews had lived in Jaroslaw, they had endured sporadic antagonism and dangerous hostility. Large numbers of Jews first arrived in the city during the sixteenth and seventeenth centuries. The settlement of the Jews in Jaroslaw was intimately connected with the vital role they played in the city's commerce. Since the sixteenth century, Jaroslaw had been an important market center offering three impressive yearly fairs. Jewish merchants, many of them dealers in oxen, attended in large numbers, thereby laying the groundwork for a Jewish community. During market times, temporary quarters were set aside to provide space for a synagogue. A Torah was supplied by neighboring congregations, thus providing opportunity for services, prayers, and learned studies. To adjudicate conflicts during the fairs, Jewish judges were appointed as counterparts to Christian judges. Jewish leaders also organized a Jewish police force to guard Jewish traders. By the middle of the seventeenth century, a Jewish settlement was established, the first synagogue erected, to be followed by a Jewish cemetery. The Jewish population increased steadily from 100 families in 1738 to 6,577 in 1921.

The welcome extended to Jews wishing to settle permanently in Jaroslaw varied. Although the relationship between Jews and Christians was peaceful on the surface, an undercurrent of hostility swirled beneath. This simmering hostility originally exploded in 1737 with the accusation of a "blood libel"—the accusation that Jews killed Gentile children to drink their blood during Passover. The aftermath prompted the suicide of one of the tortured accused and the execution of others.[1]

As Lonek's awareness of the world beyond his own backyard increased, his sense of belonging was steadily eroded by a sense of unease. He began to notice the overt and covert anti-Semitism. For one, even though Poles were employed in Jewish factories, there was no social contact between the two groups. It was as if the Jews had been planted into hostile soil and were surrounded by invisible fences. Perhaps the fences were not quite so invisible. Even as a young child, well before Hitler's invasion of Poland, Lonek had witnessed demonstrations against Jews in the big square in front of the city hall. "I remember they [the Polish demonstrators] used to give out pamphlets and paper flyers. They read: 'We want Poland without Jews. You are different from us.' All different kinds of slogans—very anti-Semitic. Also they would sing: 'Death to the Jewish people.'"

Lonek's sense of isolation increased once he attended public school. Most Jewish children went to parochial schools. Because of his parents' secular outlook, Lonek not only attended public school but he was the only one of the few Jewish children who also went to classes on Saturdays. The only allowance made for the Sabbath was that he abstained from writing on that day; he caught up with missed work on Sundays.

There were only a handful of Jewish children attending public schools and everyone knew who they were. Eliott explained, his voice rising with resentment.

"Every morning we used to pray together with the Gentiles. We were standing in line and we were to pray to God. The Jewish children didn't, but were just standing there and didn't move. The other children used to make the cross. So they knew who was Jewish and who wasn't. All the time they called us names, like "bloody Jews." I remember the many times they catch me and put me in a corner and beat me up for no reason, just because I was Jewish. There is not a day that I didn't get beat up. Or maybe every couple of days. The Jewish children always got good grades. When we would get report cards, I would hide mine. They were running after me and the other Jewish children. They was so bitter that if we got the good grades, they would tear it [the report card] in pieces—two, three pieces and beat me up and say: 'We don't want you here.'"

The teachers did not attempt to shield the Jewish children. On the contrary, they openly displayed their contempt. Eliott describes this scene: "Many times—excuse the expression, I used to pee in my pants. They [the teachers] didn't let me out of the classroom. They knew I want to go, but they didn't care—like we didn't exist." Resulting "accidents" brought shame and humiliation. Neither could the Jewish children protect themselves by banding together. With most Jewish children attending parochial schools, too few of them attended public school for them to create an effective united front. Yet by a twist of fate, having attended public school would turn out to be a lifesaver for Lonek, because the perfect Polish he learned enabled him to pass as a Gentile.

Lonek's sense of apprehension during his school years was reinforced by his parents' whispered conversations. He overheard his parents remark that they really ought to leave Poland. No matter what would happen in Germany—and this was said before the German invasion of Poland—they feared matters might not come to a good end: "It is not our land," they said, referring to Poland. "We should not be here because there is no future for us. No matter if the Poles win or the Germans win, whatever will be, we will be the victims."

Yet life maintained its usual course much as it always had, and news of the outside world barely penetrated. Lonek was unaware of the invasion of Czechoslovakia by the Germans and, in any case, would not have under-stood its meaning or impact. He did realize without too much apprehension that his father was called up to the army and, after participating in maneuvers, had been commissioned as an officer. Before leaving for the front, his father had kissed Lonek good-bye and told him to take good care of his mother and brother. With childlike confidence, Lonek had not particularly worried about his father. He simply assumed that he was to stay with his mother, enjoying the fact that all schools had been closed.

On August 23, 1939, a secret mobilization order was promulgated throughout Poland, calling men to arms because of Germany's threatening posture. Yet the Polish government felt quite confident. Some officials maintained that, in view of the Allies' commitment to Poland, the Germans would never risk an attack: they were merely bluffing. Even if they were not, the Poles felt secure about their military prowess. Poland, they felt, had a strong army with an international reputation. For over six years, Poland had invested 50 percent of its budget in the military, and the reputation of its horse artillery was firmly established.[2]

The complacency of this period was described by Jan Karski, an officer reservist in the Fifth Horse Artillery Battery (who later in the war unsuccessfully attempted to bring the news of the destruction of the Jews to the West). After his call-up on August 23, 1939, he leisurely ministered to the horses and galloped around the countryside without much foreboding. But at dawn on September 1, the army's self-confidence was literally blown to bits. The Blitzkrieg had begun. For what seemed like an endless time, the countryside was saturated with bombs. Such wreckage and ruination had neither been anticipated nor witnessed before. The soldiers and their horses were totally unprepared. The latter bolted from their stables into the countryside, abandoning not only potential riders, but also the artillery they were supposed to pull into position. The artillery was not of much use anyway, because it was not sufficiently powerful to pierce German armor. The soldiers were at a loss—orders from the command centers had ceased. Some Polish soldiers tried to return to their homes, others sought to escape to Hungary or Romania, and still others searched for functioning army units to continue battling the Germans. They wandered the countryside from town to town attempting to regroup, each time finding that the Germans had gotten there first, leaving total destruction. In addition, roving *Volksdeutsche* [Germans living in Poland] took the opportunity to shoot at the distraught, disorganized, roaming soldiers, while trains filled with troops were sitting ducks for strafing German planes. Karski recalled offering his Leica camera to a farmer in exchange for food, but being rebuffed with contempt when endeavoring to barter his valuable honorary sword. The farmer knew better than the officer that future invading armies would not value a Polish status symbol. Indeed, it might mark its owner for destruction.[3]

The Polish civilian population was also savaged. Vicious bombardments set homes with their trapped occupants aflame and strafing pilots followed those who tried to escape by foot, cart, or train. The smell of burned animals caught in their barns filled the air. People trampled each other to get on board any moving vehicle and dropped into ditches while the planes, releasing their merciless cargo, dipped low enough for the pilot to come, clearly into the view of the petrified refugees. In the hasty flight among throngs of fleeing citizens, husbands became separated from wives, and lost children disconsolately searched for parents. Wherever the Germans entered, shooting and mayhem followed, and stacks of bodies were left behind. Jewish bodies were piled high among them.[4]

Lonek knew nothing of the earthshaking upheavals taking place in most of Poland. He sensed that something might be amiss because schools had been closed ever since his father went away. The first full realization came to Lonek's hometown in the form of German paratroopers: "The Germans sent spies. They sent people from the sky. They were jumping and we saw them running and the police running after them [to find out what was happening]. This was the way we found out [that the Poles had lost the war]. Soon afterward I saw almost a hundred soldiers near our house in the square. There is a big soccer place and here came the Germans. They came with their motorcycles and trucks and bayonets. They put up their rifles, standing up three of them together, like triangles with bayonets on top. They used to take off their shirts and get washed up [outdoors], though it was September and the weather was getting cold. And then they used to eat and drink beer." This display of masculinity had its desired effect on the observers. Although the Polish population was apprehensive but did not quite know what to make of the Germans' intent, alarm and dismay spread quickly among the Jewish population. By now they had heard about what was happening in Germany. This consternation became palpable to Lonek. "My mother told me not to go near them [the soldiers], not to talk to them, not to say nothing to them. She warned me to stay at home. 'If you can't stay home, tell me where you go and I will pick you up. But don't go alone.'" The atmosphere had become ominous.

About two weeks after Lonek's father had left, he returned home exactly at noon. Lonek was thrilled to see him still looking dapper in his uniform and army cap. His father bent down to pick him up and planted a big kiss on him. The family greeted him joyously, but Lonek's father's homecoming did not lead to a lengthy celebration. Even though his father's departure for war had been very worrisome to his mother, the new dangers facing the family were infinitely more threatening.

Lonek had no understanding of the potential consequences of the Germans' quick defeat of the Poles, which had taken only two short weeks, but he was aware of the air of dread and foreboding that now surrounded him. He had noticed signs on buildings all over town requiring all returning soldiers to register. His parents were huddled in anxious conversations, trying to decide what action to take. His father had heard that anyone failing to register would be shot on sight. "So my father didn't know [what to do]. My mother told him: 'Go away! Change your clothes and go away!' But he was afraid that someone would recognize him and they would shoot him to death right away. So he said to my mother he had nothing to worry about. He didn't know that the war would be so cruel and they will shoot and gas chamber us—to get rid of the Jewish population." Lonek's father, usually so resolute, hesitated and after some reflection, decided to report to the German authorities. After all, he had nothing to hide; he could only be accused of having fought for his country. He would be reporting as a Polish officer, not as a Jew.

His father took Lonek by the hand, and together they walked about a mile or two to the German registration office. As long as he was with his father, Lonek was not particularly frightened. He did not fully grasp the threat hanging over both of them. The two, father and son, stood in line, aware of the armed German soldiers in and outside the office. A high-ranking German officer stood behind a German soldier who was seated behind a long table and who was in charge of questioning the Polish soldiers. Lonek's father stood at attention before him and gave the required information: name, rank, and serial number.

It was at that moment that the leather lash came whipping across his father's head. It was wielded by the officer standing behind the seated soldier. The officer roared: "You take off your hat when you speak to a German!" With this stroke of the whip, Lonek felt terror for the first time.

With the move of the Germans into Poland, enormous political and military events, which would affect countries and continents, were set into motion. Lonek's carefree childhood, ended by world events, would give way to fear, terror, loneliness, hunger, and want.

CHAPTER II

The Cart Rolls East

Lonek's father did not move when he was struck by the German officer. His hat fell to the ground, but his facial expression remained frozen. He knew better than to protest. On one level, Lonek grasped what he was observing. He knew that the gun-toting soldiers in front of him did not value life at all and could, without hesitation, shoot his father. Intimidated, Lonek did not utter a sound, though tears filled his eyes. On another level, Lonek understood nothing. The shocking events had no reality but were merely surreal pictures passing before his eyes, as if he were somehow caught in a nightmare. A sharp shove administered to his father by a German soldier brought Lonek back to reality. The boy was overwhelmed by his father's plight. Compassion for him drowned out all other sensations. "I was thinking that it was very cruel what they were doing to my father because he didn't have any defense. There were about ten to fifteen soldiers there. They had rifles and they could shoot him if he answered. Life was like a fly. So he was very smart to hold himself in, not to answer much, and to take it like nothing happened." In a daze and crying to himself, he saw his father, the factory owner, the respected family man now totally helpless, sandwiched between two German rifle-toting soldiers, being marched to a large fenced-in area located near the local railroad station. It was a huge empty lot, where the local boys had played soccer and other games and where the visiting circus had put up its tents. He followed his father at a distance but was not permitted inside the enclosed area. He guessed that about a hundred or so Polish soldiers were already confined. Once inside, his father called to him to run home and tell his mother what happened.

When Lonek brought the news, his mother quickly wrapped his baby brother Heimek in a blanket, and all three hurried to the fence. What they saw was not reassuring. German soldiers stood guard inside and outside the enclosed area. Lonek's father had situated himself at an end of the fence, slightly removed from the soldiers congregating at the other end. There the family huddled on both sides of the fence—mother, baby, and Lonek on one side and father on the other. Eliott described the moment: "I was crying, my father was crying, my mother was crying. We were all crying, crying. But it would help nothing. My father told us to go back to the house because it was getting late. So we stayed a few hours, we got tired and were cried out, and we left."

The little family, now without a father, sadly walked home. Heimek, the baby brother, was too young to understand, but Lonek was pervaded by acute fear. He was old enough to realize that his father was in dreadful danger. The German soldiers with guns spoke a language even a child could understand. His mother tried to reassure him, and possibly even herself, that the Germans were only rounding up the Polish soldiers to get their identification numbers. She explained that the German soldiers were just holding them temporarily, and father would be back soon.

But father would not be back soon. In fact, he would never return to his hometown. By morning, all the Polish soldiers had vanished. The family had no idea what had happened to them, and as each day passed, they grew more apprehensive. What they did not know, and only learned much later, was that all the prisoners, officers and noncommissioned soldiers alike, had been marched about two hundred feet from the former soccer field, so conveniently located near the railroad station. There they were loaded onto cattle cars, each of which contained two small windows on either side of a door that bolted from the outside. As the men were herded and shoved into the cattle cars, Lonek's father was fortuitously pushed in front of one of the barred windows, allowing him to observe the passing terrain. He fully realized that he was in danger. Although he had not yet been singled out from the other Polish officers, he knew that it was deadly for a Jewish man to remain in German hands, and even though afraid, he felt resolve. He turned to the other Polish officers and urged: "We have to jump or sooner or later we won't be alive. Now is the time. It is dark and we are passing a wooded area." Lonek's father's fellow officers objected strenuously. They held no hope for a successful escape and were convinced that if one soldier did escape, all the others would be killed by the Germans. Lonek's father simply reiterated: "We, each one of us, have to take care of ourselves." He somehow managed to push the barred door open and jumped. He heard bullets whizzing past him but it was dark, and the trees he had counted on to shield him obscured the Germans' vision. Their bullets missed their target.

Although Lonek's father injured his leg in the fall, he pressed on. With German soldiers everywhere, it was essential to get rid of his army uniform. Fortunately, near the village of Lezansk, he spied some civilian clothes hanging from a washline in front of a temporarily empty house. After stealing and putting on the most suitable items, Lonek's father decided to risk knocking on a farmhouse door—a dangerous proposition but nevertheless his only alternative. In his father's favor were his Polish looks and his ability to speak Polish fluently. He also had some money in his possession which he intended to use as a bribe. He planned to identify himself not as a Jew certain to be rejected, but as a Polish soldier newly returned from the war. The farmer who opened the door in response to the knock—whether grateful for the escaped soldier's defense of Poland or just compelled by payment—allowed Lonek's father into his house.

Fortunately for Lonek's father, the Germans had not searched the Polish soldiers before loading them onto cattle cars. Lonek's father still had sufficient money, not only to bribe the farmer to shelter him, but also to fetch his wife and children from Jaroslaw. The farmer had no idea that he was sheltering a Jewish family in his house. It was dangerous enough to conceal a Polish soldier hiding from the Germans. It is unlikely that any amount of money could have moved the farmer to brave German soldiers with a Jewish family in tow. But Lonek's father assumed that it would not be too difficult to conceal that his family was Jewish because Lonek spoke accentless Polish and did not wear traditional garb. Four days after Lonek's father had left home, the farmer went on his errand to Jaroslaw, a ten-kilometer distance.

Lonek and his mother knew nothing of his father's activities or whereabouts after they had left him behind the fence. The sinister German presence loomed over the town and petrifying fear pervaded every Jewish heart. Yet, circumstances for the Jaroslaw Jews were less deadly than in other occupied Polish areas. In many Polish cities, towns, and hamlets, Lonek and his family would not have survived a four-day waiting period for his father. In many areas, the Germans had descended on the Jewish population, beating, burning, slashing, and shooting them. Descriptions given by Jewish inhabitants from different Polish towns all reverberate with the same refrain: death. "The first Saturday during the occupation, Jews were rounded up from a big synagogue. They collected forty Jewish children of different ages and many old women, forcing them to walk naked before the gathered crowd. If anyone refused to do as they were told, they were beaten with a whip. . . . The public was told to applaud. Baker Gorowski who refused was shot on the spot. . . . The following day the commander of the city, Oberleutnant Kurt Keinz, ordered a 'relay race' with twenty religious Jews. They were forced to go down on all fours and crawl, licking the ground with their tongues. The Nazis threatened to kill the Jew who was last to reach the finish line. However, they killed the Jew who reached it first. After two weeks, new arrests, tortures and massacres took place."[1]

Other cities fared no better. A Jewish woman living in Goworowo described the arrival of the German troops: "They shot without reason through doors and windows and burned the synagogue. All men between seventeen and forty were rounded up for work. They did not trouble themselves to search for those who had hidden, but set the houses on fire. One hundred and fifty people lost their lives."[2]

The Germans' arrival in Stoczek Łukowski was equally deadly. A former inhabitant commented: "All through the night we heard shooting. In the morning, the Germans screamed that all Jews leave their hiding places or they would be shot. . . . In the evening [Rachel] went to look [for her husband and brother]. I ran after her. We found them in front of the church among other dead Jews. There were also dead [Jewish] soldiers there. It was said that they were Jewish prisoners of war. The square was red with blood."[3]

Similarly, persecution started the instant the Germans marched into Pultusk: "They fetched many for the labor camp and they burned fifty Jews behind the bridge. One [Jew] had to pour gasoline over the other and they [the Germans] set them on fire. Among them was my Uncle Izhak with his wife and five children."[4]

Many Jewish and non-Jewish Poles tried desperately to escape from the approaching Germans. One youngster, thirteen years old at the time, recorded: "[The train] was terribly crowded; there was no place to sit or stand. Kids were trampled and people walked over each other. Shouts, cries and complaints reached to the heavens. At every station, more passengers were added. Fights broke out between new and old passengers. From time to time we saw German planes. The train stopped and the crowds, trampling over each other, jumped from the trains to hide in the ditches. When the planes left, we were pushed into the trains again. Family members were separated, possessions were lost. The yelling, the cries of the children, the shouts of those robbed were reaching the heavens."[5]

The Germans were not above looting by any means. "Daily they plundered the stores. . . . The Germans took off our clothes and separated us from them. They searched for diamonds. They gave us no food for twenty-four hours and then they gave us castor oil in order to get the diamonds out of us while they beat us horribly."[6]

Whatever goods the Germans demanded, they wanted instantly. They spared no effort in obtaining whatever luxury came to their minds. The son of a former shopkeeper recalled: "One officer and two Germans came into my father's store and demanded that he make three pairs of boots for them by morning. When my father explained that this was impossible, they threatened to shoot him like a dog if he were not ready by morning. My father and his workers labored all night. The Germans came in the morning, put on the boots and didn't pay a penny. From then on, they [the Germans] came and ordered boots without paying for them."[7] It was probably the Germans' avarice that allowed the bootmaker to remain alive.

An appeal to the Germans' rapacity occasionally resulted in the saving of a Jewish life. When the Germans marched into Siedlice "my father was sent to Wegrów to a labor camp. When we found out that the overseer accepted bribes, my sister Rachela and I went there and bought my father free for ten zloty. His beard had been torn out and he looked like death because he had been starved and tortured."[8]

While the Germans were looting, the Poles waited impatiently and then they enriched themselves by stealing whatever the Germans rejected, discarded, or overlooked. "The Germans could not tell the difference [between the Poles and the Jews] but Polish youngsters and Polish women ran behind them and pointed out the Jewish stores. In return, they were rewarded with as much merchandise as they wanted. The Germans took the chocolate; the Poles took shoes and manufactured wares and carted them away in wagons."[9] An onlooker commented: "What could not be carried off, was destroyed."[10]

So far, the Jaroslaw Jews had been spared the worst of such outrages. Eliott only vaguely remembered the details of waiting for word from his father. But the dire sense of threat and foreboding, which followed Lonek continuously even in his mother's presence, remained clear in his mind. At the time, neither his mother nor he knew that in neighboring towns mayhem already reigned, but they did realize that they were in profound peril. Thus, the next event in their lives came as a beacon, breaking through the pitch darkness of fear and despair.

Eliott could still see the hay-filled wagon pull up in front of his house; he recalled the driver, dressed in dirty clothes and a weather-beaten hat, climb down from his perch; he remembered the farmer knocking on the front door and the relief on his mother's face when the farmer said: "I have a message for you." Eliott recalled the note so clearly that while relating its contents to me, he picked up a piece of paper from my desk and demonstrated exactly how the note had been folded. To disguise the message from the farmer, his father had written the note in Yiddish. "She [my mother] was crying. I asked her what happened and she said: 'Your father is okay, not to worry and everything is okay.' And the farmer was sitting outside on his wagon and my mother from this window she saw him." Pointing on a photograph of his house to the exact window from which his mother had directed the driver of the cart, Eliott continued: "My mother told him: 'Stay there, I'll be ready in ten minutes.' My father [had] told her [in the note] to come immediately—don't ask questions. Take everything and go back with him. And she took everything what she could, clothes for us, clothes for my father, bedsheets to put everything in. They took the hay out [of the wagon] and [after depositing their belongings] covered everything with the hay."

Lonek's mother now had only one more task. She took a hammer and smashed a spot in the wall of the bedroom and removed a small metal box. With astute foresight, Lonek's parents had secreted a cache of money and jewelry, some gold chains and watches, in case of emergency. The current emergency was surely worse than any his parents had ever anticipated, and so his mother quickly gathered the hoard. Lonek and his mother watched the farmer from the window until he had completely replaced the hay. Eliott recollected: "We went down and my mother left the door open. I told my mother to close the door, and she didn't answer." Without looking back, she climbed onto the cart.

By September 28, the Germans had burned down the Jaroslaw synagogue; arrested the head of the Jewish community, Mendel Reich, who was never heard of again; and ordered the Jewish population to report to the Sokol sports field and to surrender their valuables. The Nazis had not yet conceived of mass killings and found a solution that suited them for the moment:—expelling the Jewish population into Russian-occupied Poland.

Then the Germans issued an edict requiring all Jews in Jaroslaw to cross into Russian territory before Yom Kippur. Anyone who turned back would be shot immediately. At first, some of the Jews procrastinated or went into hiding, but the Germans made it clear that, within hours on the designated day, all must be gone. So they gathered their belongings in heavy bundles and commenced their weary march to the San River. There the Germans and Ukrainians spitefully, greedily, and brutally relieved them of all their belongings. Roughly ten thousand Jews crossed the border bloodied and with their clothes in tatters.[11] Only several hundred survived the war years and the Holocaust. The rest disappeared into the labor camps of Russia or were exterminated by the Germans when they marched into eastern Poland during the German-Soviet war.

In a perverse way, Lonek's father's deportation as a soldier had been a very disguised blessing. It compelled the family to flee instantly despite the intense danger. The rest of the Jewish population, less acute in awareness, and also lacking anyone who could direct them to a place of refuge, did not leave instantly. As a result, when forced to leave, these unfortunates commenced their trek entirely unprepared, and deprived of all possessions. Lonek's unsual luck arrived in the form of escaping a fate more horrific than the one he had to endure. The catastrophes he was to encounter could have been worse—worse usually meaning death. In this particular case, it was his father's deportation that indirectly led to the family's ability to flee with some possessions intact. Still, it was clear that every move Lonek's family was to make from now on would be fraught with dreadful danger. The invasion of Poland by the Germans was barely over, but Jaroslaw was already *Judenrein* (cleansed of Jews).

Tears welled up in Eliott's eyes more than once during this session. When we came to this point of the story, he suggested we stop for the day. It was impossible for him to continue.

CHAPTER III

Search for a Sanctuary

The landscape was dotted with roving German soldiers and danger pervaded the countryside. The little group had no choice but to venture forth. The family perched on the seat next to the farmer, right behind the horse. Their belongings, covered with hay behind them, were at the bottom of the wagon. Lonek was placed in the middle between the taciturn farmer who held the horses' reins and his mother, who clutched Heimek in her arms. No one spoke. The only sound was the clopping of the horses' hooves and the rumbling of the cart wheels.

Lonek had only one hope—to reach his father. Because of the proximity of German soldiers, it was essential to be as unobtrusive as possible and to stay off the main road. Still, in the end an encounter was unavoidable. To reach Lonek's father, the San River had to be traversed, and there was only one bridge close by. There was no hope of passing the heavily armed German soldiers, who were stationed at each end of the bridge, unnoticed. The risk of crossing the bridge had to be taken. "I remember all my life the whole thing. The farmer told us he will speak for us. He told my mother: 'You don't talk nothing. Let me talk.' Because, you know, the soldiers asked from which village we came, and we didn't know what to answer and it could be very dangerous. So the farmer told my mother: 'You don't talk nothing. You just use [shake] your head yes, no.'" This was good advice because when challenged the farmer intended to pass off Lonek's mother as his wife and the children as his own. The farmer planned to pretend that he was taking them home from a visit to a relative.

It was dusk. As the cart rolled onto the bridge, the brutal voices of the German soldiers made Lonek's body quiver with fear. He heard the shouted orders, the bellowed commands, the degrading insults. A nightmarish atmosphere surrounded him. As usual, when the Germans did not use actual force, they intimidated by creating an aura of ferocity, violence, and frenzy. As gun-toting soldiers approached the wagon menacingly, Lonek's eyes were riveted on the soldier whose rifle with fixed bayonet was trained directly at him. The soldier's features were solidly imprinted on Eliott's mind. "And as we were crossing we were shaking. The soldiers with bayonets, screaming and yelling and calling us names. You know like 'dirty Polak.' I remember the soldier with a helmet and," Eliott demonstrated, "holding his gun like this. I kept my head down. I was scared, shaking. So finally we crossed the bridge."

As the wagon penetrated further into the countryside, Lonek noticed a stream of trucks heading west loaded with soldiers wearing unfamiliar uniforms. He heard the men call and shout to each other and realized that they were speaking Russian. It seemed astonishing to hear Russian voices, but Lonek, overwhelmed with events, did not attempt to decipher this strange phenomenon. He was unaware that the soldiers were the vanguard of an occupation force. The wagon carrying Lonek, his mother, and brother arrived at the farmhouse at around dusk. How many hours they had actually been on the road Eliott could not remember. At the time, it had seemed forever, though he later surmised that it must have been just a few hours. On a return visit with his brother in 1992, he searched for the road to the farmhouse, which was located near Lezansk, but was unable to locate it. Too much in that area had been destroyed during the war, and much had changed since. He did recall, however, that in the final leg of the trip, they had climbed a little hill, where he spied his father, who had been waiting for his family, his eyes impatiently searching for the long-expected wagon. For a moment, Lonek had trouble matching the man who was standing in front of the farmhouse in ill-fitting, stolen, and somewhat disheveled clothes to the trim figure of the man in uniform he had last seen. But as soon as he noticed the smile lighting up his father's face, the changed appearance ceased to matter.

"The farmer, as I remember him, he was not old," Eliott recalled. "He had a cap with a brim with a snap. He was sloppy, you know. There was his wife. She had a little child she carried and she also had another child—a boy running around with the pigs. This I remember, he was beating up the pigs. We unload our things and put them inside. It was a small farmhouse. The farmer got a barn there, I remember. He got cows there. He got pigs. He got two horses there. Inside the house there was a big opening, a kitchen, living room, everything together. Very high ceiling. There were little side rooms and one of the rooms he gave us. I remember my mother and my father was talking together. I don't know, some business. My little brother was with my mother. I went outside." In the age-old manner of little boys, Lonek went to play for a while in the yard. But soon he got hungry. "It was late and they gave us some food; I was very hungry, so I situated myself in the kitchen. We went from hell to heaven, between night and day. She [my mother] was very happy."

Exhausted from the day's tension, Lonek and his family, after having fallen asleep, were jarred back into reality by angry voices emanating from the next room. The farmer and his wife were having a heated argument. The wife expressed outrage at her husband's having brought strangers to the farm. The husband argued back furiously. Lonek's parents lay quietly, frozen with fear. They began to suspect that once morning came, the wife would betray them to the Germans who were never far away. "At night we hear screaming and yelling. We didn't know what happens. My father was scared, you know. He didn't know. He said the farmer was drunk. He probably got money from my father and bought booze. So my father said to my mother: 'We have to leave in the morning, because it is too dangerous.'" As Eliott related the incident, his voice dropped to a conspiratorial whisper as if there were danger that the farmer would overhear us.

Where were they to go? They certainly could not return to Jaroslaw, and it was impossible just to wander across a countryside filled with Russian and German soldiers. Besides, they had no transportation. Yet it was clear that they could not remain in their present hiding place. At some point, the farmer might recognize that he had a Jewish family on his hands. Never conceding defeat, Lonek's father came up with an idea. Not too far from their current hiding place was the home of Sosa, Lonek's beloved former nursemaid. The family would try to find refuge with Sosa's father. Eliott described his relationship with Sosa. "She started with us she was like eleven, twelve years old to be my nanny, you understand. She was a little girl. We got another maid, but Sosa's main purpose was to watch us. She stayed with us for about six years." During that time, her father would visit his daughter and even stay overnight with Lonek's family. He appreciated that his daughter was being treated kindly and generously, and mutual respect grew between the two families. Wisely, when the Germans were about to arrive, Sosa's father sent for her to return home. In view of the two families' past relationship, it occurred to Lonek's father that his family might find refuge with Sosa's family. "My father knew her address. So he figured the best way maybe was to go to her parents, because we treat her very nice, and we sent money to her parents over the years. We ask him [the farmer who was currently hiding them] to bring us over there."

For payment, the farmer consented. Relief was experienced all around. The farmer was glad to be rid of the family, and Lonek's family was eager to make their getaway. Uncertainty, fear, and roller-coaster twists of fate had dogged the family ever since the Germans had invaded Poland. Lonek had seen his father go off to war, then gratefully saw him return, only to watch him being beaten, humiliated, and quickly snatched away by the Germans. Then after Lonek's father miraculously escaped from a transport and the family was reunited in a farmhouse, they had to flee almost immediately to avoid betrayal. Now Lonek and his family were on the road again. Life no longer offered any stability or predictability.

It was into this dangerous countryside, where German and Russian soldiers roamed, that the wagon got under way, with the farmer, as before, avoiding main roads whenever possible. For safety's sake, they had waited until nightfall. Lonek slept, woke, and fell asleep again. Occasionally, he heard his brother crying and saw his mother rocking him to still the noise. The night was filled with apprehension and unease, but morning brought an ebullient welcome from Sosa. No doubt about it—although many things had changed, Sosa was still Sosa. She stretched her arms in greeting as Lonek ran toward her. Her smiling face was framed by a brightly colored blue, yellow, and red kerchief on which were printed little blue flowers. A nostalgic warmth crept into Eliott's voice as he recollected: "Little blue flowers. I still remember this." In the years after, whenever Eliott saw a peacock, he perceived in its multicolored tail Sosa's brightly colored scarf. "She picked me up," Eliott continued, his eyes filling with tears. "She kissed me. 'Lonek, Lonek!' She didn't know what to do. She was so happy to see me because she had spent six years with me. She used to take me to the public garden. We chased rabbits, you know. There was a little sandbox. We played, building castles. So many, many memories were there. I was almost like her child, you know. So she was very happy and her parents were also happy. They took us and we moved in. I remember my father wanted to pay and took money out from his pocket, and they pushed his hand. My father told me that Sosa's father didn't take nothing. The farmer was a tender-hearted gentleman whose son had been killed. Therefore, his full devotion lodged with his only child, Sosa. 'You had my daughter,' he said. 'She is happy. She was crying not to see you. She miss you!' the farmer said."

Sosa's father was a farmer, but he was of an entirely different mold from the one they had just left. He wanted to repay the kindness Lonek's family had previously extended to Sosa. "My father was very good to him [when Sosa had worked for Lonek's family]. My father pay him all the time for his daughter's service, and he [Sosa's father] was very happy. And later from this money, maybe he bought himself a farm. My father told me he gave him a lot of money. But he knew we are Jewish. He respected us and he didn't make jokes on Jewish people. He knew with whom he was dealing. He was always happy with my father." In repaying the family's kindness by harboring them, Sosa's father risked the gravest consequences, possibly even a death sentence. Nothing that Lonek's family could possibly have done for Sosa was comparable to what Sosa's family was about to do— namely to build a refuge to conceal Sosa's former Jewish employer and his family. The Germans were not far away and extreme caution was demanded.

Eliott recounts: "He [the farmer] started right away to thinking how to keep us alive. There was a barn, and they dug out a bunker underneath the horses and put wood pieces on the sides and on top so it would not collapse. The farmer and my father built it. With a little ladder from inside, you opened a trapdoor. And the farmer covered the trapdoor from the outside, so nobody will see it. Above us, the cows were walking around. It smelled terrible from the urine of the horses and the cows. [The space inside was] about five by four. Dirt on the ground. All four of us slept on the floor, sitting up. We had sacks to sleep on. At the time, it was almost winter. It was very cold. We slept with our clothes on. No blankets. For bathroom we had buckets. The farmer brought the food over. In the morning, he brought us some milk, cheese a little bit. Whatever he had, he shared with us. There was another exit to the outside. The farmer made another hole with straw on top; not a big hole, just for emergency. He covered the top and we were underneath three to four months like this. During the day, we were sitting inside the house. We didn't go out. Never go out. We watched the windows to see if somebody come. Always my mother was watching, all the time. She was working with Sosa's mother. She prepared the food, they were washing. It was very friendly, very friendly."

Lonek felt protected. He was close to his parents, who carefully hid their tension from the children. Sosa's presence even made it feel a little like old times. But in spite of the farmer's courage and the efforts his parents made to shield Lonek, the constant suspense, the never-ceasing vigilance of the grownups, the listening for strange voices and footsteps, left him "scary, shaking" much of the time. He was aware that there were Germans in the vicinity. Although none actually ever came to the farmhouse, the potential threat was always there. The Germans might come for any reason—to search, to plunder, or to commandeer farm animals for their own use. "During the day, we were normal—almost." Probably only someone who has lived through such hellish times can refer to such a dangerous predicament as "almost normal times." "Except in cases of something happening, we were supposed to hide ourselves. They told me in case somebody visit the house, some official want to inspect, we are to go under the bed and keep quiet." Policemen did come to the house occasionally, but to Lonek's relief, they never insisted on going inside. The farmer always stepped into the yard to do whatever business he had to conduct, and the farmer's wife would field the policeman by saying that the house was not in good order so she could not invite the officials inside. The farmer had few friends and thus few people came to the door. At times, Lonek could play in the yard, dally with Sosa and his brother, see his mother in the kitchen with the farmer's wife; at other times, danger loomed acute and imminent.

Family life and the possibility of imminent death were strangely interwoven. When asked whether his parents betrayed the tension they must have felt, Eliott remembers: "No, they hide it. Was everything family. But always was fear, great fear, when we were not under the ground. It was terrible. From the time the Germans arrived at Jaroslaw, everybody got shaken up. Specially when I saw my father, how they beat him up because he didn't take his hat off for them. So I got right away a bad feeling about it, you know."

"And does that fear ever come back?"

"Sure. All the time. When, for example, I was now in Germany, when I hear the train, or the announcement or loudspeaker or something like that remind me of the past. When you hear the German language speaking, and loud, memories come back like mad." After a pause, Eliott questioned in a sad and melancholy voice: "For what reason they cut my youth out? No reason at all. No reason at all."

Over time, the Germans' presence loomed ominously, and the danger became more menacing. The Germans began to expropriate the farmer's animals. Lonek's father felt his family's position had become untenable, and after some deliberation, the family decided to journey to Lvov. A larger city would likely offer more protection than this smaller farming community so close to the Germans. Lvov, a spacious city, had been a mercantile center under the Poles. Lonek's family did not know whether Lvov would fall under German or Russian jurisdiction. There had been no way of predicting just where the Germans' authority would end. But now it seemed established that Lvov was within the area occupied by the Russians. Lvov would be the family's next destination. Once more, this time under the guidance of their farmer friend, the family mounted a cart and commenced a perilous journey.

CHAPTER IV

From Chaos to Chaos

When Lonek's family climbed onto their protector's cart, they could not possibly have suspected the extent of the chaos that had overtaken their country and pervaded the countryside. From the isolation of the farm, it was impossible to gain an overview of the conflicting forces that had been loosed onto the land.

During Eliott and his family's journey with the first farmer, the danger of the invading and marauding Nazis had been clear; Russia's role was not as evident. The Soviet Union's contribution to Poland's fate had actually been determined by the Nonaggression Treaty, which had been signed by the Soviet Union and Germany on August 23, 1939. It stated that in the case of a German attack on Poland, the Soviet Union would not side with Britain and France, should they come to the aid of Poland. The treaty also contained a section that was only revealed after the war with the capture of German documents. The segment, which was called the "Secret Additional Protocol," divided Poland approximately in half, giving the area west of the Bug River to the Germans and the area to the east of the Bug River, which contained the Western Ukraine and Western Belorussia to Russia. This area was mostly the agrarian and less prosperous part of Poland, which covered over half of prewar Poland, and contained 37 percent of the population. It had taken some negotiating between Stalin and Hitler to determine the exact demarcation line, which not only depended on Stalin's long-range political designs but also on his personal whims. The region around Augustów, for instance, was awarded to Germany by Stalin because Joachim von Ribbentrop, the German foreign minister, enjoyed hunting stags, and it was thought that this area sheltered particularly fine red deer. This deal, as well as many others made between Germany and

Russia, would prove disappointing: There were no red deer in the Augustów forest.[1]

By September 17, the Russians were beginning to swarm over Poland, though the speed of their takeover varied in different places. The exact location of the boundary dividing the Russian- from the German-occupied part of Poland was by no means clear to the local populace. In fact, the meaning of the Russian troops' arrival was difficult to decipher. Confusion and bafflement reigned among the Poles when the first Russian columns appeared. Their entrance had been so sudden and unexpected that few of the local citizenry knew whether they had come as friend or foe. An onlooker at the time described it as follows: "We were plunged into the mist of insecurity, and various, most fantastic rumors became facts for us, around which we spun interpretations and forecast the future. . . . so, when one misty September morning on the Moscow-Warsaw road, tanks, armored cars, trucks bearing the red star, cavalry, and infantry in combat gear appeared moving westward, we suddenly faced a number of questions for which we had no answers. Where was this gray army decorated with red stars going? Was it bringing us assistance or final defeat? . . . Crowds that lined up the streets and roads in villages and towns were trying in vain to solve this burdensome puzzle."[2] Even though the Polish citizenry was ignorant of the spoils the Germans and the Russians had prepared for themselves, its deep-seated suspicion of Russia did not need much fuel to be stoked. The profound mistrust the Russian forces provoked in the Poles could hardly have been surprising. Poland had been invaded in 1772 and 1792 by the Russians, Austrians, and Prussians, each time losing some of its territories to foreign powers. In 1794, a rebellious Poland disappeared entirely under the alien yoke, to find its independence again only after World War II.

To dispel Polish suspicion, the Russians promoted themselves as liberators, as brothers. Even before the Russians arrived, they inundated the populace with propaganda leaflets, announcing that the Russian army's goal was to aid the Poles in their struggle against Germany. When they entered villages, Russian army bands played Polish patriotic songs, implying that allies, not occupiers, had arrived. Upon entering towns and villages, the Russian army created a festive atmosphere, festooning their path with victory arches and flowers. A radio broadcast announced that Hitler had been killed in a coup. As even the Polish authorities had no clear picture of the Russians' intent and in any case no longer had any power over Polish citizens, and because the invading forces stressed their common cause with Poland, most of the Polish civilians were eager to perceive the Russians as rescuers. A city official in Kopyczyne announced: "Gentlemen, Poles, soldiers, we will best the Germans now that the Bolsheviks are going to help us."[3] In another case, a Polish captain announced to his troops: "The Soviet army crossed the frontier to join us in the struggle against the Germans, the deadly enemies of the Slavs and of the entire human race. We cannot wait for orders from the Polish High Command. We must unite with the Soviet forces. Commander Plaskov [the Russian commander] demands that we join his detachment immediately after surrendering our arms. These will be returned to us later."[4] Russian and Polish soldiers embraced and marched together, the latter not suspecting that they would soon be disarmed and imprisoned by their "comrades in arms."[5]

The benign attitude of the Russians was quickly revealed to be a mere pose. When the locals refused to answer the Russians' celebratory entrance with hearty welcomes or refused to display Russian flags, threats of mayhem quickly convinced the citizenry to provide a triumphal reception and to make certain that the Russian soldiers would be received with salt, bread, and flowers, the traditional symbols of welcome and hospitality.

The invading army, followed by the NKVD (Russian secret service, later changed to KGB), ruled largely by intimidation and plunder. Most orders were followed by dire threats. Thus, a Russian official ordered villagers to hand over all their grain within one day's time or the village would be set aflame.[6] Churches and libraries were quickly closed down and priests were arrested.[7] Class dissension was promulgated by dropping leaflets, encouraging citizens on the lower end of the economic spectrum to attack, plunder, even murder those wealthier than they[8] and to occupy landowners' estates.[9] According to the Russians, wealth could only have been acquired by exploiting the poor. Other leaflets goaded Ukrainians and Belorussians to grab "pitchforks, axes, saws and scythes and overwhelm the Polish landlords.[10] In despair, a landlord's family turned to a Russian officer quartered with their friends, begging him to prevent the father's arrest. The officer explained: "If he killed someone or stole something, all this could be taken care of. But if he is a landlord, I can do nothing."[11]

The Russians cleverly exploited deep-seated ethnic tensions inherent in Polish life. Whereas before the Russian occupation the Poles were the ruling class in southeast Poland, they were actually in the minority. Sixty percent of the population were of various ethnic origins—Ukrainian, Belorussian, and Jewish.[12] Over the years, the Polish government had repressed these minorities and held them in contempt, making every attempt to eradicate their ethnic identification and to root out their language. The Polish farmers who had been moved into the area to administer and pacify it were despised by the local population for their xenophobia, their sense of superiority, and their rigid, unsympathetic, bureaucratic ways. Violent uprisings by the Ukrainians against the Polish authorities had been frequent and had been met by brutal retaliation.

To manipulate these schisms, the Russians assured the minorities that the rule of their "Polish masters" had come to an end; they urged the Ukrainians and Belorussians to attack the Poles with whatever weapons they had, be they guns or pitchforks. Soldiers were urged to shoot their Polish officers and seek revenge on those Poles formerly in power.

On the whole, the Belorussians and Ukrainians had initially welcomed the Russians, believing falsely that their ethnic identification would be encouraged by the occupying forces. They did not know about the reign of terror inside Russia which had killed approximately 20 million people by 1939. They themselves were soon to experience venomous repression, but this did not become clear until the Russians were well entrenched.[13] Some of the older, more educated, intellectual, or prosperous members of the ethnic population or those engaged in commerce or trade, however, harbored a deep sense of apprehension about the future designs of the Russians. When they hailed the Russians, it was more due to a reluctant choice of one evil over another, though the Ukrainians hoped to immediately chase out both the Poles and the Jews from their enclaves.[14]

Most of the Jews were also initially relieved at the Russians' approach. From the Jew's vantage point, no one could be worse than the Germans who were trying to exterminate them. In their case, friendly welcoming of the Russians had less to do with their economic system than with the thought of survival. This was well expressed by a Jewish man: "Who cared about communism? Who paid any attention to theoretical problems of national economy, when one faced an immediate danger to life? The question of whether the regime was good or bad was irrelevant. There could hardly be any doubt that a great percentage of the Jewish population, poor and rich, workers and factory owners were relieved when the Red Army entered our town."[15] Another Jewish man characterized the current sentiment: "We had been sentenced to death, but now our sentence has been commuted—to life imprisonment!"[16]

The uncertainty created by the Germans' withdrawal and the unpredictable arrival of the Russians created a power vacuum that produced chaos. As the Polish civilian government abandoned the population, villages and towns formed their own citizen guards to fill the void, which were frequently led by Poles. Some merely sought to protect their communities from marauders, but others turned into vigilante groups and adopted the prejudicial attitudes of the former Polish government, and vented long-harbored antagonism against Jews, Ukrainians, and Belorussians.

This ethnic hatred now burst into violence as Ukrainians, sometimes with the bribed consent of the Soviet authorities, plundered Polish communities, attacking at night and killing local Polish farmers. "One evening they attacked a farm where they completely destroyed the house and practically killed people, ripping the clothes off them. Of everything that had been in the house only rubble remained. Those who had been seriously wounded and left naked were threatened that if they reported the Ukrainians to the authorities, they would come back and finish them off. Russian soldiers stood with rifles and watched that the Poles should not resist".[17] Returning Polish soldiers were in constant danger: "There were two Polish officers on the road going home to their wives and children. Some Ukrainians and Bolsheviks grabbed them . . . they were shot and the Ukrainians took their shoes and clothing. Before one of them died he said to tell his wife he was alive no more."[18] A child observed at the time: "The Ukrainians came and took away our cows, horses, pigs and even small things like my rabbits."[19]

Russians had only contempt for the Poles whom they considered bourgeois. In turn, the Poles despised the Jews, whom they described as "elegantly outfitted promenading the streets. They received bread and flour, and sugar and lard for the children. They didn't pay for shelter. They occupied themselves profiteering and lived carefree. The Poles, on the other hand suffered hunger and labored hard."[20] Actually, the Jews had no such advantages, and suffered acutely along with everyone else.

With a large part of the population under arms, not only did ideological differences spark battles, but so did long-standing personal grudges and individual greed. People were killed by gunfire, hammer blows, and axes. Opponents were flayed alive, buried alive, dismembered, dragged to death by horses, beaten to death, and buried in pits, frequently while still alive.[21]

Adding to the mayhem was the Russians' refusal to view Polish soldiers as honorable enemies according to the articles of war. Instead, the Russians considered the Polish soldiers as mere rebellious rabble engaged in a civil uprising against the true rulers of Poland—namely, Russia. Regarded as traitors to the Russian cause, Polish soldiers were arrested and frequently executed. Polish officers in particular were tracked down and slated for extermination. For instance, in Tarnopol, the Polish officers had assembled to welcome their Russian counterparts. But when it became clear that the Russians did not regard them as comrades, they tried unsuccessfully to flee in their cars, but recognizing the hopelessness of their situation, surrendered. "The Russian officer ordered them to turn around and a moment later a salvo rang out as they [the Polish officers] fell dead and those cadavers lay out in the courtyard for several days . . . the wife of one of the officers found her husband among the dead."[22]

As the Russians became more solidly entrenched, some Polish army units scattered; some tried to escape over adjacent borders; and others, joined by Polish civilians, fought the invaders. In turn, Ukrainians and Belorussians ambushed Polish soldiers as they attempted to fight the Russians or flee the Germans. The remnants of the defeated Polish army, enraged by the unsympathetic stance of the Belorussians and Ukrainians, vented their fury against these ethnic groups as well as against local Jews. Chaos reigned. In one village, Poles conducted a pogrom against Jews, and in another, they killed Ukrainians. Elsewhere, Belorussians who were harassing Polish troops were being caught, shot, and hanged by the Poles. The killings were wanton, constant, and indiscriminate.[23]

Russian officers personally encouraged the local population to commit the most heinous atrocities: "A Soviet commissar came by and shot one lawyer . . . the rest [of those rounded up] he left for the hoodlums to do with as they pleased. They were taken into the fields, ordered to undress, and were shot one after another. They threw them into pits, still alive. My father was alive when they threw him into a pit and when he stood up and shouted at them 'even if you murder us, Poland will still be here,' they smashed his skull with spades. They broke the legs of an acquaintance, a teacher, and then buried him alive. Such killings were taking place all over the area."[24]

The Russians almost immediately began arresting civilians. "At night you could hear the hard steps of the NKVD leading away people they arrested."[25] Those who had formerly worn uniforms were primary targets: The NKVD searched for former boy scouts, foresters, guards, and district administrators. A sixteen-year-old boy was interrogated for two hours, and forced to sign a sentence against himself while being pistol-whipped into eventual unconsciousness; his teeth were knocked out and his face crippled.[26]

Arrests in the countryside were frequently accompanied by the confiscation of cattle, horses, pigs, poultry, farm tools, and grain, leaving survivors to starve. In the cities, the appropriation of houses, furniture, and businesses rendered the surviving family members destitute.[27] Arrests were usually accompanied by gratuitous cruelty, such as cursing, spitting, and beatings.[28] Official paranoia added bizarre twists. Thus, an eleven-year-old boy was forced to drink thirteen liters of water to prove that the well had not been poisoned by the local population.[29]

Summary executions against former Polish officials began soon after Russian troops and the NKVD arrived. "After entering the Lerypol settlement in Grodno county, NKVD men in disguise arrested the colonists [Polish officials] and led them in the direction of the nearby forest. Suddenly we heard shots. So my older brother ran in the direction of these shots. Near the forest they saw corpses, among which was my father."[30]

Heads of villages, a particular target of the NKVD, were vulnerable, even if they had served their community well. As the village head was led out in the direction of the forest, "the people begged to let him go with great crying and lamentations. It didn't help. On the way they beat him, spit in his face, threatened that the good times of domination are over . . . They brought him to the edge of the forest. There they searched him, undressed him down to his underwear in front of the crying people, beat him with butts, kicking him and threatening that Poland will never rise again. They shot him in the chest with a revolver. They asked someone to knock out his golden teeth because it is a pity to leave them behind." [31]

At first, the Russians allowed the citizen guards to continue rampaging; however, after a time, when they were ready to assume total power, they slowly and methodically arrested the leaders and disposed of them, generally by murder or deportation.[32] They then substituted the most uneducated and have-not section of the local population to lead the citizen guards. Some of these new leaders were criminals, not necessarily considered a handicap by the Russian authorities. The reasoning was that those who had been accused of crimes were the hapless victims of a capitalistic society and had done nothing more than to repossess what the bourgeois class had unfairly wrested from them.[33] This largess on the part of the Russians had a two-pronged effect. It gave the Russians a cadre of loyal followers and showed the rest of the population that the Russians could do whatever they liked. Of course, after some time, when more Russians were brought into Poland, another round of deportations eliminated the local population from the positions in which the Russians had placed them, so that the newly arrived Russians could be put in charge.

Although Lonek and his family were unaware of the full extent of the surrounding brutality and violence, they were nevertheless filled with great uncertainty, fear, and trepidation. They were fully cognizant that Jews were not secure among the hostile Polish population and did not know what to anticipate from the Russians. It was into this threatening, unsettled world that Lonek, perched on yet another cart, headed.

The tension in Eliott's voice rose as he recalled the circuitous route to Lvov: "Sosa's father, he took us with his carriage. He put a lot of things on this wagon. Milk and a pig to give to someone in case to reward [bribe] them and then in case of trouble to let us go. He put hay on top. I remember we was walking nights. It must be two nights or three nights maybe. We rest during the day. We hide ourselves in the woods or somewhere off the side [of the road]. He [the farmer] was really taking an enormous chance." The family arrived safely in Lvov and said their grateful good-byes to the farmer. Many years later, Lonek's father revealed that he had heard that the farmer's whole village had been wiped out by the Germans during World War II.

CHAPTER V

A Failed Haven

When Sosa's father's wagon pulled into Lvov, the little group rightly felt an enormous sense of relief just to have escaped to Russian territory. Many refugees crossing from German into Russian-occupied Poland had suffered more harrowing encounters. A young girl logged her mother's experiences at the time: "The last time she tried to cross the bridge, she stayed a whole night in the water [in the river near the town of Sanok]. She was fired upon from two sides: The German and the Russian. At daybreak the firing stopped and mother crossed the river."[1]

The sense of respite Lonek's family felt upon arrival was mixed with consternation. The family always strained to attain the next goal, but once it was within their grasp, the question arose anew: "What now?"

The choice of Lvov as a destination had been reasonable. For one, Lvov was located well within the part of Poland under Russian domination. Set in a largely agricultural and primitive countryside, it had, in prewar years, been a lively city, a cultural center. Approximately 13 percent of its population had been Jewish.[2] By the time Lonek and his family arrived, the city had already been severely bombed by the Germans. After the dividing line between the Germans and Russians had been drawn, Lvov had fallen to the Russians. Lonek and his family could not have anticipated how much the city had changed under the Russians.

The invading Russians were indeed an odd looking lot. Although their tanks and guns pointed at the citizenry inspired awe, the soldiers' appearance did not. Their clothes were shabby and bedraggled; each soldier lacked some part of his uniform. Some were beltless, their guns attached by mere string; some were without shoes and had their feet wrapped in make-shift rags.[3] The cavalry horses that followed the tanks were in even worse shape than their riders. Covered with blankets instead of saddles, the horses were emaciated and looked as if they would drop from exhaustion.[4]

The soldiers' demeanor brightened when they saw wondrous items in store windows. And, indeed, every item was wondrous to them, as the occupation army lacked almost everything at home. The Polish stores were replete with goods the Russians hardly knew still existed. Deprivation and greed prompted the soldiers to walk from store to store, buying everything from pins to furniture. They cleaned out the shelves like locusts, all the while mechanically repeating in a well-taught mantra that these items were really plentiful back home in Russia but they wanted to purchase them anyway. They bought twenty watches at a time, whole bolts of dress material, armloads of shoe leather, trunksful of clothing, and, to their great delight, food. At first, they meekly asked to be allowed to purchase a few ounces of sausage. Upon learning that there was no rationing, they wrapped long strings of sausage around their necks and stuffed some into their boots to keep their hands free to purchase other items.[5]

The Russian women, who were part of the occupying forces, did not have to share the endless queues with the local population; they received preference. Any shopkeeper showing a lack of eagerness to sell was frequently fetched the next day and never heard from again.

Of course, those locals who had been even moderately affluent before the Russian occupation were immediately thrown out of their apartments to make way for party functionaries. It forced the local population, including the Jews, into the most deplorably crowded conditions.

Generally, once the Russians invaded a city, it almost immediately began to disintegrate:

> They spoiled things—depleted stocks, destroyed crops, vandalized cities. Within a week our town was completely changed: dirty all around, no one caring to keep it clean, heaps of refuse, thrown away by the army, disintegrating on the streets. The city, neat and pretty before the war, now assumed an eerie appearance: dirty streets full of mud, lawns walked over and covered with mud, lawn fences and small trees lining the streets all broken down. Display windows, unkempt and covered with dust and cobwebs, were decorated with portraits of Soviet rulers. Store billboards were mostly ripped off, with empty spaces left where they were once attached.[6]

The population, afraid that the NKVD might consider them bourgeois, assumed a proletarian look. Colors were muted, ties were considered too middle class and disappeared, and women's hats were replaced by headscarves. To remain inconspicuous, everyone walked quickly, without looking right or left.[7] Anyone too well dressed or whose hands were uncalloused could be carted off immediately.[8]

The Lvov citizens, as well as the refugees, became more and more impoverished. The Russian authorities methodically emptied the city and its surroundings of everything that was transportable. Cars loaded with furniture, clocks, wood, cattle, horses, grain, potatoes, and much more departed from the railroad station; the final destination was Russia. Houses were sometimes dismantled and entire parts of the structure, such as doors and windows, were shipped off.[9] Citizens were prevented from hiding their assets as officials noted down all their possessions. In anticipation of confiscation, property owners were forbidden to sell any listed item or slaughter any of their animals.

Ironically, as Lvov was being stripped of its material goods, streams of refugees, running for their lives, poured across the border into Russian-occupied territory. In addition, when the Germans established command over a Polish village or town, they frequently expelled the whole Jewish population into eastern Poland. Objecting to the wholesale deliverance of dispossessed Jews, the Russians refused to allow any more into eastern Poland after December 5, 1941. Still, by stealth and desperation, many Jews managed to reach Russian-occupied territory. The number of Jews in Lvov increased drastically.

Unemployment had always been high, but now with the increase in population, the situation worsened drastically. Those who had been employed in pre-Russian days in a responsible or administrative position were considered bourgeois under the communist doctrine and immediately dismissed in favor of those Poles who previously had been engaged in low-level positions. The very top ranks were reserved for Soviet citizens. The nationalization of businesses and factories meant that everyone who had previously been self-employed was now either unemployed or underemployed at substantially lower wages by the government—that is, if they were able to obtain or keep their jobs. Jews who in pre-Soviet days had been engaged in private businesses or trade found themselves out of work and therefore vulnerable to arrest for "sabotage."[10]

Some people were reduced to such poverty that they succumbed to the Russian lure and sought employment in the Donbas Mines located inside Russia. Soon they became disenchanted with the grueling working conditions, backbreaking labor, utter poverty, and freezing cold, and returned to Lvov if they were permitted to do so.

The Russians chose a number of Jews for low-level positions because, unlike the Ukrainians, the Jews were not sympathetic to the Germans. In addition, Jews were among the more educated citizens in eastern Poland. In contrast, the Ukrainians and Belorussians, frequently peasants who came from small villages, had little education. Installed in bureaucratic government positions, Jews now represented Russian officialdom before Poles who had dealings with the government. Because such contacts usually involved frustrating conflicts over autocratic and petty regulations, the Poles came to associate Jews with the hated Russian administration. In addition, because the Jews considered the Russian invasion a reprieve from the threat of a more feared German occupation, they responded to the Russians with relief; this reaction angered the Poles. These resentments, combined with long-standing Polish anti-Semitism, heightened Polish antagonism toward the Jews.

Not that the Jews remained in these government positions for very long. By 1941, as soon as the Russians had imported sufficient party hacks from Russia, they dispensed with the Jews, who first slowly, then with an ever swifter pace, were arrested and disposed of in various ways.

After their invasion, the Russians adopted their own currency—the ruble—in Poland. As a result, the Polish coin, the zloty, lost all value. Unemployed refugees became penniless as their savings instantly became worthless. In addition, daily life was made agonizingly difficult as those in charge spewed forth innumerable new edicts and rules. Bureaucratic intransigence and stupidity complicated the smallest tasks, and standing in line became a full-time occupation. The longest and most desperate lines formed outside food stores, starting at dawn. Everything was scarce. People were suffering severely from hunger as bread became increasingly harder to obtain and pantries emptied. Usually, a single family member could not serve as a representative for the whole family in order to obtain the appropriate rations.[11] Instead, the presence of the whole family was required. Obedience to the law did not facilitate matters. Underhandedness and bribery did much to advance one to the head of the line.

Both adults and children suffered in equal measure. An adolescent recorded her impressions at the time: "My father had spent the rest of his money which he took from home. We had nothing to live from. My father became a dealer. He dealt in everything: sugar, meat, saccharine. . . . We, the children, learned to stand in these lines for hours, and then sold the bread we stood in line for."[12]

Despite the influx of Jews into Lvov, the Jewish community was never-theless disintegrating. Although the Jewish religion was not forbidden outright, Jewish institutions, such as *yeshivas* (Jewish religious schools), were closed down and the output of Jewish newspapers was curtailed. Jew-ish practices, such as circumcision and the attending of *mikvas* (ritual baths), were discouraged. Jewish social organizations were no longer permitted to raise money for charitable purposes or for essential aspects of Jewish life, such as the education of rabbis and the upkeep of synagogues and cemeter-ies. Without funds for the myriads of needy, Jewish relief organizations had to shut their doors. Zionism was anathema to the state. The authorities could not see any reason why Jews should yearn for Palestine, now that paradise had been achieved under the Soviet regime.

Similar measures were taken against Christian believers. During searches of homes, holy pictures were destroyed. In public places, crucifixes were taken off walls and red flags and portraits of Lenin and Stalin were substi-tuted.[13] Officials made lists of religious statues, then methodically ordered them smashed.[14] Anyone found praying was threatened with imprison-ment or denial of food rations. A youngster described a child's funeral cor-tege in which women and children participated: "The Bolsheviks saw the procession. They came with revolvers to disperse us. But the women weren't giving in. They kept walking as they looked at the blasphemies of the Bolsheviks. A Bolshevik militiaman named Koshelev jumped in front of the coffin, pushed the women aside, took away the cross and trampled it with his feet. Behind him the militia commander by the name of Shpunov jumped in and started kicking and trampling the women who wanted to get the cross back. Other Bolsheviks dispersed the crowd."[15]

The authorities were particularly eager to root out religion among the young. They not only forbade religious instruction in schools but went to great length to convince the children that their beliefs were erroneous. A youngster described his experiences: "They drilled two holes in the ceil-ing. The commander would say into one: 'God, give me a dumpling' and nothing would happen. To the other hole he said: 'Soviet, give a candy' and candies would fall down. The commander would laugh and say that God gave nothing."[16] Teachers taunted the children by pointing out that the atheistic Bolsheviks still had their country, whereas the religious Poles had lost theirs.

Similar attempts were made by the Russians to destroy any ethnic iden-tification or nationalistic feeling. Schoolteachers had to teach exclusively in Russian. Soldiers emptied libraries of all Polish books, burned them, threw them on a garbage heaps, or used them as waste paper.[17] Whole libraries were destroyed or even burned.[18] The teachers were ordered to call the children "citizens" or "comrades" rather than by name.[19]

The secret resistance of the various religious groups to the attempted eradication of their beliefs was remarkable in view of the possible consequences. Christian women continued to pray and to hide religious medallions and holy pictures.[20] Polish children reacted with outrage: "The cursed Russians all the time tried to talk us out of Polish prayers and hymns. But it is all right. The good Lord will pay them back for this." [21] Another child commented: "They said that God was Stalin and that Stalin gives everything. We weren't listening to that because we knew well who God was. … They couldn't do anything with us because we were persevering and we didn't lose our spirit."[22]

The Polish Jews were equally as determined to cling to their religion. At the risk of starving in prison, some Jewish men refused to eat nonkosher food.[23] A fourteen-year-old youngster recorded his father's dedication:

> Father organized prayers in our apartment. During the daytime, older children came, and with covered windows father taught them from sacred books. In the evening, older citizens came and they sat together with father over the books. NKVD found out about it and they started to persecute my father. Every day at daybreak, he was called for interrogation and he was warned to stop religious practices. . . . After each interrogation, my mother cried and begged father to stop prayers and studies. Father didn't want to listen but he continued his mission with more precaution. . . . Not even for a moment did my father stop teaching.[24]

As Lonek's family entered the city, they pondered what steps to take. Where were they to go? What were they to do? Not only were they strangers in the city, but they suspected that with the influx of refugees and soldiers, housing would be scarce. As usual, Lonek's father hatched a plan: "My father always knew that in order to find some relative he would have to go to the shul [synagogue]. So the farmer took us over to the shul in the morning and he left us inside. I remember this. My father told me later that he asked somebody if he knew maybe of his relative. A man asked: 'What is your name?' My father answered: 'Jaroslawicz.' Then the man said: 'Your cousin Mendel is not far away from here.' And he told my father where Mendel is. So my father right away was very happy. And we went right away to him." The family, relieved, now felt assured that they would find shelter. True, Lonek's uncle had eight children—quite a brood—but under the circumstances, they felt certain that they would be taken in.

The family made their way to Uncle Mendel's house. The memory of that encounter left its mark on Eliott and added to his sense of disillusion:

"My uncle was a very religious type. He was with *payess* [sidelocks worn by the orthodox]. He was the opposite from my father, but you know, they didn't fight. Brothers, they was surviving and in the same boat. My uncle took my father inside. My father slept there a day and a night. The room was crowded with the eight children. And my father told me that his cousin said that a fish and a guest stink after three days. My father said he remembered all his life what his cousin told him. He wouldn't believe that his cousin talked to him that way. But that is the way it was. The war makes people animals. The war makes from a cat a dog. Survival."

Of necessity, Lonek's father approached some other families living in the same house, just one flight up. "We found some neighbor from our hometown who said: 'If there is room for two, will be room for another one. For three. Or four.'" Pointing to a photograph of the house, Eliott traced their steps. "From here, we went inside and here in the corner in the backyard was a little hall. The room was not so big, maybe ten by fifteen or twelve by fifteen. And there was about five or six families. So the guys that my father knew from somewhere told him: 'You can stay. We give you a little space.' So he gave us a little space and my father left his cousin. We went upstairs. I remember the door that was leather, white leather on the inside."

As Eliott described the door to me, his voice rose with excitement. In 1992, when he revisited Lvov with his brother, they had searched for the house and found it—unchanged. As the two men strode through its halls to reach the room they had shared with so many others fifty years before, Eliott suddenly put his hand on his brother's arm, and breathless with anticipation predicted that a white leather panel would cover the other side of the door they were facing. True to Eliott's word, as they opened the door, there was the white panel, right where it had been so many years ago. "The same thing. Didn't change!"

Years of memories flooded back at the recollection of sighting the door, bringing in their wake details of the time the family had been crowded into the small area they had shared with other generous refugees.

"People slept on the floor. There was no bed, there was no bench there. Everyone was sleeping on the floor. I don't know how they cook outside. And what was the cooking? The bread came ready. And a little water and the salt. The salt was what people ate those times. Maybe some coffee or tea with sugar if you were lucky. And nothing else, because it was the war. Bread and sugar and tea with salt. You had to stay all day to get food. We used to stand three or four times in different lines. I would stay in one line, my mother in another. So one day we stayed for a little bread, one day we stayed for a little sugar, for a little flour, because after two hours it disappeared. You had to wake up about five, six o'clock, because the day before was advertised that in this and this store would be a certain kind of food. So we had to stay in line."

Eliott recalled the torturous difficulties of obtaining food during his 1992 visit to Lvov when he lined up behind twenty or thirty people at a bakery. The result of the wait was an unappetizing, very sour piece of pumpernickel bread wrapped in a piece of newspaper. Yet, Eliott reflected how happy he would have been in 1941 to receive a piece of pumpernickel, no matter how sour. "I imagine in those times if I would have had the bread we would have been so happy, but today. . . . The memory makes me cry."

In contrast to the farmer's bunker, Lvov seemed acceptable to the eleven-year-old. Lonek did not see any Germans around, and he began to acquire some sense of security. The presence of Russian soldiers and Russian airplanes flying overhead reassured him. At that time, the Russo-German pact was still in effect, and there seemed little danger of a German invasion. Life even had some pleasurable aspects. Lvov was a prominent city, striking in appearance. Lonek remembers its wide streets, parks, and the theater that was located near the house where he lived. Streetcars led from their home to parks.

Lonek's father was among those fortunate refugees who obtained employment as a civilian worker for the Russian army. His job was to organize a unit transporting food and clothes. As a result, Lonek's mother was able on occasion to ride the streetcar with the children, and take them to a park to play. At home, Lonek played with his cousins or spent time people watching from his balcony. He lived entirely in the present, never giving a thought to the possibility that the Germans might overrun the city. "I was not thinking about it. I was a child. Maybe if it was now! In those times I was thinking how to go to the park. My mother was very helpful. She took me with my brother. See, on this street [pointing at a photograph] the electric car was stopping. So we were one stop from the park. If you look at this building [pointing at another photograph], we were not far from the theater. This was beautiful. Across the street from our house was a wide street, a lot of strollers, and shops."

The opportunity to attend school and the reassurance gained from seeing his father work again infused Lonek's life with some sense of normality.

In contrast to his experiences with the Germans, the drunk farmer, and the hollowed-out bunker, his life in cramped quarters, even with strangers, seemed luxurious.

Yet underlying a patina of predictability remained a constant aura of trepidation and fear that only increased with time. Lonek sensed that nothing was what it seemed. The Russians ruled the occupied country with an iron hand. That iron hand, however, was wielded by local citizens. From the very first, the local population was warned in no uncertain terms to obey every command without a murmur and without question.[25]

The Russians dictated and strictly outlined every aspect of life in the city. The accelerating arrests of former officials left the population in a constant state of anxiety, for any unforeseen transgression could trigger instant arrest or even execution. Literally every movement was supervised, including school calisthenics, which were designed to familiarize the students with aggressive behavior which might prove useful in wartime. Children were encouraged to report any failings on the part of their elders. In contrast to the underlying tensions, the city constantly reverberated with celebrations of communist anniversaries, victories, and cultural events, such as concerts, choirs, and ballet performances.

The initial relatively benign attitude of some of the ethnic minorities faded as they were forced to eliminate signs of their own culture. The population was told what they could talk or think about; any transgression was severely punished, frequently by death. For instance, one man was brutally separated by Russian soldiers from a friend he was chatting with on the street and then questioned about the topic of their conversation. Had his report about the conversation not tallied with that of his friend, the soldier would have surmised that they had discussed some anti-Russian topic, and both men would have been arrested on the spot.[26]

Conditions worsened as arrests increased. People disappeared in all kinds of ways. Often, they were simply rounded up on the street and never seen again. They were collected in large groups of similar classes, such as "officers and NCOs of the Polish Army, policemen of all ranks, landowners large and small, teachers, entrepreneurs and businessmen, politicians, local government officials, lawyers, civil servants, better-off peasants, Ukrainian Belorussians and Jewish activists, ex-members of the Communist party and ex-sympathizers." Estimates of the number of arrests vary from two hundred fifty thousand to five hundred thousand.[27]

Prison conditions were appalling. Because prisons were filled beyond capacity, other spaces, such as cloisters, office buildings, and even pigsties, were commandeered. A man recalled mistaking imprisoned lawyers, doctors, civil servants, and businessmen for serious criminals and suspected they had been incarcerated for years. Actually, none of them had been imprisoned for more than three months. In fact, after prisoners had been jailed for just a few days, their rapid physical deterioration made it impossible to discern whether they were forty or seventy years of age.[28]

The NKVD quickly ferreted out some of the most renowned members of the Jewish community. Soon after, others quickly went underground or attempted to flee into neighboring countries. Paid informers soon tracked them down. By 1940, the Russians widened their net and ever increasing numbers of Jews disappeared.[29] Denouncing neighbors or business associates became commonplace. The Russians kept dossiers on all citizens and arrested people under various pretenses. Poles were usually sentenced under the guise of being counterrevolutionary, and Jews tended to be marked as speculators.[30] Any pretext, or frequently none at all, could serve as an excuse to carry people off, particularly because it provided an opportunity for the arresting officers to "purchase" the furniture of the accused.

Eliott remembered an incident that, though frightening under any circumstance, highlighted the refugees' constant awareness of the tenuousness of their existence. "One day my parents told me to take my little brother out for a walk. He was about three years old. The street was very wide, and on the other side was like a little shopping center. In the center were stores and people walking. There were a number of roads leading from the middle. We went outside and somehow Heimek, he got lost. I was maybe ten to fifteen minutes calling and screaming for him." At the recollection of the horror of the moment, Eliott's face contorted with pain.

"I decided I would go home to tell my parents. And I was crying. I came home crying, you know, a little child. It is not my fault. So, anyhow, I came without my little brother. My father took out his belt, put me on his knees, and beat me up. I remember the belt, the belt from the Polish army. My mother was crying. She didn't let him. 'Why are you doing this? It's not his fault.' Suddenly, after a couple of slashes, my brother was knocking on the door!" As if the toddler were standing before us, Eliott began to laugh with seemingly immense relief while dabbing at his tear-filled eyes. "Heimek was very smart. 'How you came back,' I asked him. He said: 'I don't know.' Who knows? Three roads on this side. Two or three roads on that side." The family could not even guess how the little tot had retraced his steps. (As an adult, Heimek had no memory of the incident.)

What made Lonek's father, who had escaped from the Germans with cool deliberation, seemingly lose control over his emotions when Lonek returned home sobbing out his story? It would have been much more appropriate for him to rush out into the street and search for Heimek than to release his anger and waste time by punishing Lonek. One can only surmise that Lonek's father's reaction was not due to the dismay, fear, and consternation any parent would feel at the thought of a small child roaming by himself through city streets. It was more likely that Lonek's father was overcome by the fear, frustrations, and apprehension that went into the daily effort of keeping his family together. For months, existence had been a daily challenge. Lonek's father knew that quite frequently people simply vanished from the streets of Lvov. No one could determine the cause of such disappearances. Eliott reconstructed the incidents: "This was during the war. People disappeared. My mother's stepbrother disappeared on his way to work. Her sister disappeared, too. On the street, people suddenly disappeared. We didn't know what happened. For some reason, the Russians took them away or they killed them. Never heard from them again. They disappeared at different times. By themselves."

The disappearances indicated clearly that whatever seeming constancy existed in the family's life could cease in an instant. Its stability was tenuous, a facade, an illusion. Anything could happen at any time. Yet, when calamity did strike with unanticipated swiftness, Lonek's family was as unprepared as all the other refugees in Lvov.

CHAPTER VI

The Knock on the Door

The threat of arbitrary arrest, incarceration, and even execution hung over each citizen as an ever-present menace. Now a new danger began to loom—wholesale deportations, which meant the systematic roundup of whole classes of people, even of entire populations. The Poles' apprehension about possibly being deported was quite understandable. From the early years of the Russian revolution, millions of people had been shifted and exiled en masse on Stalin's orders. Mass deportations could occur for many reasons or for no reason at all. For example, when Russia claimed territory near the Bug River, the dividing line with Germany, local residents were capriciously given only forty-eight hours to abandon their homes and all of their earthly goods in preparation for relocation to distant villages and towns that offered only unemployment and starvation. Although the citizens were transformed into refugees under the guise of establishing the new German-Russian border, the beneficiaries of their misery were barely disguised: The edicts yielded the locals' apartments and household goods to the Russian administrators and officials pouring into the recently claimed zones.

The Polish Jews correctly interpreted as ominous the exhaustive efforts of the Russians to register the whole population of Russian-occupied eastern Poland. They believed that the Russians were planning large-scale, systematic arrests and subsequent deportations of the non-Russian population. Because most people desperately attempted to avoid registering to maintain a certain amount of anonymity, Russian officials resorted to crafty ruses to flush people out of hiding. Names were collected from archives and organizations in existence before their takeover. Ration cards were required ostensibly to institute a more equitable method of food distribution. However, the true purpose of the cards was to locate and interview registrants who had been missed in previous surveys. This more sinister motive was revealed by the detailed nature of the interviews, sometimes lasting for hours, about every possible detail of the registrants' personal lives, their possessions, their livestock, and their household goods.[1] The detailed information gained about every citizen in eastern Poland by the authorities gave the Russians total control over the population. The atmosphere grew more menacing every day.

The names on the list of registered voters made it possible for officials to check that every citizen participate in a plebiscite which was to take place on October 22, 1939, and which was to determine whether the western Ukraine and western Belorussia should be absorbed permanently into the Soviet Union.[2] This would automatically turn all the residents of eastern Poland into Russian citizens. Of course, the result of the voting was determined by the authorities well in advance.

The Russians set about to prepare the citizenry for what was expected of them. An immense propaganda machine went into action. Night after night, after a full working day, the population was forced to attend meetings in which anti-British and anti-French slogans were repeated ad infinitum, and the virtues of Russia were praised to the skies.[3] Participants, exhausted and bored, and compelled to neglect their own households, spent hours feigning interest. Lack of attendance brought dire consequences. "They [the Russian authorities] said openly that anyone who didn't vote or spoke against it, are enemies of the Soviets and there are prisons, Siberia and mines for enemies.[4]

The refugees fought tooth and nail to avoid Russian citizenship. For one, it often came with the dreaded "paragraph 11," which prohibited citizens from dwelling within one hundred kilometers of a border or a major city. They would subsequently be banished to desolate areas deep within Russia that offered a tenuous existence at best. In addition, citizenship would forever bar refugees from returning to their former homelands, even in postwar years.

On election day, officials made the rounds to catch slackers who avoided reporting to the polling station. An observer recorded: "The Bolsheviks led [voters] with drawn guns [to the polls] and if someone protested, he would not be there the next day because they would arrest him."[5] Another voter observed: "The voting looked like this: They led the people into the hall. They gave them a card and ordered them to throw it in the urn. You couldn't do anything else because there were guards all around and militiamen with bayonets. Every person from fear of arrest or deportation put their card into the urn. If [the guards] noticed that someone spoke up and demanded the freedom he was promised, that night that person was no more."[6] The urns were even carried to hospitals so that the sick were forced to vote.

"After the voting they [Russian authorities] announced the 'rightful' annexation of occupied Polish lands to the USSR as the freely expressed demand of the population."[7]

To test the loyalty of the population, the Russian authorities organized another deception. It began with a Russian announcement that a German commission would register all Polish citizens wanting repatriation to lands under German rule. Those not wishing to return could apply for a Russian passport and Russian citizenship.

Soon after, eight thousand people registered to return to Germany. This number swelled to seventy thousand following the May arrival in Lvov of a representative of the German commission. Astonishingly, a large number of applicants for repatriation were Jews. With a passionate eagerness to avoid deportation into the heart of Russia, these unfortunates volunteered to jump from the frying pan into the fire. Ironically, while thousands of Jews were desperately clamoring for entry into Russian-occupied territories, other thousands were pleading with the Germans to allow them to return to their former homes in Poland.

The fearful decision, whether Germany or Russia would offer a better chance for survival, haunted many Jews right from the beginning of World War II when the Germans and Russians carved up Poland. Many of the Jews living near the Bug River, the dividing line between the two conquerors, were at a total loss in which direction to flee. Some remembered the deadly pogroms in Russia and, therefore, recalling "German Kultur" of the past, opted for German-occupied Poland. Others were more familiar with Nazi philosophy and actions and sought to flee to or remain in Russian-occupied Poland. Not knowing which desperate choice to make, many religious Jews, following customary patterns, decided to obtain rabbinical counsel. They turned to Rabbi Simcha Zelig Ryger, supreme rabbinical judge of the Brisk community court in Poland. After pondering the question, the rabbi released the following statement: "Recent events were without precedent in history. The bestial treatment of Jews defied human understanding and therefore could not be analyzed. No Torah ruling could be issued on matters as they were beyond human comprehension. Each person's action had to be dictated by personal decision.[8]

Now under the Russians, new lists of petitioners, desiring to return to Germany, were constantly generated, and preparations for imminent departure began. A black market developed to procure a number on the repatriation list for those who could not obtain one legally. A petitioner recalled that while waiting at the German offices, a military officer warned the crowd: "Jews where are you going? Don't you realize we are going to kill you?[9] The petitioners quickly changed their mind, and remained in Russia.

Suddenly the German commission departed without explanation. Left stranded and caught unawares were those who had rejected Soviet citizenship for German repatriation. The Germans also left behind for the Russians lists of other supplicants. Now the Russians could easily identify these "traitors." Their disloyalty would be avenged by banishment to Siberia—though it must be noted that by now, the Russians eyed all the Poles who had fled to eastern Poland as fodder for new huge forced labor camps in Karelia, Siberia, Murmansk, and along the shores of the White Sea. In addition, Russians won the cooperation of neighbors and co-workers of potential victims through intimidation that crushed personal loyalties and citizen solidarity. In a land now riddled with informers, maintaining constant vigilance in relationships had become a matter of life and death.

Different classes of people were selected for each transport. For instance, the first transport, which left on February 10, 1940, for forest-clearing projects in Siberia, consisted of former Polish, Ukrainian, and Belorussian government officials. It also included foresters, the only prisoners who might be genuinely useful on such a project. Leaving on April 13, 1940, the second transport contained a high percentage of family members of those dispatched on the first transport. They landed in Kazakhstan and were condemned to build railroads. In addition, many Jewish leaders were also dispatched on the first two transports. Leaving in June 1940, the third transport was dominated by professionals who had fled German-occupied Poland, a high percentage of whom were Jewish. The last transport, containing thousands of Jews, departed on June 20, 1941, about ten days before the Germans invaded Russia.[10] The professions of the deported spoke to the arbitrary nature of their incarceration. Next to each name was listed an occupation: peasant, landowner, cadet, locksmith, sergeant, store owner, attorney, pharmacist, priest, shoemaker, merchant, high school student, and so on.

The procedure for deportation was always the same. The police typically surprised and subdued their quarry as quickly as possible. Because sufficient police were unavailable for such large-scale roundups, civilians were frequently conscripted to assist. In the middle of the night, as is the custom in dictatorships, doors were made to fly open, and men rushed into the bedrooms of sleeping, unsuspecting families. Usually the head of the household was tied up or put against a wall and ordered to stand still at the risk of being shot. The soldiers then searched for nonexistent weapons. It was as dangerous not to possess them, as to have them. A thirteen-year-old boy was ordered to hand over his father's weapons or his father would be shot. When the boy could not find any, they shot his father anyway.[11] After disposing of the weapon search, soldiers ransacked the homes for valuables and jewelry; if any were found, they disappeared in a blink of an eye into the pockets of the searchers. Frequently, the guards spied inviting morsels of food or usable clothes, which they stole.

An order of deportation was then read in stentorian tones to the terrified deportees, and an announcement was made that everyone was to get ready to leave immediately. The women were instructed to gather the infants, children, the old, and the sick. The amount of time granted for packing some necessities varied from commander to commander: from no time at all to twenty minutes, to forty minutes, or occasionally up to two hours.[12] In many cases, so little time was granted for preparation that whole families were loaded half naked into wagons. As to the quantity of goods allowed, this also depended on the commander's whim. Some deportees were allowed a few items, some 50 kilos, others as much as they could carry; a few lucky ones were permitted 100 kilos per person.[13] In their desperation and confusion, victims searched for any available money and grabbed whatever was at hand. Under such intense emotional pressure they did not necessarily choose the warm clothes essential for survival in the Siberian climate.

In many cases, the arresting soldiers willfully misled their prisoners by permitting them to pack several bundles and promising that they would be returned at the end of the journey. Of course, all such baggage disappeared.[14] At times, the frightened families were pacified by being told not to carry anything because on arrival they would receive everything they needed.[15] This reassurance was intended to mislead the victims to avoid any unpleasant lamentations, but its consequence was frequently the demise of those who froze to death in their skimpy clothes on their way to or in Siberia.

Children caught home alone were shown no mercy. A thirteen-year-old recorded his experience: "My brother and sister were about five years old. My father was a prisoner in Germany and my mother went to grandmother's. They took us at night and loaded us on a freight train. My mother came. They didn't want to let her on the train and we went off alone.[16]

The deportees did not necessarily know their destination, though many suspected it. Arresting officers sometimes revealed that destination, but others attempted to hide it. (For instance, Lithuanians were told they were being delivered to Lithuania. Once on the trains, they realized that they were traveling in the direction of Siberia.)

Trucks, carts, and vehicles of all kinds filled with deportees converged in lines over a mile and a half long from every direction into the railroad station, the collection point. Horrified onlookers saw the traffic jams and heard the wails, moans, sobs, screams, and cries of the passengers, which were interrupted only by gunshots that reverberated throughout the countryside. A fourteen-year-old recorded the moment: "Passing through the streets I saw a great commotion. Cars and wagons were driving through the streets and on all of them sat people with bundles. Long lines of these cars were aiming for the station, as was our car and I understood: it was a roundup organized on a large scale.[17] In summer, horses and carts were used. In winter, the shivering deportees were collected on sleds that were driven in such haste that on occasion they overturned.

Eliott recalled the sequence of events that led to the family's deportation in June 1940. A few months previously, his father, together with the rest of the refugee population, had been handed a harmless-looking questionnaire. According to Eliott, potential deportees were asked to decide between accepting a Russian passport and staying inside Russia or retaining their Polish passport with the idea of returning to German-occupied Poland after the war. Other Jews had no intention of ever returning to Poland, but thought that their request to do so would prevent the Russians from expropriating their passports.[18] For Lonek's father, the decision was rather simple. The idea of going to Germany was too ludicrous to be considered. At the same time, the idea of going farther into the Soviet Union was a fearful proposition. As a result, Lonek's father requested permission to remain with his family in Lvov.

Thus, Lonek's father became a traitor. As far as the Russian authorities were concerned, his refusal to accept a Russian passport made him an enemy of the state. The Russians, having skillfully exposed such "traitors," would now gather them and ship them off. Actually the Russians had eyed all the Poles, including the Jews, who had fled the German-occupied part of Poland into Russia as fodder for their labor force; they were then arrested under one pretext or another.

Then one night, a rumor that the Germans were about to overrun Lvov spread like wildfire through the Jewish refugee community. The authorities instructed the refugees to remain indoors and not to light their usual

Friday night candles. The Jewish population went to bed full of fear and apprehension.

In fact, the Germans were not about to overrun Lvov. The Russians had only spread the rumor to consolidate the refugees so that the deportation roundups could proceed, and the net could be pulled in more easily. The Machiavellian ruse worked well. The Jews were all found in their homes.

Eliott recalled: "Five o'clock or four o'clock [in the morning]. There was a lot of people in this building. In our room there was many people and there was many rooms. The soldiers knock on the door like this, you know with a bayonet. Almost breaking in. We asked: 'Who is it?' because they woke us up. So they say: 'Russian soldiers.' So at least we were happy." (A clearer indication of the tenor of the times can hardly be cited: If one recognized the soldiers breaking through one's door as not being from the German enemy side, it was sufficient reason to be happy.) "We opened up. People were sleeping half naked on the floor on straw mattresses. And waking up like four or five o'clock in the morning was terrible! I remembered all my life. They chased us out. They didn't let us take anything. The people started to dress. My mother tried to put a little bit in a bag, but the soldier pushed her away. My father also tried to take things with him. What could my father do? He couldn't fight. It was very brave for him to keep quiet. Because you see, little punks like seventeen, twenty-year-olds with bayonets like mad dogs were chasing us out. There were families that could be parents to these soldiers. All older, and the soldiers chased them out. I was terrified. It's absolute . . . it's a nightmare . . . a nightmare! A soldier pushed us downstairs. He was screaming: 'Get out! Leave the place! Otherwise we burn this.' Was brutal, very brutal." Eliott's voice had risen in outrage and indignation. His words tumbled out of his mouth in half sentences to describe the affronts, indignities, and humiliations that were once more being heaped on the hapless refugees.

"Outside were waiting trucks—open trucks. They push us about like cattle. We were terrified and mad. Everyone was talking. This was like being animals. They treated us worse than animals. My father was mad. They were screaming, but nothing could help. They were the people who conquered us. We didn't have a choice. They brought us to the train station. We didnt see my uncle. He was maybe in another train. Each truck went to a different train. They took out a whole city. Lot of Jews were there. Many of the refugees were Jewish people who had escaped from the Germans."

The horror of that night stayed with Eliott all his life. It would appear that nothing much worse could happen than banishment to Siberia via cattle car. But as usual, Lonek's "good fortune" tended to come in the shape of avoiding worse calamities. If it is possible to speak of good fortune in reference to being deported, the June transport had one great advantage: the weather was not cold. True, it was hot inside the boarded-up cattle car and thirst became unbearable, but at least deportees did not freeze to death while traveling to collection points, or after boarding the trains.

Perhaps it also should be noted that it was "fortunate" for Lonek to be deported because at a later date the Germans did invade and drive out the Russians—but not before the Russians ruthlessly murdered hundreds of refugees who had been "lucky" enough to have so far escaped the transports. Hundreds of others who had been imprisoned for no particular reason were shot in jails. The bloodsoaked condition of these prisons shocked the civilians who later viewed them.[19] Sometimes the Russians had used guile to convey the prisoners to places of execution. A mock pardon was read to the summoned prisoners, who were then handed their clothes. Under the guise of being freed, they were driven to a forest where they were shot, and after being relieved of their clothes, buried naked. Long columns of prisoners, as young as fourteen years of age, who had been directly taken out of school, were marched toward the Russian border, frequently to be shot and killed on the road or upon arrival.[20] One such column under German air attack was divided into criminal and political prisoners, and roughly fifteen hundred "politicals" were machine gunned while the criminals, after burying the "politicals," were set free.[21]

In later years, mass graves and obviously tortured bodies were found by the hundreds in wells and other remote places. In fact, during the years 1939–41 while the Russians occupied a smaller part of Poland than the Germans, they killed far more people than did the Germans during that time. By the time the Germans attacked the Russians on June 22, 1941, 1.25 million Poles had been forcibly placed in labor camps or in prisons or had been forced into settlements scattered over the Soviet Union.[22] Thirty to 40 percent of all deportees were Jewish.[23] Although eastern transports from Russian-occupied Poland did not mean almost certain death as did eastern transports from Germany, the chances for survival were bleak.

When Lonek and his family, overcome with fear and misery, were herded into the cattle car, they were unaware that they had narrowly escaped the deadly mayhem created by both the retreating Russian forces and the invading German army. At least every member of the family was still alive.

CHAPTER VII

The Icy Void

The cattle trains stretched endlessly along the platform; each unit was boarded up, leaving only one or two spaces open for air.[1] Up to sixty deportees were stuffed into each car by bayonet-wielding guards. That task accomplished, the doors were forcefully locked in anticipation of departure. But even with the doors closed, the trains did not move. They continued to stand in the station, in winter in the freezing cold, in summer in the burning heat, and at night in total darkness. The prisoners stood inside the nonmoving trains sometimes for two days, sometimes three, sometimes even for a week.[2] They were not told how long this torturous delay might last, nor were they given water or food. Because of lack of air and agonizing thirst, the dying began rapidly.[3] In their desperation for water, children licked the frost that had formed on nails inside the cars; they pushed their hands through the small window and attempted to reach the snow on the roof.[4] The prisoners became stuck to the icy walls and to the floor of their prison, and they kept dying.[5] When well-meaning citizens approached the trains to bring some succor, horse and foot militia chased them away.

When the train finally departed, the prisoners' condition did not improve. The lack of water continued to torture them. On some trains, evil-smelling, oily water was drawn from the locomotive and issued as drinking water. On other trains, women were allowed to fetch water once a day because the general assumption was that men would prove more likely to escape. Although there were wells at every stop, the prisoners were prevented from drawing water by their guards. Meals were sparse and rare. A watery, sour liquid passed as soup, and small amounts of moldy bread were distributed very occasionally; in one case, only five times in fourteen days.[6]

As the trains traveled on and on, the temperatures became more extreme, in winter dropping as low as −70°. The few stoves that actually worked presented a serious fire hazard in the crowded cars.

Not only hunger and thirst tormented the deportees; it was also the appalling hygiene. Tightly packed together, the prisoners could only sit or sleep with their limbs interwoven with each other. With large numbers of ailing people onboard, the odors soon became unbearable: "The worst was the bathroom. We had to go in front of everyone into a hole in the floor of the wagon. In the beginning the people were extremely embarrassed, especially the women."[7] Because they could not wash, lice soon became a torture. The riders suffered from foul air, hunger, thirst, dirt, tormenting lice, heat, cold, sickness, darkness, and mortal fear.[8]

Some trains had an attached refrigerated unit to receive the bodies of those who died during the journey; other trains did not have such conveniences. In those cases, bodies rested among the living until the train came to a stop and then they were unceremoniously tossed out and left for the locals to bury. Between long stops, mothers were forced to throw their dead children through the window bars.

The length of the journeys varied from two weeks to four months, and different seasons presented different horrors. Lonek was fortunate that his transport departed in June. The officials did not need to go from car to car collecting the bodies of frozen babies as they did on winter transports. On the other hand, the captives on the winter transports were able to gather snow to satisfy their thirst while Lonek had to wait parched for rainwater to satisfy his.

Eliott shuddered at the memory of the journey. "When we arrived at the collection point, the cattle car right away was opened and they push us inside the cattle car, about twenty, thirty people and lock us. We could only stand. This way they let us stay for a few hours. Inside like you were choking. It was terrible! Screaming and swearing. We want to get out. It was terrible. Some people want to go to the toilet. Some people was thirsty, wanted water. Nothing. No one pay attention. And we was hot. Was a little window in the corner. I remember I stick my head out. The train was a big, long train, maybe two, three hundred cars. You couldn't see the end unless the train was going in a circle. Then you could see the end. I remember to me it looked like miles of train. Once a day, they open the train. They gave us a little water from the engine, hot water for tea. They gave us a little soup once a day, boiling water with a half potato swimming inside with a little bread. A piece of bread was like a square, two inches by three inches. Hard like a stone. We cut small pieces. You didn't know which corner to start to eat because we was afraid it was for the whole day. We was starving to death."

Eliott's father managed to fashion a bucket for collecting human waste from some debris he found on the road. Eliott believed that about once a day or so the train would stop, and different families would take turns trying to clean the car with leaves or whatever makeshift utensil they could find.

The train rumbled on and on, an endless journey into hell. "We was the lucky ones; we had a corner with the window. The car has two windows and one door in the middle. Little air come in. So many times people push us just to get a little breath of air. My mother was holding my brother. Was in the car not many children, so the others let my mother stay near the window. It was terrible! Terrrrible! It was yelling and screaming for two weeks. We was worried, we ask where are we going? They say: "We will let you know." We was waiting so hungry every day for noontime; the train stop and we can stretch ourselves and get a little borscht. The Russian soldiers didn't care. They was not in touch with us. They just was screaming and yelling: "Go inside, we leaving." If someone was sick, they didn't care. I don't remember if anyone died. We didn't know where we were or where we were going. We was in some desert in Russia. Once we got there, it was worse. At least on the train we are together. We are like a big family. Everybody tried to help each other. In a situation like this, I imagine people geting more stronger. Each one more polite to each other because we are in the same bad boat. If we don't cover the hole, the boat will go down and nobody will be left."

Eliott seemed to be exhausted by his recollections, and it might have been good to stop our session at this point. However, he seemed caught up in the past, and the words continued to tumble out as he visualized the train rolling across a vast, unfamiliar countryside to an unknown destination. As he was reliving his arrival in Siberia, he searched on the map for the place where he finally left the train, after what Eliott estimated to have been about two weeks' traveling time.

"Here, here is Sverdlovsk! This is the first impression when we arrived. The train stopped and we took all our possessions—nothing."

Eliott recalled arriving at his final destination: "We were sent to a little village. And there were already prisoners from the time of the czars, from long time ago. The communists took them to Siberia during the revolution, the new Russia. It was a labor camp. There were towers outside . We saw a couple of guards with dogs. I remember the towers, I don't remember the surroundings. This was like a desert, not a hot desert, a cold desert. It was a wasteland; the whole thing was woods. You could go through miles of woods and you can get lost in the woods. When you fall down, you cannot get up. Like sand."

"You mean like a bog or quicksand?" I asked.

"Yes, like quicksand. And on that part was also a river on one side. Wide, that is impossible to cross it.

"And the first day I remember when we arrived there, we saw little houses, built from wood, one [piece of wood] laying on the other."

"Log houses?" I suggested.

"Yes, exactly, log houses."

"But how did you know where to go when you arrived?"

"They showed us. These are the houses. 'There you are going,' they said. Empty houses. The prisoners before, they built houses all the time for prisoners coming in. And," Eliott added sarcastically, "they always have prisoners from against the government coming in. In this hotel everybody will be ready! My father asked where he could get a number or something like this." Eliott commented again caustically: "Which suite is there for us? They divided out with the list. They called out the names, and this one goes to this-and-this room and that one goes to another room.

"My father went to the first house he saw. He talked to the man in the house. My father spoke Russian, I told you. So he spoke to the man and the man told him where he was from, and already about twenty years staying there in this accommodations, in this vacation home! I heard him say something like: 'You will die here. They will never let go of you in your life.' This I remember. He said: 'This is your last stop.' I was shocked to hear that we came here to die. His wife, he chased her out. I remember like today. And my mother said: 'Why did he chase out the woman?' And my father said: 'Because he was afraid that she would talk to the Russian government officials against him if he talks against the government.'" Lonek had just witnessed an aspect of the communist state that pervaded every part of Russia, its conquered territories, and its prisons and labor camps, and that contributed to the prisoners' total sense of helplessness: the authorities' determination to manipulate the citizens into destroying each other. Human relationships were undermined as the population recognized that mere survival frequently depended on the denouncing and betrayal of others, no matter how closely allied. Power changed hands constantly as the leaders fell under the scythe of the ever-changing, fickle rule of those above them. Because laws, rules, and the party line were arbitrarily and illogically altered, there was never a way of identifying what act, what mere phrase, could lead to one's demise. Thus, the government not only ruled by killing, deporting, and imprisoning but also by undermining dignity, self-respect, all trust, all close relationships, and the ability to predict the consequences of one's actions, no matter how innocent.[9]

"We were very shaky. We were very scared. My parents were scared. They couldn't run away. Where could you run away? There was no way to go. They was very depressed. 'Eighty percent of the people die in this place,' the man said. 'You never leave alive.' The man was right. From hunger you couldn't stay alive."

Frightened and dispirited the families proceeded to their assigned log house. They were devastated by what greeted them. The conditions of the shacks were appalling. The prisoners saw "a falling down mud hut without windows, without doors, with a hole in the roof over the chimney and a mud floor. In case of rain, water leaked through the clay roof dropping together with pieces of wet clay. As for furniture, nobody would even have dreamt of it."[10] Another deportee recorded that "there were such bedbugs in the barracks and so many of them that at night if you struck a match your body was black and the walls were gray with bedbugs."[11] Another scourge were the biting mice "as big as cats,"[12] which jumped over the sleeping deportees at night and bit them. [13]

Lonek's family had to share their quarters with two other families: a young couple and a family with two daughters. The hut contained no furniture only an iron stove for cooking and a pot, which mostly contained only potato peels. Because Lonek's family arrived in summer, fresh air streaming through holes cut in the walls made the temperature quite bearable. In winter those gaping holes were another matter. For sleeping, there were sacks of hay. But little Heimek refused to lie down at night. He knew that children go to sleep when it is dark outside, but because the sun remained high during the summer months, he cried and refused to go to bed. For bathroom facilities, there was an outhouse, and the families sharing the hut took turns carrying water from outside in a big drum. Later, his father built a bench and, together with another prisoner, a carpenter, he constructed a bathtub out of wood.

After the harrowing cattle car journey, after the shock of arriving in a most inhospitable countryside and being assigned to barely livable quarters, the deportees were given no more than a day, or at the most two, before being commanded to report for heavy labor. The work schedule for the prisoners in Lonek's camp rarely varied. The guards, who were not allowed to speak with the prisoners, knocked on the door of the houses at about five or six o'clock in the morning. The prisoners asssembled in long lines waiting to be told to march to their work site which could be as much as ten to fifteen kilometers away. In summer, they worked long hours. Twelve to fourteen hours was the norm. In winter, when days were very short due to the proximity to the North Pole, the men worked only a few hours a day, occasionally continuing their work after dark.

Both men and women were assigned dangerous, backbreaking work. Men, who had never done physical work, were now felling huge trees from dawn to nightfall. Women were employed in such tasks as carrying heavy logs and planks, digging ditches, carrying manure, scything, and clearing railroad tracks.[14] When a woman pushing a dumpster in a mine begged to be given lighter work, the director replied: "There is no lighter work for masters [referring to the Poles as the rulers of the Belorussians and Ukrainians before the Russian invasion], and you will be working in the mines until you die."[15] At times the women, for lack of other resources, carried their infants to work; in winter, the infants died of cold.

Children were also forced to do hard labor; the starting age varied according to different commanders' whims or the family's need for a wage earner. In some camps, even ten-year-olds were marched several kilometers to a work site where they were compelled to work twelve-hour days. Children were assigned highly dangerous work, such as driving tractors, sawing wood, grinding grain by hand, and carrying heavy boards from the sawmills. Some described their working conditions: "I was twelve years old and very little. I was not strong enough. I worked everywhere even on tractors with a trailer. I weeded wheat and vegetables and I scorched in the sun all day."[16] A particularly hazardous job was rafting: "They took all the boys and girls to work on the so-called rafting. That is very dangerous because you can drown. You had to go across the river from bank to bank. There were no planks or bridges. And it was all done through a floating forest. You jumped on a trunk and ran. When you jump, you can't go back because the forest is no longer behind you. So you stay on two logs and float with the tree. When the tree floats to the bank, you must jump as fast as you can."

The official workday still did not yield enough returns to prevent starvation, another former child laborer recalled: "Being fourteen, I started working to support the family consisting of six persons. After 16 days of sickness I had to get up in spite of the illness and tiredness and I had to go to work. I was the oldest in the family. Father and mother were very ill for two months. . . . I worked twelve hours without lunch and at home after work I would fix shoes to try to earn a morsel of bread and some clothes, because we walked around in rags."[17] A six-year-old explained that his father had died and his mother was ill, so "I gathered grass. . . . When I was hungry because there was nothing to eat, I went in the field to look for [steal] potatoes."[18] With remarkable resourcefulness, a starving youngster thought of a solution, which unfortunately did not last long: "There was no kitchen in the new settlement. One had to walk several kilometers to get the soup. I went to fetch soup [for other people] and for each portion I received three spoonfuls. Because I was bringing five or six portions, I was eating soup every day. Once I almost froze to death on the way to the kitchen. My hands froze and I could not move for several weeks. I was forbidden to bring soup anymore. At this time my brother got sick and in a few weeks without medical help, he died. We buried him in the middle of the forest."[19] In their despair, children were forced to beg: "I went from cottage to cottage and sang. . . . I was shaming myself a lot but it couldn't be helped. One had to go because mama and brother were dying of hunger."[20] Food was an overriding need and could wipe out former values and standards. Stealing for some, who would never have considered such a step in their former lives, became a way of life. "In the camp we had to steal because if we had not we would have died."[21]

Supervisors mercilessly set work quotas too high to be reachable. In some areas, the allotment was 800 grams of bread and a slightly thicker soup than usual for the felling of twenty-two trees. Because the required task was beyond most people's capabilities, the prisoners usually ended up with a mere 200 grams of bread. When they could, they tried to include the previous day's production in each day's tally, thereby risking punishment for lying. Occasionally, it was possible to bribe a supervisor, who was himself a prisoner, to accept less wood than the assigned quota. Sometimes the prisoners managed to bring some wood home for fuel. But on the whole, they had to fulfill their norms before the guards would provide their families with starvation rations. Children were shown no greater mercy than adults: "When I rubbed my ears or nose at work [in the freezing cold], the foreman yelled why I wasn't working." Unable to fill their work quotas, children were forced to plow on for extra hours beyond the lengthy assigned workday.[22]

There were no extenuating circumstances, not even illness, for incomplete quotas. Failing to turn up for work could land the culprit in prison for "vagrancy," which meant that bread rations were reduced to the starvation level of 200 grams and 50 percent of the pay was deducted.[23] But it could be worse. One man was sentenced to eight years in prison for being late: it drove his wife mad.[24]

Inmates of the camps were given minimal pay to buy their starvation rations. To afford a plate of soup, two people had to pool their earnings.[25]

Frequently portions or all of the measly wages were withheld under various pretexts. Officials failed to record the numbers of work hours logged to avoid paying for them. People resorted to eating dogs, horsemeat, and weeds. A youngster working in a mill simply ate the raw flour.[26] Those who had been able to bring anything sellable from Poland attempted to trade these items for food with members of the local population: "We traded for very low prices because the natives, despite their own shortages of clothing and footwear, couldn't give us more. They didn't have anything to put in their mouths themselves. A few more things were sold, the last pillow pulled from under the head of a sick child. . . . Then began slow death from hunger and cold."[27]

In theory, the deportees were to be paid for their work so that they could buy food. Food rations varied from camp to camp and were always insufficient. Pleas to the commander elicited responses such as: "You should either get used to it or die."[28] At times mothers gave their own food to their children and thereby starved to death.[29] At other times, survival fell on the children's shoulders. A thirteen-year-old reported mournfully: "Mother and sister died April 7, 1942, and April 21, 1942. . . . My older sister and I buried almost the whole family in the course of a month. Not long after, my father died. We were left two orphans. Death by hunger looked us in the eyes, but I defended myself as best as I could to stay alive so someday I could tell how they mistreated us Poles in Russia. Not just my family died of hunger, but many others died. I remember that in one *kolkhoz* [collective farm] there were seven families that died of hunger. All that was left was one two-year-old child. The child cried when I went into the house and said to me: 'Daddy doesn't want to get up. Zosia cries and cries.' The child really was hungry, because it turned out the parents died the night before."[30]

Hygienic conditions were practically nonexistent. "A small muddy stream flowing through the kolkhoz served as a well, lavatory, laundry, and watering place for cattle."[31] No wonder that such illnesses as typhus, dysentery, scurvy, pneumonia, malaria, pellagra, and ulcers were rampant. Mostly they were left untreated, with the expected results. Even if a hospital were nearby, commanders frequently denied permission for the use of a horse to transport the patient.

Not that it was necessarily an advantage to be in a hospital. Even there, there was a shortage of everything, including blankets and food. An already weakened patient quickly froze to death. The wards were so overcrowded that the sick were placed on tables and floors amidst dirt and lice. When a doctor made his rounds, he carried with him a wooden box for supplies that contained nothing but cotton and bandages.[32] The staff paid scarce attention to prophylactic measures. Children with one type of contagious disease were not separated from those with other ailments. The same unsanitized spoon was used for dispensing medicines to all the patients on one ward. Syringes were neither sterilized nor airtight. "Mother went to the hospital and they didn't treat her. She came home and died of hunger."[33] A twelve-year-old recorded his experiences in the hospital: "They were performing surgeries without even putting any ointment on. They took a knife and started cutting. It was very painful."[34]

Lonek became acutely aware that hunger overrode all loyalties. "I remember the newlywed couple," recollected Eliott. "They were sleeping at night. The husband stole the bread from his wife. It was terrible when this happened. All my life I remember this. As a kid I was watching them."

Eliott also remembered the two teenage girls, about twelve and thirteen years old, part of the family who shared their space. The girls seemed to suffer because of the lack of privacy. "They used to be embarrassed. They used to hide themselves. Be modest."

Because there was no opportunity for seclusion, there was not much opportunity for sexual contact. Eliott guessed there was not much desire for it either. "From all the unhappiness, you lost your appetite for sex. This was not the time. Not a problem. It was so sad, so terrible, the whole thing. You didn't have any appetite to think about sex. You were thinking just to get a piece of bread or a piece of sugar that you can drink with tea. This other thing, this was luxury." It would seem that the families Lonek lived with were more discreet than some others. Other children reported that the grim situation led some adults to lose all restraint.

That the families Lonek lived with managed to stay on good terms with each other, even though they were hungry, melancholic, and in continual close proximity to each other, was surely to their credit. "The women had to take turns using the stove. They got along. In a situation like this, people tried to help each other. They did not get on each other's nerves because we were all in the same boat. But, you know, still sometimes there was an argument. I imagine like in every good family."

Lonek's father instantly grasped that felling trees was such heavy labor that it might threaten his survival. He therefore claimed before the authorities that he was a metalworker, a much-needed skill. As a result, he was assigned to sharpening knives and the like, a much less physically exhausting job.[35] While Lonek's father worked, his mother tried to look after the children. She sewed if she could find some material and cooked whatever food could be foraged. Although there was little contact between the Polish and Russian prisoners, the Russians managed to caution the Polish prisoners to prepare for the terrible, freezing, sunless winter. As a result, Lonek was sent to the woods to collect mushrooms and berries. The Russian prisoners, who had been exiled much longer than the Jewish and Polish arrivals, advised them how to avoid the poisonous ones. Lonek's mother stretched a rope inside the house and hung mushrooms to dry for the winter. Lonek also combed the woods for red currants. They were a little sour, but when his mother could obtain some sugar, she made jam out of them. There was no hope of obtaining meat. Lonek was proud of being able to help the family survive, but he battled bouts of fear and terror when he roamed the woods for food. The threat posed by dangerous bears wandering through the forest was heightened when Lonek occasionally lost his way. "I was scared. How I go back? How I go back? So I remember my mother told me that when you're lost, remember to go with the sun. When the sun goes down, you know where to come back."

Lonek's father, ingenious as usual, constructed a fishing basket that could be lowered with a string into the river and immediately trapped any fish that entered it. On lucky days, the basket was so heavy that Eliott had to drag it behind him, but on other days, the basket remained empty, particularly during the harsh Siberian winter when a hole had to be dug in the ice through which to lower the basket. Then, his mother would encourage him again and again to walk scantily dressed into the freezing cold through an ice tunnel the family built, and stand at the river's edge, hoping that a fish would land in his homemade container. Eventually, the dreadful Siberian winter began to threaten. The people owned only the clothes they had had on their backs when they were rounded up in Lvov. Later, they were given a parka, a hood, and tire-soled shoes to manage the cold as best they could. The snowfall was deep and endless. Eliott shuddered as he conjured up those dreadful winter months: "The winter was very heavy there. If you went outside, your fingernails grew numb; right away you were frozen. Lots of people lost their toes in cold weather. You spit and in midair it turned to ice. I remember as a child the snow covered me up to the neck." At times, the snow would accumulate so high that the front door could be pried open only with great force.

People died like flies from cold, hunger, and disease. The bodies were placed in the river unless the ice was too thick. "In Siberia, 60 percent of the people died from cold weather, from malnutrition. Was terrible. You go around with twenty or thirty layers of *shmattes* [rags] around you." Eliott pointed to a small plaza in front of our window: "The river was like the distance from this house to there You know when I go there I came back frozen—like a piece of wood." His voice revealed the outrage he felt, the wonder that life can be so horrific: "The situation like this, you don't know. . . . Sixty percent of the people die!" He drew out the word *die* to convey the feeling. "Diiieeeee! You imagine!"

Wood for heating was essential, but spotting loose-lying timber in the snow-filled landscape was a strenuous task. One day, when Lonek was unable to detect any, his mother asked him to cut some off a tree. The saw slipped, cutting him severely. Somewhere his mother found a nurse who ministered to him. Nevertheless, he carried the scar the rest of his life. Yet Lonek never faltered in his quest to help the family to survive. As Sholem Aleichem remarked: "You have to survive—even if it kills you."

Although Lonek felt a strong sense of pride in his ability to help his family survive, the days were difficult, dreary, and depressing. For one, there was no school. Lonek's mother tried to teach him by reciting the months of the year in Russian, telling him stories, and reading him books when she could lay her hands on any. But Lonek recalls: "It was sad, so terrible the whole thing." His little brother became ill and without medical care, his mother tried to restore him to health by feeding him little bits of bread. All kinds of unfamiliar and deadly diseases plagued the prisoners. One of the worst was "cynga," possibly due to a vitamin deficiency, which painfully affected the flesh of the gums.

Everyone, including Lonek, felt hopeless. Most of the time, he cried. His parents' personalities had changed. They had lost their happy demeanor, their smiles, and their chatter, and it was clear that they were angry at their fate. "Everyone didn't know why this happened to us. After all, what is the reason? We weren't the enemy of the Russians. We just wanted to stay in Lvov. My mother was even working for the Russians there. We didn't do anything. We didn't steal, we didn't kill nobody. Why did we deserve this? What is the use to bring us so far, traveling for two weeks and to come to Siberia for no reason. My parents were trying to survive. They didn't know what would be the next thing. And there we were, I believe almost a year there. The guard told us: "This is your last stop. Here you only come out with a box or they throw you in the river." That's what they told us from the beginning when we arrived. They were right. Another year or two, nobody would be left alive."

Death from overwork, malnutrition, climate, and disease stalked the camp. The indifference and cruelties of the overseers worsened an already desperate situation. A thirteen-year-old girl described her father's death while laboring: "My father felt weak while working. We wanted to save him. But the overseer said that nothing was wrong with him. All eyes were watching. Without help he died in the forest. In the evening, when we returned from work, we were brought my father's body. All night, my mother and the children stood over my father's body and chased the mice away. In the morning from several shirts we sewed a 'cape for the dead' and buried him"[36]

Lonek had no tales to tell of anyone in authority ever extending a kind word or look. Under such crushing circumstances, Lonek's parents had no optimism to offer their son. Lonek saw people dying every day. He was fearful of the future, contemplating that his father, mother, little brother, or perhaps he himself might die. After all, this was to be their last stop.

Then one day, a miracle occurred, a miracle so astounding, so unanticipated that no fiction writer could ever dare to suggest such a turn of events. Truth was indeed going to be stranger than fiction. Lonek and family would, in spite of all the dreadful prophecies, be able to leave Siberia—not in a box—but alive. Siberia was not to be their last stop after all.

CHAPTER VIII

The Gates Open

The news that the prisoners would be released came suddenly. Eliott's voice was filled with wonder and amazement as he related: "I remember one day in spring or summer of 1942—it was like a big holiday—everybody started to walk outside the house. I asked my father: 'What is it?' He said: 'We are going back. If we want, we can go.' They gave us passports and food stamps so we could go where we want in Russia. All of a sudden we got out. Like you don't eat a couple of weeks and suddenly you get food as much as you want. Unbelievable! I remember we went outside to see what happened to the guards." At this point, Eliott, almost hugging himself, smiled and laughed, his being flooded with relief at the memory. "We didn't see any of the guards! They didn't let the Russian prisoners outside. We were on this side and they were on that side, they didn't want us to mix together. So all the left side was open. There was nobody there on the towers, only on the Russian side. My father said to me: 'See, we can go wherever we want.' I was very happy, very happy."

The Poles and the Jews among them were suddenly set free to go anywhere in Russia. What could have catapulted the deportees to freedom so suddenly, so precipitously? As abruptly as they had been rounded up and deported, so as suddenly and seemingly without cause they were released. There was a cause, and its roots lay in faraway London, where in response to the German advance into Russia, the Polish Government-in-Exile had begun negotiations with the government of the Soviet Union, which led directly to Lonek's gaining freedom. As on previous occasions, Lonek's and his family's lives had been decisively affected by faraway political negotiations and intrigues.

After their release, the family learned the reasons for their deliverance.

Eliott explained: "Russia was very occupied with Germans. It was fighting for its life, and the Russians needed more soldiers because every day the front got bigger and bigger because the Germans were deeper inside and so the Russians needed soldiers. In order to get the release of the prisoners, the Polish Government-in Exile promised they would go into the army."

Eliott was correct. His change of fortune was brought about by the turning of the tables on Russia. After the Nazi-Soviet Pact in 1939, the Russians and Germans had carved up Poland between themselves. But on June 22, 1941, the Germans marched into Russia—and Stalin went into shock. In London, General Wladyslaw Sikorski, prime minister and commander-in-chief of the Polish Government-in-Exile, had watched the Russians devour and devastate the part of Poland they had occupied. With the Soviet Union's very existence threatened, the Polish prime minister seized the timely moment to negotiate with Stalin. After all, both countries were now on the side of the Allies.

Sikorski had a number of reasons for opening negotiations with the Russians. Most important, he wanted to free the Poles who were languishing in Russia's prisons. In addition, he hoped that Poles fighting with the Allies under a Polish flag would lay the groundwork for the restoration of a free Poland after the war. The British government supported Sikorski's efforts because they hoped to use the Polish soldiers in their hard-pressed fight against the Germans in Africa. There were up to 1.5 million Poles— about 400,000 of them Jews—in Russia, including those who had fled to Russian-occupied territory of their own accord, as well as prisoners-of-war and vast numbers who had been arbitrarily deported by the Russians. Without some rapprochement with Russia, these unfortunates would be lost forever.

The Polish Government-in-Exile hastily took advantage of Stalin's precarious military position and bargained for the release of all the Poles who had fled to Russia after the German invasion and all those who had been taken prisoner by the Russians. On July 30, 1941, Poland and Russia signed the Sikorski-Maisky Treaty, becoming strange bedfellows indeed. The treaty entitled the Poles to open an embassy in the Soviet Union, as well as welfare centers from which its delegates could fan out to offer some assistance to the exhausted exiles.

Possibly one of the most significant and consequential stipulations of the agreement was the granting of "amnesty" to all Polish prisoners in Russia. Although amnesty is usually granted to guilty parties, in this case the Russians used it as a face-saving device for releasing innocent men, women, and children. Not only did General Sikorski obtain their freedom, but he laid the foundation for a semi-independent Polish army in Russia. Instead of fighting under Russian command, the Poles would serve under the Polish flag and under Polish command.

Could a plan that provided for a modicum of independence for Poles on Russian soil be sold to Stalin? Was it conceivable that this bloodthirsty tyrant would permit an incarcerated mass of people at his mercy to escape his clutches? The bait was the need for more manpower to fight the Germans. The Poles, with the support of Britain, persuaded Stalin that a great deal of manpower was being wasted while able-bodied Polish men lingered in prison camps. The Poles promised that if these men were released they would be incorporated into an army.

The inconceivable happened. Stalin, desperate in the face of Germans swarming into Russia, not only agreed to the formation of an army of Polish men inside Russia, but also consented to the Polish army being commanded by a Polish general, though under the High Command of the Soviet Union. On August 12, 1941, the Presidium of the Supreme Soviet of the Soviet Union officially granted "amnesty to all Polish citizens who are at present deprived of their freedom on the territory of the USSR either as prisoners-of-war or on other *adequate* (italics mine) grounds."[1] The groundwork for this decree had been laid by the Sikorski-Maisky Treaty and included both military personnel and civilians. It gave Lonek and his family another chance for survival. As on previous occasions, the amnesty came none too soon. It is estimated that by the time it was proclaimed, half of the prisoners were already dead.

Among those released from the infamous Moscow Lubianka prison was Wladyslaw Anders, the Polish general, who was selected to lead the Polish army. Immediately he began to organize a Polish army in southern Russia. Hundreds of thousands of Poles emerged from prisons from all over the Soviet Union and began to stream toward the south to General Anders' headquarters. They headed to the warmer regions of Russia not only for patriotic reasons, but also because joining the Polish army removed them to some extent from Russian jurisdiction. As they left, the survivors mourned over three hundred thousand victims who had succumbed either during deportation or in the camps.[2]

It was no simple matter to make so lengthy a journey under wartime conditions. The obstacles were numerous and formidable. To begin with, the prisoners had to be informed that they were permitted to leave. In some cases, this was done immediately, but sometimes considerable time elapsed. In the worst instances, the news either did not reach or was intentionally withheld from the prisoners. Resentful of losing free labor, com-

mandants at some camps simply ignored the order for months and prisoners labored on in ignorance. There were incidents in which the inmates
learned of their freedom through shreds of newspapers in which some items
arriving at the camp were wrapped. The commander of one camp had
known of the new edict for two months, but had craftily hidden it from the
prisoners. The inmates went on strike in order to be released immediately
and were threatened with withdrawal of food. It did not move them. High
government officials who had been summoned to break the strike attempted
to persuade the prisoners that, because of the danger of being bombed by
the Germans while traveling, it was in their interest to remain at the camp.
Failing to elicit a response, the officials then conjured up a picture of flooded
roads that would impede transportation. Undaunted, the prisoners replied
that they would walk to their destinations. Finally allowed to leave, they
arrived at the railroad station, only to find that they had insufficient funds
to board the trains. Infuriated, they insisted that as they had been brought
to Siberia without a railroad ticket, they should be allowed to return in the
same manner. Their complaints fell on deaf ears until by chance a Jewish
army lieutenant heard of their plight and referred them to a nearby Polish
official who came to the prisoners' aid.

Many unreleased prisoners realized that unless they took matters into
their own hands they would never escape from their commandant's clutches:
"We asked when we could leave and this went on for two months. Then I
met one of the foreman and he tells me whoever wants to leave the settlement has to spend time in prison. After this conversation I said to my
brother that we have to escape and this was what happened. On November 13, 1941, I, mommy and my brother escaped."[3]

The authorities resorted to various pretexts to detain their quarry.
One man was told that having received Russian hospitality for two years
he was now a Russian citizen and bound to Russian soil. He fled, walking
five days to the nearest railroad station.[4] Two older Jewish men were declared "religious offenders" and therefore in need of special release papers. Fortunately, they encountered a Jewish NKVD man who arranged
matters for them.[5] Even more devious trickery was used by a commandant who before informing the inmates of the amnesty gathered them
together and presented them with a contract to work in the forest for a
year. When the assembled prisoners refused to sign, he finally admitted
that, yes, they were free to leave the camp, but they were to stay in Siberia. The prisoners, joyful on hearing about the amnesty, paid no attention and departed en masse.[6]

Commandants in still other camps, afraid of a potential labor loss, began to fawn on the prisoners, promising them land, potatoes, seeds, utensils, wood, construction material, and even a cow for every family. Their earnest advice, that the future outside the camps was too insecure compared with the prisoners' current lives, not surprisingly, failed to sway the inmates. Some camp commanders resorted to another convenient, though not unusual tool—anti-Semitism. They proclaimed that amnesty did not apply to Polish Jewish prisoners, just to ethnic Poles. It was only due to the Jewish inmates managing to reach some authorities superior to the camp commanders that the Russian pharaohs finally "let the people go." Yet some commanders' malicious treatment of the Polish Jews continued to the last moment when they distributed food and clothing to the departing Poles, but none to the Jews.[7] A fourteen-year-old described the situation succinctly: "In September 1941 the moment of which everyone dreamed took place: the amnesty was proclaimed. But it was difficult to break away from the hell, because the red devils having caught a man alive let only a corpse leave. So we only got documents on February 20, 1942 and left for the south."[8]

The deportees had to reach a railroad station, but the commandants were frequently spiteful and uncooperative. In one camp, the commandant refused to lend the prisoners horses, forcing them to walk 30 kilometers with their belongings to the train station.[9] Inmates of a different camp walked 100 kilometers on foot in deep snow, also carrying their pathetic bundles.[10] Another group waited for five days for a boat to take them to a train station where they waited for a month for a train. In fact many prisoners walked for days or even weeks with barely any food and money to reach transportation or a Polish outpost.[11]

The prisoners were besieged by dangers. Many straggling travelers were intercepted by government officials and sent into Central Asia to labor once more under harrowing conditions. Robbers waylaid them to deprive them of their essential documents and the little they still possessed. Such unbridled violence resulted in the death of some of the helpless victims.[12] In spite of all barriers and impediments, a stream of thousands of Poles, among them thousands of Jews, many in rags and some even shoeless, wended their way slowly toward General Anders in the south of Russia on the border of Afghanistan.

Not everyone was able to reach a station or board a train. Those left behind frequently vanished forever, and many of those who entrained did not reach their goal. As on the previous journey, disease, hunger, and pure exhaustion snuffed out their lives. Children and the elderly were among the most vulnerable.

Lonek and his family decided to go to Tashkent. Probably one of the most fortunate aspects for Lonek was that his father was on that journey at all. Among the former Polish soldiers heading toward Tashkent, there were only several hundred officers, though roughly eleven thousand had been expected. General Sikorski and General Anders were baffled as to the whereabouts of the missing men and besieged Stalin with questions. The latter calmly assured General Sikorski that wartime difficulties were delaying the officers' arrival and that a number of them had escaped to Manchuria. The truth lay elsewhere—partly in the Katyn Forest where at a later date, the bodies of five thousand Polish officers were found.

The devilishly crafty manner in which the Polish officers had been led to their deaths was recorded by a physician who narrowly avoided such a fate.[13] Outstanding in his recollections was the day in March 1940 when the Polish prisoners were informed that they would be released in groups to return home. Their joy knew no bounds. There was one detail, which though barely noted, caused some unease. The men to be released did not depart by the main gate of the prison camp but, accompanied by grim-looking soldiers, were sent through a small, previously unnoticed exit, to an area behind a wall where they could no longer be seen by their comrades, loaded onto a series of trains under the usual excruciating conditions, and ferried through zigzag paths to various camps and finally to oblivion.

The rumor of returning home had purposely been planted among the officers to foster their cheerful cooperation. It was not a matter of lambs being led to slaughter. Rather like the Jews who had been misled and trapped by the SS, so too were the Polish officers ensnared by a well-oiled killing machine.

Like the other ill-fated Polish offers, the physician departed through the gate with high hopes only to find himself brutalized by the guards. He spent agonizing days, provided with only pieces of bread and herring and lacking water, transported in dark, toiletless, airless trains that crisscrossed the country aimlessly in order to confuse the inmates as to their destination.

Relatives of prisoners noted with concern and trepidation that between April and May 1940, all their communications went unanswered. The families were unaware that, much as the Nazis had decreed the Final Solution at the Wannsee Conference in Germany, the Soviet Politburo ordered the execution of Polish officers. The process was quickly and efficiently put into effect. The officers were brought by train and special trucks to locations prepared for the event. Then each officer was hauled to a ditch by two NKVD men and finished off by a third who fired a bullet into the soldier's neck. One of the locations for the killings was the Katyn Forest.[14] The doctor was fortunate enough to have been sent to Griazoviets, a prison camp. Probably Stalin decided that with the eyes of the world upon him, it was important to keep some Polish officers alive.

The lives of Polish soldiers had indeed been held cheap by the Russian military who executed many Polish officers, not only because of Politburo policy, but frequently based on personal whim, sometimes singly, other times in small or large groups. A captain's capricious mood was reflected when he remarked to a captured Polish officer: "This will teach you to be a professional [officer]" and then coolly shot him in the head.[15] From a group of five thousand surrendering Polish soldiers, six officers, eight non-commissioned officers, and one hundred fifty policemen were arbitrarily selected to be shot. In another incident—and there were many—about five hundred surrendering military men and policemen, including their commander, were locked in a town hall. In a sudden, unanticipated attack, they were machine gunned and pelted with hand grenades.

It had taken an amazing number of coincidences to keep Lonek and his family alive. Each trial ultimately saved them from the even more threatening events that followed. It was Lonek's father's deportation by the Germans that precipitated the family's swift departure from Jaroslaw and removed them from the grip of the SS. Likewise, the family's deportation to Siberia from Lvov spared them the bloodbath that marked the end of the Russian occupation and the deadly German invasion that came on its heels. Similarly, the seeming victories of the Germans over the Russians prompted Stalin to release the Polish prisoners, thus saving the family from probable death in the Siberian labor camp.

Underlying all these ironic, lifesaving turns was one particularly fortunate twist of fate: Lonek's father had initially been deported from Jaroslaw by the Germans as a Polish officer. Had they recognized him to be a Jew, they would have dealt him a harsher fate. The Russians deported Lonek's father as a Polish Jew. Had they recognized him to be a Polish officer, he would most likely not have survived.

Now Lonek could count himself fortunate again. His camp commandant had quickly released his prisoners.

Fortunately, Lonek's camp was located only a few miles from the railroad. Eliott described: "I remember my father make himself like a little carriage. We put all our possessions and we helped him move the little wagon on the dirt road until the railroad, about three or four miles away. It was like somebody comes from the dead!" The family was ill-prepared for the journey: They owned almost nothing except documents enabling them to travel and some ration cards with which to purchase food. Yet they were undeterred. Lonek's father focused on putting as much distance as quickly as possible between himself and his former prison. The family yearned to experience a warmer climate once again and decided to go directly to Tashkent, located in the province of Uzbekistan. At this point, Eliott showed me a map to demonstrate the enormous distances covered in their journey: From Poland to Ukraine, from Ukraine to Siberia, and now somehow they would travel from Siberia to Tashkent.

The trek south took a good deal longer than Lonek's parents had envisioned. The distance on the map looked considerably shorter than the actuality. Eliott could not recall the exact length of the journey, and it is not possible to ascertain its length from other travelers because the time experienced varied from one to two weeks up to several months. Hunger stalked the journey. When the train made either scheduled or unscheduled stops, the travelers would leave their carriage and forage in the fields for carrots, potatoes, and even grass to stifle their constant hunger. In some cases, the train would pull out leaving the despairing traveler behind. The dead were removed from the trains during halts at the station, a sight particularly dreaded by the children.[16]

To Lonek, the trip south seemed interminable. The train rambled on remorselessly day and night. Yet even though the cattle cars crawled through an endless landscape and came to repeated unexplained halts, Lonek considered the journey better than the one to Siberia. After all, the family was not headed for an unknown labor camp but away from one. Surely conditions in Tashkent could not be worse than the ones he had just experienced. Lonek recalls passing endless miles of cotton fields; the train would occasionally stop near fields of watermelon and honeydew, which he gathered as quickly as he could. Most of the travelers on Lonek's train were Polish Jews. The passengers did not encounter anti-Semitism from the local population. Eliott did not ascribe this to any particular friendly feeling on their part, but believed that their attitude reflected the immense depression and weariness that seemed to have settled over the countryside. There did not even seem to be enough energy to hate. "It was wartime and everybody was for himself." As the days wore on, relief gave way to worried anticipation. As Eliott put it: "The thought was of where will we go? What will be there was constantly on our minds."

"Did you feel anxious all the time?" I asked Eliott.

"What means anxious?"

"Well, did you worry all the time?"

"All the time. You worry all the time. You grow very quick when you are a child in a situation like this. You grow every day. You are almost like a big man."

Lonek had plenty to be anxious about, and his worries were not to be resolved by his arrival in Tashkent. The city, which conjures up pictures of veiled women and wonderful tales of old, was now merely another brutal city with milling refugees.

CHAPTER IX

Tashkent

When Lonek and his family arrived in Tashkent in 1942, the city bore little resemblance to its former self: a center of Islamic culture and an educational oasis boasting theaters, museums, and a university. Now it was overrun with destitute refugees who needed places to live, food to eat, and money with which to buy it. No government organizations to help or guide them existed. An observer noted: "People were dying of hunger. [Crews] would then ride through the streets and pick up the corpses with a pitchfork and throw them on the sleighs and drive them outside the city. Then they threw them on a pile, pour crude oil over it and burn it." A thirteen-year-old Jewish boy described the appalling conditions in Samarkand, which duplicated those of Tashkent: "It was hard to believe the poverty in Samarkand. Neither bread nor work could be gotten in the city. We sold everything for a piece of bread, for which we had to stand in line. . . . The worst thing was the typhoid epidemic. Thousands of people died in hospitals, hundreds dropped in the streets because they couldn't find a place in the hospital."[1]

A twelve-year-old noted: "In Samarkand we met many refugees. My father tried to get into the Polish army but because he was Jewish they didn't want to take him. Three weeks we wandered in the streets in Samarkand without a roof over our heads, until father and mother got sick with typhus."[2]

Three hundred Polish relief offices, which had been established under the Sikorski-Maisky Treaty and were under the direction of the Polish Embassy, worked to locate, inform, and aid Polish refugees. Another vital responsibility was to find Polish orphans and place them in Polish orphanages. The difficulties were daunting. One official Polish report states that only one third of the 1.5 million refugees, scattered in remote regions of Russia and Siberia, were located. The Polish delegates also distributed food and medicines contributed by the United States and England.[3] There was particular concern about children, the elderly, women with dependents, and the sick, as well as those with large families. The work was complicated by the dearth of local goods. Blankets, clothes, and medicines had to be imported from abroad because local merchandise was scarce or nonexistent. Money had to be raised for their purchase in Britain and the United States; this was further complicated by the British's own gross shortages. Moreover, transporting goods across waters swarming with U-boats, floating mines, and subject to vicious air raids was a daunting task. One of the biggest shipments, 2,002 tons of merchandise, was sunk when the *Steel Worker*, a large ship, took a direct hit during an air raid in the port of Murmansk. Once goods did arrive, they had to be conveyed to their destination by the most primitive and cumbersome means—for instance, on the backs of donkeys and camels.

An additional barrier blocked the delivery of goods to the very needy Poles: Russian xenophobia and paranoia. For anyone in Russia to be involved with foreign funds and to make constant contacts with foreign officials aroused the worst suspicions, even though the Russian government had granted permission for such activities. The Russians frequently put roadblocks into the path of the dedicated Polish delegates, some of whom contributed a percentage of their own salaries to helping the dispossessed. In fact, as early as the summer of 1942, most of the Polish delegates had already been arrested by the Russian authorities.

A constant threat was the NKVD's roundups of the homeless, who were then forcibly sent to collective farms. Conditions there were appalling. Exhausted, starving workers dressed in rags attempted desperately to fill their work quotas to earn minimal bread rations. However, conditions on the street were so ghastly that some former Siberian prisoners even resorted to volunteering to be sent to the "relative safety" of collective farms. Frequently, even such desperate moves were in vain because the members of some of these farms expelled newcomers when food supplies were exhausted. It must have been total despondency that drove one man to write a letter to President Roosevelt pleading for help. In short order, the writer was rounded up by the NKVD, and his wife died of typhus.[4] Some refugees preferred even their former imprisonment in Siberia over their current state.

The Jewish Poles confronted another obstacle—the intransigent Polish anti-Semitism of some of the Polish relief delegates, who withheld goods from them and blocked their path to General Anders. Although the Polish government issued directives advising the delegates to help all entitled Polish citizens, individual officials frequently violated such orders. They preferred to shunt the scarce funds exclusively to ethnic Poles.

As a result, the returning Jewish prisoners were on their own. Some found shelter in stables and barns—others in cellars, lean-to shacks, and mud huts. Still others lived under open skies and slept directly on unpaved alleys in freezing temperatures. As in the camps, whole families were ravaged by epidemics of dysentery, pneumonia, malaria, and typhus. For those lucky enough to survive, recovery could take weeks or months. Parents tried to nurse their children and each other. Youngsters attempted to save their parents' lives by caring for them or begging and crying at hospital doors to have them admitted. Often such efforts failed and the children were soon orphaned. The sight of scattered bodies of young and old was so common that even children became inured to the sight. Those who died in hospitals were sometimes buried so speedily by the authorities that relatives never found their burial places.

The ex-prisoners' vulnerability to illness was, in good part, due to their half-starved condition. The price of food in general, and bread in particular, skyrocketed. The Jews living in the city tried to help the newcomers, but were usually too poor themselves to be of much assistance. Some ex-prisoners were fortunate to find employment in menial jobs, such as carrying sacks of flour or bricks. But the monthly quota of bread was below subsistence level, and wages were usually less than the price of a loaf of bread. Bribery was rampant, and at times Jews lining up for their ration quota would be pushed out of line by Uzbeks who, to add insult to injury, cursed the Jews. In their desperation, refugees sometimes stole from each other, and the more sophisticated local Uzbekians stole from the refugees. Some enterprising refugees even risked buying items, such as bread, tea, or soap from black-market connections, and then selling those products for minimal profits. Sometimes children were used as vendors because they aroused less suspicion and if caught could claim they were orphans, thus not endangering their families.

Lonek's parents were fortunate to find small, very cramped quarters in Tashkent. At least they had a roof over their heads. Eliott glanced around the moderately sized study where we were working: "The whole room what we have was like half the size of this room. Maybe six by seven, maybe six by eight. Very little room. This side my brother with my mother were sleeping; the other side my father and I were sleeping." Yet the newcomers preferred their new quarters over the camps in Siberia and still hoped that life would not be quite as bleak as before. This was particularly true for Lonek who found fulfillment of a heartfelt wish: He found a friend. Eliott reminisced: "The people, they were all Moslems and they used to wear little yarmulkas like Jewish people. One day, I remember I got one friend, a little boy, and he used to take me to his school and introduced me to his parents as his friend. And I learned the language from him. I spoke Uzbek. Children pick up language very quickly."

"Do you still speak the language?"

"No, no, only one word. I remember the word *apricot* in Uzbek. That's all. My friend used to take me home. He used to give me some food. One day I came to his home and saw—like in the Mediterranean, and in India too—it is like half round on the top and it's like when you send children to camp."

"A trunk?"

"Yes, but the trunk is round and on the top it has a nice design and inside it was full of pita bread. And he gave me three or four pieces, and I came home and said to my mother: 'Mother, you won't believe what I saw today' and she said: 'What did you see?' And I said, 'I saw a whole coffin with this pita bread!' And this was a big deal!"

It was indeed a big deal. Lonek had never imagined so much bread in one place. Even now, as Eliott described to me the hoard of bread he had spied in his friend's home, he spoke as jubilantly and excitedly as if he were currently glimpsing the treasure. "All their lives, some people remember they saw a whole coffin with gold. This is what I saw. This is what I remember! I have a sickness. I don't throw out food. My children know about it. They never throw out food. Sometimes I see someone throw out bread, it's terrible. I am like a sick man every time that bread gets on the floor."

His words were now tumbling over each other as he pointed to a morsel of bread on the table. "I remember, a piece of bread like this; I would give my life for it. Even if the bread is hard, you understand, I don't throw it out. I use it for something. It is maybe a sickness, but it is the sickness of my life. It is a part of the jungles that I was in."

To avoid starvation, it was essential to supplement the rations. Violating the law, the refugees collected peanuts and boiled them for soup. Those not bound by Jewish dietary laws searched for and cooked tortoises.

Lonek supplemented rations by cutting the bottom off a bottle with heated thread and fishing with this contraption in the river. Because fishing was illegal, Heimek was forbidden from mentioning his brother's activities to a soul. But keeping such a big secret was too hard for a little boy unable to foresee the terrible consequences of discovery by the authorities.

When his parents learned that Heimek had revealed the secret to outsiders, they spanked him, a memory that stayed with him through adulthood.[5]

Then a new tragedy fell. Lonek's father became very ill. Now there were no able-bodied men in Lonek's family who could, by dint of effort, increase the family's ration. The most important member of the family, whose resourcefulness and ingenuity had been critical to the family's survival, was now laid low by sickness. Because the Russians stuck to the dictum that he who does not work does not deserve food, illness was a virtual death sentence.

While Lonek's mother looked after her husband and Heimek, it was now up to Lonek to forage sufficient food for the family's survival. "I don't want to be a hero, but this is the truth that without me the family could not survive. About five o'clock in the morning, I used to go in the field with a little pail. It was a farmer's field from a collective farm, and the farmers had already harvested the field. They didn't allow you to go there, but at night and in the very early morning, nobody was watching. They took out the potatoes already, but what was left over? I saw leaves and underneath I used to pick out potatoes." Eliott's voice seemed to echo the excitement of the challenging task of foraging for potatoes. "I used to make a little shovel from wood and dig a little deeper. Maybe I find another potato. And I also pick up some nuts the farmers left. My mother make soup from those nuts, and every time I eat nuts now, I remember the soup."

Lacking a fishing pole, Lonek, imitating his father, fashioned some artful contrivances for fishing. Eliott recounted: "I went to the river and I pick up fish. The river was very narrow and was not deep. I used to stand, I remember, on the side of the river and I put branches of the tree there. And then [when the fish] tried to sneak near the branches because they want to go through, I make like a little Niagara Falls and when the fish fall through, I snap them up with a piece of wood. I was always thinking how many fish I can catch to feed my father. So maybe Mommy could make something good for him to eat. Maybe I can save his life. Every time when I have five or six fish speared with a piece of string, I was so happy. I was running home. 'Here, Mommy, I have something for catch for today.' Tomorrow was another day, but we were thinking just to survive today. We were not thinking about tomorrow, just for today. My mother made soup and cake and many things from the fish."

And when there were no fish, his mother improvised. "Maybe there was something left over. We have some peanuts that I took from the farm, some potato I went and stole at four or five o'clock in the morning. I took a big can. I remember the can. I fill it up and I bring it home. My mother always encourage me. She always said: 'When you go out, you always bring something. You never come empty-handed.' It's true. I never came empty-handed. All their life, twenty, thirty years later, my parents remember that without me they couldn't survive. In a conversation with somebody, my mother always said: 'This is my son and he saved my life.'"

Lonek's mother also supplemented the family's diet by buying what Eliott remembers as camel food. These items resembled bricks made of grass: "Just grass pressed like brick they used to give to camels. And my mother would break it and make soup from this. I remember we were not allowed to eat it uncooked because it has poison. You have to boil it." In addition to food, cash was needed for other essentials of living. Without alternative means to earn cash, the family—like many others during this period—turned to the black market. Of course, the family no longer owned any possessions or valuables that were exchangeable for more practical goods. Whatever jewelry they had managed to hide from the German troops was long gone. Yet Lonek's mother—as ingenious as her husband—somehow managed to obtain linens to trade secretly. To avoid detection of her illegal sales, she wrapped the linens around her body and under her clothes, and then hired a horse and buggy to take her across the river where she would be less likely to be recognized and arrested. On one occasion, the crossing cart capsized and the rushing current swept it away. Lonek's mother, landing in the water, struggled desperately as the watersoaked linen nearly pulled her under. But the merchandise was too valuable to forfeit and the strong-willed woman managed to reach the shore. The driver had run away, but undeterred, she spread the linen in the sun, dried it and herself, and went on to sell her goods.[6]

Lonek's mother also augmented the family's wages by somehow obtaining a large piece of soap weighing ten to fifteen pounds, cutting it into small pieces, wrapping them in newspaper, and selling them in the streets through the illegal black market. Such efforts required Lonek and his mother to rise early in the morning, put Heimek into a neighbor's care, and set out for the five- or six-mile walk to town. In order to remain inconspicuous, Lonek's mother would leave Lonek on a street corner with the bulk of the goods, keep a package or two of the soap on her, and after selling them, return to Lonek to replenish her stock. Lonek, though recognizing the necessity of this pursuit, was nevertheless petrified of arrest. He would stand on the corner, searching for his mother's return but always apprehensive that the police would arrive first. "I was scared. They could send me to jail. But it was a question of survival." With tears running down Eliott's cheeks, he laughingly mocked his childish pleas: "When we go home, mommy? I want to go home."

Eliott talked about his mother with something akin to awed admiration. "She was a strong woman. A very strong woman. When I look at today, what she went through! To have children and to have a husband who is dying. She must be made from steel. From some supermaterial that does not exist. To go through what she went through in order to feed us, to cook, and to figure what will be." But in spite of Lonek and his mother's resourcefulness and dedication, the family remained hungry. "You ask me how is it to be hungry? It's like ticking like a clock."

"What do you mean: 'Your stomach feels like it is ticking?'"

"You are hungry. It feels like an empty stomach."

"You mean contractions?"

"Yes, contractions. Yes. Like an empty stomach. You feel the tongue want to go out, want to eat something. You try to drink water to fill up your belly. And that is all you are thinking all day; you are just thinking about food. People don't think of anything else but: 'How can I get a piece of bread?' Even if you are a little not so hungry, you put something in your pocket. Maybe you have it for later. You always worry. You always keep supply. You never stop hunting because you may be thinking in an hour or tomorrow you won't have nothing. I remember many times I went to bed and there is nothing I can do. If I complain, nothing will help. My mother didn't have, my father didn't have. Whatever she could, she gave me. My father was sick. My mother was very helpless. She didn't know what to do. Even I was the main supplier, but still I was a burden. No matter how I help, still. . . ."

Hunger was not the family's only constant companion. Illness also stalked the family. Without a doctor, Lonek's mother administered to sick family members her own primitive form of what Lonek called "penicillin." To do so, she would soak a piece of bread with cold water and put it on the patient's head. Due to malnutrition, Heimek lost almost all his teeth. "Every time one of his teeth was bad, they pull it out. Like an auto mechanic. It's like they pull a nail out of the wall." Heimek frequently suffered from various infections, which at one point impaired his hearing.

The family's circumstances worsened as Lonek's father's health deteriorated. "My father, he didn't talk. He was laying hopeless on the bed and he got fever, he got sweat. I don't know what kind of sickness. We asked for the doctor; they said they don't have one. Then came the nurse and she gave him a couple of pills. It didn't help nothing. I see it now. I see the bed, like a bench he was laying on. He was never complaining. No matter how bad he was, how he suffered, he never complained. You could see all the pain in his face. The only thing he asked once in a while that somebody give him a cigarette—he was a chain-smoker. My mother used to go out with me to the city to get some medicine. She asked some friends where she can get any herbs or something, but nothing. We were very worried. I was sure he wouldn't survive. I was thinking how many fish I can catch to feed him. So maybe Mommy could make something good for him to eat. Maybe I can save him. I remember I used to change the towels, put cold towels on his head, all the time. Make one wet, put one in the river to make it very cold and then bring it home and put it on his head." Even applying cold compresses was no simple matter in Tashkent!

As time went on, Lonek simply lived from day to day without any thought about the future. He hoped that life would continue in this desperate but still manageable routine. "I was the main supplier and my mother was taking care of my father and my father didn't know what had happened to him." As Eliott thought back on these harsh days, his voice suddenly became subdued, sad, almost secretive. As a rule, his words followed each other so rapidly that he dropped syllables and left sentences unfinished. Yet suddenly he spoke slowly and hesitatingly and his explanations came in fragments: "It was terrible. My father was sick. My mother was very hopeless. She didn't know what to do. Even I was the main supplier but still I was. . . . Another child is to feed another mouth. . . . No matter how I help, still. . . . One day my mother decided to. . . . I don't know how to say. . . . She went in the market. . . . Somebody was there from Siberia and told her that they are taking children of Polish soldiers in a camp, [long pause] in orphan home. My mother went home. I don't know . . . she spoke with my father. But anyhow the next day. . . . Another child is to feed another mouth." At this point his voice trailed off.

A disaster, one that was worse than all of his previous trials, was about to descend: What Eliott was trying to tell me, but was too painful to say, was that in her despair his mother had decided to put him in an orphanage.

CHAPTER X

Abandoned?

Twelve-year-old Lonek stared blankly at the passing vista. Most of the time, he cried. Although he was only vaguely conscious of the other children around him, he was acutely aware of the seemingly endless miles that were distancing him ever farther from his parents. How could he have been so suddenly wrested from his parents without a word, without an explanation, without a good-bye to his mother, his sick father, and his tiny tot of a brother? How would they ever know where he was being sent? How would they ever locate him again?

The events of his last days with his family had developed at such a furious, unexpected pace that, in retrospect, Lonek could barely sequence them. Two days before his lonely journey began, Lonek's mother had decided to place him in an orphanage. He remembered walking the 10 kilometers to the orphanage with his mother. "We walked there from the morning around ten o'clock. I remember the yellow land, not dark; like desert. I don't know exactly. I remember crossing a river. I imagine in winter was water there. But at the time almost nothing—maybe an inch or two of water. We crossed this."

"Did you know where you were going when you went with your mother?"

"She prepared me all the way. She was talking to me that: 'I need to give you away because it's terrible to see your father is sick, and I cannot do nothing.' And she was crying all the way we was walking." And Eliott, his voice expressing infinite sadness, repeated a refrain again and again: "I remember all my life. I remember!"

"How did you feel walking and hearing her explanation?"

"I was a child, what can I do? Your parents tell you, you listen—you don't say nothing."

When telling his story, Eliott recalled the smallest details of events—the shape of a tool his father made, the color of a door in his house, the sequence of events long past. Moreover, his reminiscences skipped from one episode to the next, so that frequently I would have to guide him back to our original topic. By contrast, when he was asked about his feelings, his answers tended to shorten, and he would return to the main thread of his story as quickly as possible. Although Lonek appreciated the importance of reflection, introspection about emotions was apparently more difficult for him than describing concrete events. Yet, though his words frequently failed to express his emotions, his voice invariably betrayed his sentiments. His speech would accelerate with excitement when describing happy occurrences, become labored and slow when recalling grievous events, drop to a whisper when citing moments of rejection, rise in outrage at the unfairness of life, and reflect inexpressible sadness at losses. His voice reflected emotions more intensely than his words might signify.

"But how did you *feel?*"

"I felt terrible. My mother took me to the orphanage and she spoke with the people there, and they say they don't have the room, they don't have where to put me. Children are already sleeping in the hall. She said: 'I don't care nothing. Take him.' They say, 'We don't have room. We are already overloaded. We don't know where to put the children.'" Eliott's voice was sad, even melancholy: "My mother said, 'I don't care. I cannot take him back. Do whatever you want with him.' That's what she told them. Was terrible. And she left." At this point, Eliott sounded so pained as if he were saying: "Yes, I am telling you of these events, but in truth the blow, the distress was so great as to be indescribable."

"And I was feeling like someone threw me into a deep hundred-foot pit. All my life, I remember this. And I was crying, but I couldn't do nothing. My mother went."

"Did your mother say good-bye?"

"Yes. She kissed me. She say, 'You stay here. They take you. Don't worry about it.'" By now Eliott was extremely agitated. "And I said, 'Mother!' but she ran."

"You must have felt terrible!"

"Terrible! All my life I remember this. All my life I remember this!" The tears were coursing down Eliott's cheeks as he continued: "She left me like this. It's terrible. All my life I remember this."

"Were you angry at her?"

"I was angry all my life, all my life. And many years later I find out that she was standing not far away until midnight. It was dark."

"You mean you were outside the orphanage?"

"Outside. They didn't even let me inside. I remember, near a wall was a bunch of tomatoes. I remember I took the first tomato that I ate in my life. I pick up the tomato and I was thinking it is an apple or something and I put it in my pocket. I never saw a tomato before."

"You mean you were standing in the dark?"

"Outside, dark, crying."

"And you didn't know your mother was there?"

"I didn't know. I was standing or sitting. It was an old big, huge building. Was yellow. There was a door and I was standing on the right side facing the building. And there was a long hall inside. And they put me in the hall. We slept on the floor because this way you can push many children in."

"They finally took you in?"

Apparently late at night they opened the door and allowed Lonek into the home. The house was devoid of furniture. The floor was covered with sleeping children.

"Who opened the door?"

"I don't know."

"Anyone say anything to you?"

"Nothing. They just open the door and let me in. Later my mother told me when she saw me inside, she left."

Years later, Eliott was told by his mother that she had pretended to leave to force the administrators to accept Lonek in their very overcrowded, overextended orphanage. She had, however, waited in the dark until she saw that Lonek was safely inside.

"What a feeling it must have been for you and your mother, too. Terrible."

"Terrible." Both of us fell silent.

"Dreadful memory," he began again. "Later, when we was in the United States, she always was crying, kissing me. She always said, 'Forgive me. I was many times crying my heart out. I didn't have another choice.' It was terrible. I have never forgiven her!"

I was taken aback by the last remark. Elliot had always described his mother with great affection—how capable she had been when they first fled their home in Poland, how she had cared for the family in Siberia, how she had encouraged and praised him when he had foraged for food. How was it that Eliot, aware of his mother's dedication to him, failed to recognize that his mother sent him away for lack of a better alternative—that she acted out of desperation. I was particularly surprised by

Eliott's bitter reaction because it conflicted with those of many other Jewish escapees from Austria and Germany that I had previously interviewed. Sent in 1939 by their Jewish parents on *Kindertransports* to unknown destinations in England, these escapees realized that their parents had sent them away because they had known that even the worst home in England would be preferable to the prospect of life, and probably death, under Hitler. Although many of these *Kinder* grew up in very unsuitable and uncongenial settings, almost all admired and appreciated their parents for having made the sacrifice of relinquishing them. Rather than resenting their parents for abandoning them, they were grateful for their lifesaving choice. I wanted to learn more about Eliott's very different feelings toward his mother.

"You have never forgiven her? How come? Do you feel that your mother should have kept you?"

"I don't know. It's hard to judge. Who am I to judge? I was not in their situation. Maybe she felt that she couldn't do nothing."

"Maybe she felt you would die of hunger or malnutrition."

On the surface, Eliott agreed. "Die or something. I am sure she was thinking that I would get food in the orphanage. I would get clothes and everything."

"But are you still angry with your mother?"

"I have some bittersweets for my mother." Eliott's voice descended into a mutter, as if he did not want me to discern his ambivalence about his mother's actions. "Was terrible, you understand. I never told this story to people. When I told my brother when we was on the trip to Poland recently, I said, 'You don't know my mother deserted me when I was little.' He said, 'What?' I said, 'Yes.' He didn't believe me. I said, 'I would not make up stories about my mother. I love my mother.' He said, 'Maybe she didn't have a choice.' That's what he told me. 'If our mother didn't keep you, then she didn't have a choice.' Even my wife said the same. I told her a few days ago. I never spoke to anyone."

"Did you feel disloyal talking about your mother?"

"Right. My mother said a couple of times, 'I didn't have another choice.'"

He had only told his brother about his feelings about a year or so ago and his wife even more recently. Obviously, he considered his mother's action shameful, and by carrying the secret with him for years, he was protecting both her and himself.

In the middle of our next session, Elliot suddenly interrupted our discussion and brought up his mother. He had evidently been thinking about the topic. My speculation that his mother might have placed him in an orphanage solely because of concern for his well-being, or indeed his survival, and that the decision might have been excruciatingly difficult for her, had given Elliot food for thought. Clearly, he wanted to discuss it further.

"I want to clear up a little bit [about my mother]. It's a little bit strange. When I talked to you, I got to thinking more and more like this: What was my mother thinking?"

I commented, "You know, it is fortunate that you or I never had to be in the position of your mother."

"Right. It's not so easy for her." But his distrust and ambivalence about his mother's actions resurfaced. As if to justify his anger at his mother, he quoted a conversation with his brother on their recent their trip to Poland. "I remembered just now, my brother told me when he was sick [as a child], he told her: 'Mother, remember you sent Loneki away. If I was sick, who would take care of me?'" The implication was that in view of his mother's placing Lonek in an orphanage, Heimek feared his mother would not want to accept the burden should he, Heimek, continue to be sick. Eliott laughed sadly as if to say: "You see, I was right about my mother in the first place."

Elliot was speaking more to himself than to me as he wrestled with a problem that had vexed him for a long time: "I don't . . . I never . . . but it's still . . . but it's still a little bit puzzling me, how could she . . ." His voice sank almost to a whisper, as if his mother were currently in the room with us and had to be shielded from overhearing Eliott's remarks. As he mumbled and repeated phrases, I could hardly hear him. Trying to ease the pain of his memory, I suggested some alternative rationales to the one that distressed and grieved him, namely, that his mother had abandoned him. "Perhaps," I began, but he did not appear to hear me. He continued: "She tell, she say: I cannot survive with Lonek. Or better she use a diplomatic word for it. But if you translate this, she left me and said: 'Take him, I don't want him.'" At this point, his voice, while plaintive, assumed a definite finality.

He was plainly so troubled that I could not let the matter rest: "You see," I said placatingly, "I think there are some people who would look at this situation differently. Some people feel that for a mother to give up her child for his sake is the most heroic deed a parent can undertake. The feeling was maybe, 'I can't survive—'"

At this point, Eliott eagerly broke in to finish my sentence: "So I give a chance to my child. This is one way to look at it." He seemed relieved at that thought, but after a short pause, added: "There is another way to look also, she throw me away. I . . . I. . . . A coin have two sides. One side I look at it, she thought maybe I am not . . . I don't. . . . Believe me, I cherish my mother. I see looking on one side that she don't have a choice. Without me, it was much easier."

"You always put it that it was much easier for her," I remarked. "You ignore the possibility that it was primarily better for you. Because her feeling might have been that if you are in an orphanage, they will feed you and you will have some sort of a chance."

"She didn't know. She didn't know whether they would feed me." Elliot tended to repeat phrases when he was upset.

"Maybe she guessed?"

His voice rose with great intensity as he declared vehemently: "But at least if I was with her, somebody will hold me, somebody will . . . in bedtime somebody wipe my tears, somebody will worry about me. Then she didn't know who will be looking after me. . . . Nobody knew for sure."

I started to remind him of all the dangers he and his family had gone through: "To give you the opposite possibility. You had told me that 60 percent of the escaping Jews died" But he would not let me finish, jumping at me angrily. "No, this was not Siberia. In Siberia maybe she was right. But here was a warm climate. It was on the south side—at least I catch a little fish, I brought her some potatoes, a little nuts. We have some . . . we didn't die, you understand. I [even] had a friend. From this point was not Siberia; [where there was] the cold weather and we didn't have nothing, nothing."

"What about your father being sick? What about her thinking if he dies how can I possibly. . . ."

He broke in again, though the reminder of his father's illness kindled some positive thoughts about his mother's motivation.

"This is what I told you before and this is the only way I feel that this is her thinking: My father die and she survive with two children, this very hard for her."

"You see you always say. . . ." He interrupted again, but this time I would not let him. I was too eager for him to consider that his mother's actions were based on concern for him rather than herself. "Wait, wait, you see you always say if your father dies, it would have been hard for your mother. Might she not have thought: 'If my husband dies, Lonek may have a better chance in an orphanage than here where we don't have enough to eat.'"

"Could be, I don't know. It's very hard to judge. It is a possibility. I don't judge, but I have a little grudge, you understand. This is a bad thing—because the memory was haunting me all my life." As tears welled up in his eyes, he sadly said: "Wherever I see some children gathering, I look on them and see sometimes myself standing on the side like this."

I continued to attempt to alleviate Eliott's almost lifelong distress by promoting a sympathetic interpretation of his mother's choice. I asked: "What was your mother like aside from this one particular situation? Was she caring?"

"Very caring, she was very caring. She was always, like I told you, when we were on the market we was selling soap or other things that we sold there—shoes—whatever, just to survive, yes. I remember, she always came back with something. In Russia they take from pickles the water and sell it in the street, like sodas. She always bring me something to drink because she knew in the hot days I need to drink. This I remember."

"So you see my point, here is a situation which you can judge from two sides."

"Right, right." Eliott seemed eager again to hear the positive side.

"When you judge a person, you have to consider their actions beyond a particular situation, in the context of their overall behavior. Now, it would be a different story if you said to me: 'My mother was a self-centered person, and she was not very caring. Therefore, I think in an emergency she just took care of herself and forgot about me.' But if you say that she was always very protective of you, then I would say, that most likely, in the situation under consideration, her aim must have been to protect you. It's out of character for her to have acted only in her self-interest. Do you get my point?"

"Yes, I get your point. In wartime, people see different angles. She didn't know what would happen to me. Nobody knew. I just remember, that many times, no the few times I talked to her, she said: 'I was many times crying my heart out that I let you go.' It was on her conscience, you understand. She didn't do it because she want to get rid of me. But she did it because it was wartime and nobody knew what happen."

Yet, Eliott was not entirely reassured. Although he apparently wanted to believe in his mother's goodness, his concern about his mother's conscience reflected continuing ambivalence.

"You know these are Solomon-like decisions."

"Right. Absolutely right," he responded, sounding somewhat relieved.

"It's very hard."

"Was terrible."

"Yes," I sympathized. "Terrible. A terrible feeling. It's just fortunate that you and I don't have to make such decisions."

"Right, life and death. Life and death. I imagine people in camps and in Germany also had to make decisions. Give the children [when] the mother cannot survive, so the child can survive. They chose to save the child and the mother will die."

Evidently preoccupied with thoughts about his mother, he returned to that subject from time to time. Once he commented, "I tried to hide it, to block it out because I was not sure how she was thinking. But I think of her always in a good way. Even if I have a little reaction. Sometimes behind me there was a dark side. But the years passed, and I more and more started to think on the other side. I see the other side of the coin—that my mother was right."

Yet his sentiments wavered. Although his recognition of his mother's possible selflessness grew, his tortured feelings never quite rested. Once, he asked me about my own experiences.

He said, "I imagine you went through a lot of things."

"Yes. But not like you."

"I feel like my story I believe is unbelievable." With a voice reflecting great perplexity and sadness, Eliott explained, "Someday, somebody will ask: 'No, do you lie? Your mother left you?'"

It seemed to me that Eliott's doubts about his mother's decision haunted him all his life. Was his inability to give his mother the benefit of the doubt based on deeply felt suspicions developed by a lifetime of observing the treachery of humankind? Was it due to the fact that his brother had remained with his mother while he was sent away? Yet many of the Austrian and German *Kinder* who had been sent away by their parents also left siblings behind. Did the *Kinder* tend to admire their parents more than Lonek because they faced more immediate threats of death? Whatever the cause, the haunting suspicion that his mother had abandoned him weighed heavily on Elliot and had certainly contributed a certain melancholy to his life.

In the middle of our sad reflections, Eliott suddenly surprised me by saying: "The next day they [the orphanage] took us to a Russian port."

"Wait," I said. "The next morning you got up and all of a sudden you are leaving for a port?"

"Yes, breakfast and they say we go. I remember they took us in groups with the buses to the train."

Fate, with its long list of unexpected twists and turns, foisted another surprise on mother and son. Unknown to Lonek's mother when she left Lonek, the orphanage was scheduled soon to leave for Palestine. She had walked the long road back to her home in the dark. Then later, she returned to the orphanage to deliver some clothes to Lonek only to find, to her horror, that the whole orphanage had pulled out for points unknown.

CHAPTER XI

General Anders' Army and Lonek

As stipulated in the Sikorski-Maisky Treaty between Poland and Russia, thousands of Polish orphans scattered throughout Russia were to be collected and attached to General Anders' troops. All along the way, Polish children had lost their parents—on their trek to Siberia, in labor camps, on their journey south, and on the streets of the southern cities. It was estimated that of the Polish orphans, one thousand were Jewish.

Jewish leaders hoped to deliver the Jewish children ultimately to Palestine. However, for the time being, no one had any clear idea how to achieve this goal. At present, the most important task was to get the children out of the Soviet Union as quickly as possible. Unknown to Lonek's mother, the orphanage in which Lonek had been was scheduled to be evacuated from Russia together with the Polish army.

Arranging the exodus of Polish soldiers and civilians had been a Herculean task. It was almost miraculous that Lonek would be a part of it. But it was probably even more miraculous that seventy-eight thousand able-bodied men and thirty-five thousand dependents actually slipped though Stalin's iron grip.[1] For shortly after Stalin consented to the formation of the Polish army, his fortunes along the front improved, and he apparently began to regret his decision. Stalin's support of the Polish army waned in exact proportion to his successes on the battlefield. Therefore, speed in selecting and organizing the Polish army's departure was of the essence. Who could tell when Stalin would reverse his decision?

Indeed, in quick time Stalin made a pharaoh like about-face. He suddenly declared all Jews, Belorussians, and Ukrainians who had originated from the Russian-occupied sector of Poland to be Russian citizens. These former Poles—now Russian citizens—were forbidden to join the Polish army. Polish citizens who originated from the German-occupied sector of Poland were still allowed to join Anders' army. Stalin was making the long-range point that the area of Poland under current Russian occupation was now a part of Russia and would never be Polish again.

This edict caused utter despair among those Poles and Jews who suddenly found themselves to be Russian citizens and in the clutches of the Russian authorities. It eliminated all hope of joining General Anders, serving under his command, and possibly returning with him to Poland after the war. The last chance of these former Poles to flee had vanished.

After his release from Lubianka, General Anders immediately set about building an army from the one-hundred-eighty-thousand prisoners of war and the fifteen-thousand men of military age who had been impressed into the Russian army. The condition of Anders' fledgling force was appalling and training conditions primitive. Although Stalin had promised to supply Anders' men, his increased confidence in the Russian army made him entirely indifferent to the condition of the Polish men. The pledged rations of food, clothes, and armaments rapidly diminished, leaving the Polish soldiers famished and in tatters. Forty thousand food rations were provided for up to one hundred thousand people. But even this number was erratic. At one point, the allotments were reduced to twenty-six thousand. After much urging by Polish leaders, they were finally raised to forty-four thousand, still less than half of what was needed. At times, soldiers were reduced to roaming potato fields barefoot, gathering whatever was left in the ground. Outside the Polish army camps, Polish children gathered, begging and searching through the military garbage for food.

These deplorable conditions made it practically impossible to build an effective fighting force. As a result, General Anders urged Stalin to allow him to evacuate his army to Persia where the British would help furbish it. Certainly General Anders was only too eager to rescue his army from the Russians, fearing that his men might end in gulags rather than at the front. Stalin was not fooled: "I am a person of experience and of age," he replied. "I know that if you go to Persia you will never return here.[2] The British also pressured Stalin to allow Anders' troops to go to Persia, where they would support the Allied armies. What whim convinced Stalin to consent will probably never be fully revealed, but consent he did. The evacuation was organized at breakneck speed in the fear that Stalin might change his mind again.[3]

The Jewish Poles faced an additional familiar obstacle to joining the Polish army—anti-Semitism. At first, the Poles accepted Jews into the army, but when Jewish men volunteered in large numbers, the Poles blamed the Russians, hinting darkly that the latter had purposely released Jews to inundate the Polish army. With the number of slots in Anders' army limited, recruiting Polish officers wished to eliminate as many Jews as possible and reserve their places for non-Jewish Poles. At some recruiting stations, Jews were categorically rejected. Those already in the army suddenly were disqualified by Polish officers on such pretexts as lack of physical fitness, even when the contrary was blatantly evident. Jews were dismissed from officer training schools under the guise of not meeting standards. Undaunted, Jewish men continued their pursuit of enlistment by going from recruiting station to recruiting station. Occasionally, Polish officers "arranged" matters for a price. A former volunteer described: "The scenes familiar from Poland before the war were reenacted here. The Poles were automatically included among the ranks of the army; the Jews were graded type D—unfit for active military service—and even those who had already been accepted were expelled for trivial reasons. Finally, my turn arrived to appear before the committee; appearing with me was Richterman, a swimming champion. Both of us were graded type D."[4]

Another Jewish volunteer complained that though he was rejected under the pretext of poor physical condition, "maimed, crooked, hunchbacked and one-eyed Poles[5] were accepted." On the whole, the Jews who managed to enlist were those who were fortunate enough to encounter officers who were not as anti-Semitic as most of the Polish military. In addition, preference was given to the professional classes and those with special skills.

The Jews blamed the Poles for their many rejections. They had plenty of reasons for suspicion because, in fact, anti-Semitism was as much a fact of life in General Anders' army as it had been in the regular Polish army. The Russians encouraged the Jews' suspicions of the Poles, pretending sympathy for the Jews at the same time forbidding General Anders to accept any men who had lived in what was now Russian-occupied Poland. In turn, the Poles put the blame on the Russians.

The Poles found many rationalizations for their rejection of Jewish volunteers. One was the claim that Jews were cowards and unfit fighters. General Sikorski expressed this idea to Stalin who, himself an anti-Semite, agreed and replied curtly: "Jews make poor warriors." Another reason was that the Jews had been less antagonistic than the Poles to the occupying Russian forces. At that point, most Jews decided that, regardless of previous Russian pogroms, the Russians were a lesser evil than the Germans. Nevertheless, the Poles considered the Jews' stance as treason. The "disloyalty" of the Jews served as an excuse to discriminate against Jewish volunteers and for their mistreatment even when accepted.

General Anders was ambivalent about his position vis-à-vis the Jews. In his book titled *An Army in Exile*, he wrote: "I was greatly disturbed when, in the beginning, large numbers from among the national minorities and first and foremost Jews, began streaming in to enlist. As I have already mentioned, some of the Jews had warmly welcomed the Soviet armies that invaded Poland in 1939."[6]

Nevertheless, he realized that the pervasiveness of anti-Semitism in the army reflected badly on the Polish Government-in-Exile and interfered with diplomatic relations with Britain. The Poles frequently resented British support of the Polish Jews. Jan Stanczyk, a minister of the Polish Government-in-Exile, commented: "The outcry [of the Allies] concerning anti-Semitism in the Polish Armed Forces might bring about an even more severe reaction of the Poles." This statement implied that unless the Jews accepted anti-Semitism with good grace, they would be punished by increased anti-Semitism. At another point, Stanczyk commented: "I do not want to deny, and I admit, that an anti-Semitic mood prevails among the population that returned from Russia and in the Armed Forces. I note this in pain, but the fact cannot be changed by decree.[7]

In the face of British protest, General Anders declared that the selection of Jewish soldiers should be based on objective measures, and that officers ensure that Jews were treated as equals, as they possessed the same rights as Polish soldiers. He emphasized: "I order all my subordinate commanding officers to fight relentlessly against any manifestation of racial anti-Semitism." Despite Anders' worthy sentiments, suspicion of his sincerity was certainly raised by his release of a second, very different order. This second order explained that General Anders was sympathetic to his men's hatred of Jews. However, the time was not propitious for expressing such sentiments due to the British advocacy on behalf of the Jews. However, the soldiers should be assured that payback time would come. The order read: "I well understand the reasons underlying anti-Semitic manifestations in the ranks of the armed forces." Referring to the Polish Jews' hostile and disloyal behavior during 1939–40, the declaration continued: "I am consequently not surprised that our soldiers, those ardent patriots, regard the matter so seriously. . . . Our defense of the Jews might seem incomprehensible or historically unjustified and even inconsistent." Nevertheless because of political reasons such a policy must be maintained. "I therefore recommend that our position be explained to the units in a suitably discreet manner. . . . However after the battle is over and we are again our own masters, we will settle the Jewish matter in a fashion that the exalted status and sovereignty of the homeland and simple human justice require."[8]

Was this implication (it suits us now to be nice to the Jews, but we will get them later) a reflection of General Anders' own anti-Semitism, his staff's anti-Semitism or was it a fraud perpetrated by an anti-Semitic staff officer? Was the message issued due to an insurrection by his staff against a sympathetic pro-Jewish stance? General Anders vowed that he had never sent the message—that in fact he had been out of the country when it was distributed. He declared it a forgery. Whether such an order could really have been promulgated without his knowledge is difficult to say. Discrimination within the forces remained, expressing itself in many ways, such as subjecting Jews to insults, assigning them undesirable tasks, and failing to investigate any of their complaints. The conditions for individual Jews depended to a great extent on individual officers and their outlook. Some proved to be fair and even helpful, but many capitalized unnecessarily on the second Russian directive and found other spurious reasons for Jewish exclusion. Only a few Poles spoke out openly against the discrimination and intervened to whatever extent they could.[9]

Perhaps the attitude of the Polish officials can be summarized by the words of a Polish liaison officer, Andrzej Jenicz: "The evacuation of Jews from the Soviet Union was unpopular with the Polish public and army, and was restricted to the barest minimum in keeping with the position taken by the Soviet authorities."[10] In the final tally, only about thirty-five hundred Jewish soldiers and twenty-five hundred Jewish civilians were included among the over one hundred thousand Polish evacuees.

Nevertheless, despite his shortcomings, General Anders' organizational skills were quite remarkable and his achievements extraordinary. By dint of immense effort, political finagling, and by exploiting propitious events, he managed to form an army before relations between Russia and Poland permanently deteriorated. In a war-torn country where supplies were practically nonexistent, transportation was barely available, and Stalin's hostility was increasing, between April and September 1942 General Anders managed to deliver one hundred thousand soldiers and civilians to Persia. Among these were about six thousand Jewish men, women, and children. Among these were approximately one thousand Jewish orphans.

One was Lonek.

CHAPTER XII

Bereft

Through the open window of the train, Lonek glimpsed the country-side drifting by. Each passing minute additional miles between himself and his family. Bewildered, frightened, and lonely, he sat frozen in his seat. Lonek felt abandoned, destitute, alone in a crowd of children. "I lost my parents. I didn't . . . My mother . . . . What can you? . . . . When happens? . . . . I didn't know what happened to my mother because I didn't have any connection with her. Terrible, what can I tell you!"

In spite of his shyness, Lonek eyed the children around him. They seemed friendly enough, but they were all preoccupied with their own sorrows and fears. Many had entered an orphanage of their own volition and despite parental objections. They recognized the orphanage as their only means of survival for themselves and their families. One youngster whose father absolutely refused to consider an orphanage, joined one secretly in order to prevent her family from starving: "Each evening I carried a piece of bread home to keep my sisters alive. When father asked where I spend my days, I answered that I am working with a Jewish man in Samarkand."[1]

The children streamed in to join General Anders for a multitude of excruciating reasons. Some had lost their families along the way. A woman recalled: "There were nine of us children, six brothers and three sisters. In the beginning, five siblings escaped to the Bolsheviks and four stayed in Germany. Afterward, three returned to Germany, and two were sent to Russia: me and my oldest brother, Israel. On the returning road, I lost my brother and in this way, despite all my siblings, I myself, was alone."[2] Other children had been found abandoned and were placed in orphanages. Many had traveled or walked starved, frozen, and frequently alone over long distances. They later recalled how they had obtained money to reach an orphanage: "I sold my shoes and wrapped my feet in rags. . . . was dying from hunger." "I marched from the collective farm to a Polish orphanage near Samarkand. I walked barefoot through the snow."[3] In various states of exhaustion, they had begged their way across the country and pleaded to be admitted.

Some children had originally traveled from Poland to Siberia with relatives or even strangers who had taken them under their wings. When the authorities in Siberia discovered that children and foster parents bore different names, the children had been arbitrarily removed and sent to orphanages. Some of these children had now been sent to accompany the Polish army, but most of the children, like Lonek, had originally fled with their parents to various parts of Russia from which most were shipped to Siberia. There, many had been haunted by deaths, clinging to their families until one by one each member died, sometimes leaving one child, sometimes leaving a set of siblings to shift for themselves. One of those children gave a brief but telling account of her gradual abandonment: "My father got dysentery, but the hospital did not want to accept him and he died the next day. Two weeks later, as my mother and older brother worked in the field, my little sister Fejga died in my arms. We feared that this would be dreadful for mother, so we carried her into the field and buried her. When I think of my mother's despair. . . . When my mother came down with typhus, I begged the commandant of our collective farm to get us a conveyance to take her to the hospital, but she died on the way. We came back and buried her near my father and Fejga. When my younger brother Herszel became ill, I didn't want to take him anywhere. My older brother and I sold everything and left the collective farm. At the station Kitab where we waited for the train, all our money was stolen. . . . The next day we were brought to the orphanage."[4]

Another child recalled: "My father died of hunger. My mother sickened and also died. I and my twelve-year-old brother went to Buchara where they accepted us in an orphanage."[5] It was all very usual.

Another child recalled the death of her father, the mainstay of the family. Because her mother could not meet the work quota, the family was driven off the collective farm where they lived. No work meant no food. The starving drove out the starving. Who can tell how culpable the laboring members of the farms were when they were also dying of hunger? They were probably too weak to take on the burden of others when they could barely rescue themselves. The mother and her two children wandered over the countryside, trying to walk to Samarkand, eating grass and chasing dogs for food. Finally the mother was accepted in a hospital. The children pretended to be orphans to gain admission to an orphanage. They commented: "[In the orphanage] malaria and typhus were rampant, but after a while it got better."[6]

To pretend that living parents were dead was one of the subterfuges children resorted to in order to gain acceptance by an orphanage. It did not matter if illnesses were endemic and the food barely above subsistence level. Whatever limitations the orphanages had, at least they offered a place to lie down—even if it was on the floor—with a roof overhead and some food. The counselors recognized the children's ruses and tried to tease the truth out of them. A woman described an incident that occurred when she left her parent's home as a twelve-year-old: "Hearing stories how well off the children were in the orphanage, I took my siblings and the four of us rode to Dzalabadu. We stood on the street in front of the orphanage and cried for many days. They didn't believe us that we were orphans. They gave us candy and toys so we would tell the truth where our parents could be found. But we kept on stating that they died and we didn't have a father or mother. Seeing that we were stubborn and that they couldn't get anything out of us, the men in the orphanage finally accepted us. After a few months we left for Teheran. We didn't say good-bye to either father or mother and we never saw them again."[7]

At times, this deception made it impossible for the children to visit their parents ever again, forcing them to lose track of one another forever. In other cases, they managed a farewell, but only occasionally and in secret.

Like Lonek's mother, many parents were forced to decide whether to hold on to their children and risk starvation, illness, or death or try, at whatever cost, to get the children to a safer place, such as an orphanage. A woman recollected: "My father made every effort to enter my brother and myself in a Polish orphanage. Our two sisters remained with him. We never saw them again."[8] On the other hand, if the parents were to be arrested or killed or starved to death, what would happen to the children? Better to let go of the children intentionally than to leave it to chance. However, some parents adamantly refused to part with their children even under the most extreme circumstances. We shall never know how many families that stayed together survived and how many died together.

Some children's decisions saved their parents' lives. "We received four hundred grams of bread [in the orphanage] per day. We were afraid that our Papa would die of hunger. So my little brother and I only ate half of our rations and gave the rest to Papa. Because of that Papa did not die."[9]

Under such circumstances, honesty was not a particularly cherished value. Survival had greater merit. Not only did the children lie in the hope of escaping hell, parents also used every conceivable pretext to rescue their children. When parents and children realized that younger children were more likely to be accepted by orphanages, they lied about the youngsters' ages. It was easy. Due to malnutrition and general neglect, youngsters in their teens looked like ten-year-olds. Skill in deception was vital and had to be developed early. The children by now could lie with equanimity: "In the Polish homes they did not accept fourteen-year-olds. So I said that I was ten and that both my parents were dead." [10]

One particular deception helped save Jewish lives—the pretense of being non-Jewish. The orphanages, run by Polish administrators, had a finite capacity. Just as General Anders' army favored non-Jewish Poles so, too, did Polish directors of orphanages. As a result, Jewish children were up against a stone wall. Jewish parents, driven by despair at seeing their children hungry, ill, and in rags, placed crucifixes around their necks and passed them off as Christian. They then handed them over to Polish nuns and priests in charge of Polish orphanages in the hope that disguising their own youngsters' Jewish background would put them on an equal footing with the non-Jewish Polish children. [11] A little girl recalled wandering around the streets of Samarkand, a cross around her neck, shadowed by her father as she begged a Polish official for help. The latter was indifferent, having heard similar stories from others. Finally, a nun at an orphanage admitted the child. Her father smuggled a note to her, reminding her never to forget her Jewish heritage. This was the last she ever saw or heard of him. [12]

But even when children finally found places in orphanages, their circumstances did not necessarily improve dramatically. Although such homes provided shelter, they lacked food and clothing. In addition, deadly illnesses remained a constant threat. One youngster remembered that each day four to five children died; in a few weeks, eighty of them had succumbed.

The ever present anti-Semitism oppressed the Jewish children. It was endemic in Polish culture, so that Polish children were imbued with it at an early age. As a result, they blamed their misfortunes and difficulties on the Jews and made the life of Jewish children miserable with taunts, name calling and unjust accusations. The Jewish children were constantly the butt of jokes, referred to as "dirty Jews," and characterized as smelling of onions, though no one in the group was fortunate enough to have seen, let alone eaten, one within recent memory. The Polish children's antagonism sometimes turned into violence. In a particular instance, when a ripped holy picture was found, two Jewish children were immediately considered culpable and beaten so badly that they were incapacitated for several days. The intervention of a concerned Polish counselor saved them from worse. Greatly outnumbered, the Jewish children rarely received such assistance.

Jewish children commonly suffered discrimination from the adult staff of orphanages. At a time when every morsel of food mattered, this bias was often expressed through the distribution of food. Frequently the Polish children were given more plentiful portions or a thicker soup, much to the dismay of the Jewish children.[13] Compounding the children's anxiety were some teachers' threats that any infractions of the rules would eliminate the child's chances of leaving Russia.

Devoted Polish counselors who protected their Jewish charges were affectionately remembered by the children: "Our teacher would not permit the [Christian] children to beat or insult us." "Our teacher was very good and she saw to it that no harm came to us." "The Polish children treated me badly, but the counselor interceded for me." In contrast to prejudiced teachers who forced Jewish children to cross themselves and pray as Christians, sympathetic teachers permitted Jewish children to say their own prayers.[14]

Some Polish counselors and priests went to great lengths to help the Jewish children depart. When the leader of a Polish orphanage to be evacuated refused to include a handful of imploring, wailing Jewish children, their counselor hurried from railroad car to railroad car, begging the organizers to accept them. As the train prepared to pull out of the station, the children were hastily pushed into one of the railroad cars, leaving without any possessions and without being able to say good-by to their loved ones, but leaving nevertheless. In another case, a priest actually managed to have a departing train halted, so moved was he by the anguished cries of the Jewish children left on the platform The Jewish children were then allowed to board.[15]

In Samarkand, a Polish commandant prevented the Jewish children from boarding a train. The rest of the Polish staff became so incensed that they threatened to prevent the Polish children from entraining unless the Jewish children were given permission as well. A Polish priest persuaded the commandant to reverse his decision.[16]

The Jewish children endured the hardships of orphanages—illness, minuscule rations, dearth of clothing, anti-Semitism—to save themselves and their families. They remained focused on what actions were necessary for survival. One girl commented about the ceaseless taunts and indignities heaped on her by Polish children: "We tolerated it because a little soup and a piece of bread was for us more important."[17]

As time passed, tensions escalated as the Jewish children were left in the dark about their prospects of leaving Russia, frequently until the last minute. They were not even assured that when the orphanage did leave, they would be taken along. Quotas for the transports were weighted heavily against the Jewish orphans. Three transports departed from one particular orphanage without including a single Jewish child. The organizers of the fourth transport, which was filled with three hundred and twenty Polish children, finally accepted twenty Jewish ones. Another orphanage selected only ten Jewish children by lot and excluded ninety others. Another orphanage departed, leaving behind its Jewish members—four sobbing and pleading children. Because of the capricious manner of selecting Jewish children, brothers and sisters were often separated, sometimes forever. Children who had lost whole families except for a single sibling became desperate when faced with such separations. A girl, whose brother had been allowed to board the train, borrowed his cap, which identified his orphanage, and slipped onto the train wearing it. Later in the journey, she ran into the Polish director who recognized her as a stowaway and ordered her off the train.

Even when children were scheduled for a transport, the daily nerve-racking insecurities continued to gnaw at them. Suffering from typhus or some other disease, many children were left behind, forever missing their chance to escape. To avoid such a fate, one sick girl secretly fled from the hospital to join her departing transport.[18] Those who pretended to be Christian lived in constant dread of discovery.

Stealing an opportunity to say a last good-bye to surviving parents was a luxury many members of the orphanages could not afford. As a result, many children left without leave-taking, knowing that they would probably never see their parents again. Other children faced the anguish of leaving starving parents behind. A woman who joined an orphanage recalled: "On the day of departure they gave us a new pullover. My youngest brother Saul carried ours to our parents so they could buy bread for it. On the way, he was attacked by hoodlums who wanted to grab the sweaters. They hit my brother, but he did not let them tear the pullovers away from him. He knew it was the last help he could offer our parents."[19]

Last, but not least, looming over the children was the ever present shadow of the NKVD. After Russian-Polish relations deteriorated, the NKVD was eager to thwart the Polish exodus. Their men swept into the Polish orphanages and arrested the Polish staff. As many as twenty-five

Polish teachers were rounded up from one orphanage alone and sent to prison, where many died. The NKVD commandeered the orphanage's wagon, food stores, and clothes. They searched the orphanages to locate older children and carry them off as laborers to collective farms. Jewish and Polish adults, as well as children, attempted to deceive the NKVD in every conceivable way. During the day, the older children avoided setting foot outside the orphanage. One orphanage director hid the older children in the cellar pretending to the NKVD that the home housed only young children. Realizing that relinquishing their Polish passports would doom them to a life in Russia, the children resisted NKVD urgings to accept Russian passports. Instead, they claimed they needed their passports to join their fathers who belonged to the Polish military.

Pressure from the NKVD continued until the last moment of departure. As recalled by one participant:

> We received the news that they [NKVD] were coming to fetch us during the night in order to send us to a collective farm. We cried and decided we are not going on our free will. The director consoled us and said she would do everything to save us. When the NKVD did appear we children barricaded ourselves. The NKVD declared they would take us by force. But the director was not intimidated. The negotiations lasted all day long and the director ran to all kind of offices and made special appeals. When she returned at night, the teachers were awakened and the typewriters began to clatter as lists of children were drawn up. We didn't sleep that night and one of us children continually ran to the director to kiss her hand, so that she would give us the news. But she only repeated: "Everything will be all right." In the morning we were told that we can leave Russia. We jumped into the air out of joy, danced and sang. It is hard to describe. Each one of us received three blankets, a pair of shoes, a sweater and some other things. At night we slept in our clothes. At four in the morning, July 21, 1943, we were awoken. . . . At the border the Russians wanted to take our things from us. They liked our blankets the best, but we fought for each piece and did not allow them to take anything. Passport control lasted all day and towards evening we were allowed to depart.[20]

Some of the children managed a final agonizing glimpse of their families as the train pulled out of the station. One youngster boarded the train despite her father's objections: "I felt badly, but I recollected how horribly we suffered from hunger and I decided not to return home. . . . My stepmother held my little sister in her arms. The little one stretched her little arms out towards us, so we should take her with us. We all sobbed."[21]

With such harrowing experiences behind them, the children remained somber as the train moved into unfamiliar territory. Eliott recalled the pervasive sense of melancholy on the train: "We was, you know, each one, sad. Everybody was occupied with his own thoughts. Maybe the father die in Siberia, or the mother die and the kids was a burden to them. Everybody had his own *tsores* [troubles]." Then a small incident occurred that pierced the thick enveloping gloom and and suggested to Lonek that perhaps he was not entirely deserted. A counselor handed him, as well as all the other children, a little box that appeared to be a tin of sardines. Inspecting his new possession, Lonek realized with infinite delight that he was holding an almost unfathomable delicacy, a treasure, a bonanza. The box was filled with chocolates, wonderful, dark brown chocolates, in the shape of sardines! And with that, the world began to look a little brighter. Because, if the train was taking Lonek to a place where such treasures could be obtained, then perhaps the people on the train might just turn out to be well disposed toward him after all. "Everybody opened the cover like sardines and put the tongue in and licked the chocolate. This was like you find a mountain of gold. We didn't know where we were going. But we know we are going to a better place, because as they gave us chocolate, we figure it must be better. Every time I look on a sardine today . . . !"

Lonek thought he was going to England. He had been told that the Gentiles were headed there, possibly because the Polish Government-in-Exile was located in London. He believed that the plan was to drop the Jewish children off at the same time. But unknown to the children, they were heading for the port of Krasnovodsk on the eastern shore of the Caspian Sea.[22]

There a Russian ship was to ferry them to Pahlavi, which was located on the southwestern shore. But while lingering on the beach for two days waiting for the ship's arrival, no proper amenities were provided. Food was scarce and sanitary facilities were unavailable. A child commented: "There was no water and for three days we drank seawater which was salty and stank of gasoline."[23] By the time the ship arrived, the children had begun to develop dysentery, trachoma, and other infectious illnesses.

Facilities on the ship improved only minimally. Toilet facilities were overcrowded, and the young children had to make do with overflowing chamber pots, with no place to empty them or to clean themselves properly.[24]

An onlooker retained an indelible impression of the children who came onboard:

> They were pale, gaunt and famished. They had a haunted expression in their eyes. They suffered cruelly from various diseases, which took a heavy toll of death among them. They were like little battle-weary soldiers, exhausted by gunfire, expulsion, imprisonment and wandering across Siberia's endless, forgotten wastelands to Uzbekistan, Kazakhstan, and other places whose names they had never heard until they were dragged through them like beasts in cattle trucks. Man, nature and disease all vented their cruelties upon them.

Another onlooker described the children:

> A rheumy-eyed horde, bleary with the inflammations that were wreaking havoc with them, riddled with boils, ringworm, scabies—I saw them defecating in public, unable to control their bowels because of intestinal and stomach diseases. I saw them standing in the long queues for a piece of bread, a little soup. . . . [They were] shuffling along, in the rows of displaced people straggling from the internment camps in the north to Central Russia. [They clung] to each other's hands, trying to maintain contact with a brother, a sister, a parent—even when the hand had long since grown icy in death.[25]

When Lonek boarded the ship to Pahlavi in Persia, he paid little attention to its condition. He was only aware, with a sinking feeling, that he was about to leave Russia. With the ship setting out to sea, the pulling up of the gangplank might as well have been the lifting of a drawbridge. He was about to leave behind everything that was familiar.

CHAPTER XIII

A Rubicon Crossed

Crossing the Caspian Sea, a large body of water, reinforced Lonek's hopelessness at ever reuniting with his parents. He was inconsolable. Every lap of the journey seemed to throw up new barriers to a future reunion: "I went to the top of the ship and I was crying all the time. I remember the corner where I was sitting. The ship had a little anchor. They put a rope around a piece of steel, a steel drum, two feet tall and one foot wide, round. This I remember. I was holding myself tight to the top [of the drum]. The children, they tried to chase me. I said: 'I don't want to go.' I cried and they let me be." A note of amazement crept into Eliott's voice at my naïveté in asking whether any of the adults made attempts to soothe and comfort him. "Nothing, nothing. They left me alone." In the confusion of the parting, there was little time for the counselors to comfort each child. Eliott's voice was sad and his eyes filled with tears: "I was sitting on the ship and I was crying. I remember I didn't want to eat and they came with food. I didn't want to eat nothing. Was crying all the time, all the time! Memories are very sad: The memories of my mother; that I left my parents. Was a terrible thing. These feelings were haunting me all the time. I don't forget."

After roughly twenty-four hours, the children disembarked in Pahlavi, Persia [present-day Iran], the first step toward their goal—Palestine. They were jubilant to be out of Russia. A yellowing document in the American Jewish Archives lists Lonek as arriving in Pahlavi with a group of children from the Orphan Asylum at Lunaczarsk near Tashkent. Among sixty-nine children listed for his orphanage, he was child number 32. The number of Jewish children arriving from each orphanage varied. The orphanage from Samarkand delivered 151 youngsters. The one from Dechkoncbocki delivered only 1 child, while those from Besszkent and Jakkobak each brought 3. Notations next to some children's names tell of lost and scattered families: "Mother died in Russia, father in Warsaw"; "Orphan; parents died in Russia. Trace of brother Berko lost after reaching Russia"; "Parents, brother and sister are in Russia;" "Trace of father lost after escape to South Russia"; "Mother and three sisters are in Russia"; "Orphan, sister Ida is in Russia."[1]

Accommodations were primitive during the children's two-week stay in Pahlavi. The youngsters lived in tents; food was scarce and medical equipment minimal. A five-year-old girl recalled waking in the morning, her eyes closed shut because of developing trachoma. Blindly, she stumbled to the waters of the Caspian Sea to wash off the dried pus. As a result, she arrived late for breakfast, and because of the chronic food shortages, she was unable to find enough scraps to satisfy her ever gnawing hunger.[2]

The tedious land trip from Pahlavi to Teheran lasted several days. Pandemonium arose when the sick children were assigned to trucks separate from the healthy ones so that they could be tended with special care. Panic-stricken, the healthy siblings refused to leave their brothers and sisters. Life had taught them to remain wary of supposed brief separations—many of which ultimately became permanent.[3]

The route initially followed the southern coast of the Caspian Sea. The trucks wound along a narrow road, sandwiched between sand dunes and enlivened by an occasional palm tree. The dunes had their practical side. Whenever an enemy plane was spied, the children hopped off the trucks and hid among the dunes. A five-year-old was petrified in her hiding place, fearing that the caravan might suddenly depart without her. She had witnessed the exclusion and near exclusion of Jewish children before.

The roofs of the trucks were loaded with tents that were erected each night. The children washed themselves in the sea and ate what little food was available. At one spot, the friendly local population distributed some goodies, which the children eagerly stored next to their seats. Though the little five-year-old had not been quick enough to obtain some morsels for herself, she spied some grapes near her neighbor's seat. She had never seen or tasted any in her short life, and curiosity, as well as hunger, drove her to pick one and devour it. The experience was disappointing on two counts. The grape's taste did not match its heavenly appearance—it was probably too sour. In addition, the owner of the grapes, not used to possessing such luxury, had counted each grape and quickly identified the thief. Bigger than the five-year-old, his vengeance was swift and sure, expressed as a box on the ear.[4]

Lonek found the trip to Teheran confusing, disorienting. "It was like something in a dream; a bad dream. Suddenly you wake up in another place and they chase you to another point. That was my youth. Even now it looks very terrifying, but then I was not thinking as an adult. I was mixed up with many things." But as a child, Lonek's mood could swiftly change to optimism. "I was happy that I have the little box of chocolates. That was enough."

There was another reason why Lonek's veil of misery was occasionally pierced by rays of hope. Although he was exceedingly shy, he had begun to bond with the other children. "There were about four hundred fifty children, and each of the children had his own story. Lot of children cry. You are in the same boat. You see somebody else cry. You are not the only one in a bad situation. You see smaller children; you see some children I imagine was sick. You see somebody who is worse off than you and this makes you feel a little better. If you stay alone in a room, nobody is there to care. We were sitting with each other, telling stories from where you are, from what city and where your parents are. Some parents, for example, die in Siberia; some of them got in the hospital in Russia, somewhere, I don't know where. Some of them got lost. Each one has a different story. I remember I went with some children and later was told their parents knew mine from the same area in Siberia."

The counselors, though only in their twenties and quite inexperienced, had by now gotten to know the children better and were able to offer them greater care. "The people that took care of us did it for love. They didn't do it for money. So they make the situation better for us. They saw me crying; this was all what I could do. I couldn't do nothing more. So they came over with a little hand, a soft hand on the shoulder and smiled to help us."

Besides the chocolate and the knowledge that other children were in the same boat, an additional factor helped ease Lonek's spirits. It seemed miraculous to Lonek, but he had found a friend. In fact, he had created a small surrogate family for himself. Lonek had made only one friend since leaving his hometown of Jaroslaw—the little Moslem boy in Tashkent who had shown him his treasure chest of pita bread. The new boy not only brought with him the virtue of friendship, but he also had a sister, who was a motherly little girl, and a younger brother. As Eliott reminisced about the little family, his voice sounded jubilant, filled with warm recollections, his laughter ringing with nostalgia and happiness: "There was a guy Krauss. I remember his name all the time. He got his brother and his sister. The sister had red hair. And the brother was a little brother. She was holding him like he was four or five years old. I associate like it was my brother. And this was my bigger sister. She was older than me. I remember she was tall—a teenager, with a ponytail on the back and she gave me something good, always. She was like a little mother to me. We were together all the time. All the time. Till they separate us later for some reason." As recently as ten years ago, Eliott spent two days in Tel Aviv searching for Krauss. He never found him. When I offered to advertise in the Israeli *Kindertransport* newsletter to find Krauss, Eliott eagerly accepted.

During the war years, Persia was a hotbed of intrigue. Supposedly neutral, it served Russia, Britain, United States, and Germany as a meeting place for spies. Arriving from Siberia, Lonek thought that Teheran seemed almost miragelike in its modernity. Never before had he seen a metropolis with substantial buildings, homes, and well-stocked shops. Lonek marveled at the display windows filled with food and other delightful and desirable articles. "For money," observed Eliott, "you can buy whatever there is. After Siberia and Tashkent, was like heaven."

Nevertheless, by most measures the Children's Camp in Teheran, referred to at the time as either "The Jewish Orphanage Home" or the "Jewish Children's Home," was a very long way from heaven. Two representatives from the Jewish Agency and Mrs. Zipporah Shertok had been sent to Teheran to lend whatever assistance they could. Mrs. Shertok was the wife of Moshe Shertok, head of the Jewish Agency's Political Department, and was later referred to by Henrietta Szold as "an angel of mercy with a good head on her shoulders." In October 1942, Mrs. Shertok reported to the Aliyah Department of Jerusalem in some detail:

> The children are housed in one big hut and six big tents. In the big room sleep 98 small children up to age eight. They sleep on the floor, on thin mattresses and cotton cushions. Each child has three woolen blankets. Under the mattresses are spread mats. . . . In the isolation room children too sleep on the floor. There are a few white sheets, but mostly they sleep on dark blankets.
>
> The children over age eight sleep in the tents, but they do not have any mattresses or cushions but only blankets and mats. The tents are torn and cold and rain penetrates and the children are often sick. The autumn has already set in and it is chilly. The children complain that it is cold.
>
> The children receive food from the kitchen three times a day. In the morning $^1/_2$ kg. bread per child for the whole day, a dab of butter, a bit of jam and an apple. At noon: soup and cereal. At five: tea and an egg. Some get extra rations by

medical prescription. They eat in the tents, without a table or a cloth, on the blankets. Some children built themselves tables of brick.

The children are shorter than their age, underdeveloped and pale, some of them very pale. . . . Twice a week they take a warm shower and one of their blankets is disinfected. Some of them have skin rashes and sick eyes and one child has pneumonia. Some two hundred children go barefoot; others have worn out shoes and very shabby and insufficient clothing.[5]

A nurse described the children as "exhausted and feverish." Lonek recalled the monotonous diet, dominated by pita bread and dates: "They open a big square sack of dates, and they broke that in little blocks and gave everybody a piece. Every day almost it was for lunch, dinner and breakfast."

The Jewish camp was separate from and vastly inferior to the Gentile children's quarters. The days were hot, and the nights were somewhat chilly. When it rained, the tents flooded. A contemporary description graphically pictures the harsh conditions in the Jewish camp: "On the hot desert sands, under tattered straw mats, the [Jewish] children lay, ill, feverish and scantily dressed. Nearby lived the Christian children in tents, healthy looking, sun-tanned, and quite content. . . . They frequently abused the Jewish children. Ever so often a sick child broke out crying when he was hit by an object thrown at him by his Polish neighbors. Every half hour a sullen security officer would make his rounds and bellow gruffly: 'Quiet, Zhids [derogatory term for Jew].'"[6] Toward evening, all the inmates of both camps were required to emerge for roll call and evening services which were conducted in Latin and Polish. They were mandatory and included the Jewish children. Officers, cursing and screaming, hauled the sick Jewish children from their sickbays to attend the services.

A change of fortune occurred when the Polish legation in charge of all those evacuated with General Anders, and probably pressured by the British, gave permission to the Jewish community to establish an independent orphanage. The children proudly planted a flag inscribed "The Teheran Home for Jewish Children" in the middle of a parade ground they had laid out. Jewish organizations of all kinds went into high gear. The Jewish Agency in Palestine dispatched two representatives, Reuven Shefer and Avraham Zilberg, who opened the Palestine Office. They offered help with food and clothing and provided some sewing machines. In October, Mrs.

Shertok took charge of running the home. Youth Aliyah, the Society for the Immigration of Jewish Boys and Girls into Palestine, a youth organization located in Palestine, did all it could to help. From the United States, Hadassah mobilized a $500,000 fund-raising campaign to benefit the children.

Although there was a drastic improvement in the children's level of comfort, the Jewish children continued to be taunted by insults and stones hurled by the non-Jewish children. Eliott recalled the difference between the Polish and Jewish accommodations: "The Gentile children were in a separate camp with a gate that was closed. Ours was open. We were in tents and they were in big houses. Rich family houses. No one was allowed to go there. Was a guard there. Our place was a block away and standing with tents."

From the large group of released Polish Jews, fifty-eight young men and women were recruited to care for over eight hundred children. The head counselor was a very capable young man named David Laor. A former officer candidate of a Polish military school, he supervised a staff of young and inexperienced counselors either his age or junior to him by only a few years. To run the camp efficiently, he created departments, such as food, storerooms, sewing, cultural work, and so on Because of the children's poor emotional state, more counselors were urgently needed. Youth Aliyah, however, was unable to send more because the Persian government denied any additional visas to Palestinian Jews. As a result, adult Jewish refugees and young Zionist pioneers, who had arrived with the children, were put in charge of the children.

These youthful counselors, half-naked and barefoot, were young enough to need some mothering themselves. Yet, they now faced extraordinary responsibilities and almost insurmountable obstacles. Their living conditions were extremely primitive. Without mattresses, cushions, or sheets, some slept on the floor of the storeroom or in the laundry or offices. One counselor even made his bed on an office table. Food was minimal. Yet these counselors not only shepherded the children under their care, but busied themselves locating those Jewish children who had not been relinquished and were still residing with their caretaker nuns and priests.[7]

A counselor recalled the search:

> Our work was strenuous. Though we were empowered by the
> Polish legation to gather together all the Jewish orphans,
> even those who had been admitted into Christian asylums,
> the priests and nuns did not easily give up their "redeemed

or redeemable souls." In many cases we had no difficulties, especially with the older children, who were considered by the clergy as "lost souls." But we had to wage a vigorous fight to save the little ones. There were cases when we had to "abduct" them stealthily and hide them. Often we lodged sharp complaints in writing, to which we received favorable replies, but in the meantime the children concerned disappeared. We even took the officials to court to prove that the children whom they held in custody had been born Jewish and should be released to us.

The struggle of the Catholic clergy to keep the Jewish children took on various guises. They inveigled their wards by promising that they would find their parents. They intimidated the children by telling them that their food rations would be diminished. They frightened the children by maligning us, by telling them that we were Russian agents who had come to bring them back to Russia. It took us a long time and much effort to repudiate their deceitfulness and monstrous lies. Often they denied to the authorities that Jewish children were housed in their monasteries or convents. However the young non-Jewish inmates knew no wiles and with contempt pointed out the "Zhids" to us. Indeed owing to their help, I was privileged to remove many crosses from the necks of children who had already undergone conversion.

Alas, sometimes we were too late. We knew of eight young children who were dispatched to India or Africa before we got wind of them. . . . It is quite likely that many children were permanently lost to us without our knowing their names, their parents, or their whereabouts.

Once I was riding in a carriage with a six-year-old on my lap. On each side sat older children. I had removed them just in time from a railroad car bound for Africa. They had already experienced what it meant to be a Jew—the deprivations, scorn, and physical suffering. When I finally won them over and took them home with me, they broke out in torrents of tears. One of them, a boy, told me of the beatings he had received, the constant gnawing hunger and spiritual pain he had experienced during the last few weeks. He wept as he told me: "Once they beat me because of my Jewish nose, another time because the smell of onions was on my breath and a third time because I did not know the prayer to the Holy Mother." The children inquired, "In the children's home where you are taking us, are the teachers Jewish? Do they speak Yiddish? They don't hit and don't steal bread from the children? And will we go to Eretz Yisrael? When? And what of our parents? Will you also bring them there?" I had to wage constant, valiant struggles to obtain their release. Most of the children came to us ill and sore and often bloated from hunger.[8]

Besides the retrieval of Jewish children, a multitude of important issues bedeviled the counselors. Among these were the unbearable hot climate and serious health problems. Eighteen children died in the first month after arrival in camp. Many others required hospitalization for such serious ailments as scabies, ringworm, tetanus, and dysentery. Eye inflammations, aftereffects of starvation, and all kinds of skin problems were also common.[9] A physician representing a medical commission commented: "What are you delivering to me? Children or corpses?"

There was very little money for medicines. Even simple dressings were scarce. The only room available for infectious diseases should have housed eight patients. It sheltered eighty. Because professional nursing staff was not available, the *halutzim* and *halutzot* (male and female pioneers headed for Palestine) helped care for the sick children.[10] Little children, unaccustomed to having their protests heeded, silently and without protest held out their emaciated arms to allow nurses to vaccinate them. Infested with lice, the children's heads had to be shaved, giving them a particularly pathetic appearance.

The children also lacked clothing. Their wardrobes consisted solely of what they had on their backs, which was often malodorous and torn. Although a Polish official was assigned to distribute apparel, the Jewish children were the last to receive any. At times, when the counselors tried to obtain their children's share, they were beaten up instead.[11] They were told that the Polish children had priority over the Jewish children because they needed to be dressed appropriately for their journey out of Persia. One day, one of the counselors noted that a package had arrived from America that was specifically marked for the Jewish children. It was only after a long argument that the counselor obtained a part of its contents.[12] The local Jewish population contributed as much clothing, food, and necessities as they could, but they did so furtively, frightened of how the Poles might retaliate if they saw the Jewish children receive some unexpected benefit.[13]

Most important, the children had to be restored to emotional health. Until now, they had lived in hostile, unpredictable environments, always aware that they were being considered inferior at best and, at worst, sub-human. They had been beset by fears, anxiety, and chaos for years. Suddenly the children were expected to trust the adults around them and fit into a predictable structure when before no one had been trustworthy and nothing had been predictable. Even their parents had unexpectedly disappeared without a trace. How could they possibly believe that all was not ephemeral and that tomorrow would bear a resemblance to today.

The children often expressed their lack of trust by their behavior. The counselors responded by providing continual care and remaining vigilant for unexpected problems in even the most mundane areas of life. For instance, some children hoarded and hid their food; others gulped their rations out of fear that they might be taken from them. One girl refused to work at all unless she was rewarded with food. Many children were haunted by nightmares and needed comforting at night. To earn money for emergencies, some children attempted to sneak out of their tents at night and sell their blankets to the soldiers guarding them. A potential danger was averted when counselors noticed that a few of the soldiers guarding the children offered them money for sexual favors. Many children mourned their parents and siblings who had accidentally become separated. There was, for instance, a boy who was the only survivor of his whole family, all of whom had been buried alive by the Germans. The group also included an inconsolable little girl who had been separated from her father for some weeks, but then had suddenly glimpsed him out of a train window just as the train was pulling out of the station. A boy, having been separated from his brother during the journey from Tashkent, searched for him continually.[14]

The young, inexperienced staff struggled with the overwhelming task of persuading the children that they would continue to be provided for, that want and threat were not lurking around every corner, and above all, that there was hope and a future for them in Palestine. Patience, empathy, and total dedication had to be the bedrock of the counselors' relationships with the children.

Slowly life began to take on a certain routine and organization. A group identification was established by assigning each cluster of children a number matching the tent in which they resided. The children were grouped by age. A particular counselor, who helped instill a sense of pride by ensuring that the children kept their tents clean, was assigned to each unit. Lonek

An aerial view of Jaroslaw, Lonek's hometown.

Photo: M. Wideryński - KAW

The house in Lvov where Lonek and his family stayed in 1939. The building housed hundreds of fleeing Jews, cramming several families into a room.

Heimek, Lonek's brother, at eight years of age with his parents.

Henrietta Szold, the founder of Hadassah, the Women's Zionist Organization of America. At the age of 74, Szold became personally involved in organizing the reception and placement of the Teheran Children in Palestine.

(Photo from the archives of Hadassah, The Women's Zionist Organization of America, Inc.)

General Wladyslaw Anders in May 1946. Under the terms of the 1941 Sikorski-Maisky Treaty, he was released from the Moscow Lubianka prison and allowed to form a Polish army-in-exile. As a result, about 100,000 Poles trapped in the Soviet Union were led to safety in Persia. This number included about 6,000 Jews, the Teheran Children among them.

(Photo from the Pilsudski Institute Collection)

Tamar de Sola Pool (*above left*), the national president of Hadassah; Denise Tourover (*above right*), a lawyer on the National Board of Hadassah and its Washington representative; and Gisela Warburg (*right*), chairman of the National Youth Aliyah Committee, an offshoot of Hadassah. Together the three women successfully maneuvered the diplomatic feat of getting the Teheran Children out of Iran.

(Photos from the archives of Hadassah, The Women's Zionist Organization of America, Inc.)

Photographer: G.D. Hackett

(Yad Vashem)

During their journey the children lived in tent cities such as this one in Teheran.

(Yad Vashem)

Some of the younger Teheran Children in Karachi with their counselors. While in Karachi, the children were given tropical helmets and clean, though ill-fitting, clothes.

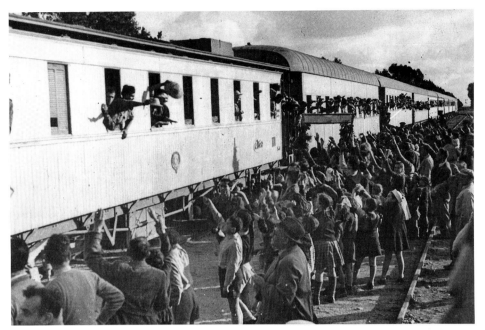

In February 1943, the Teheran Children arrived at their final destination — Palestine. The crowd that had gathered surges forward to welcome the children.

The arrival of young Teheran Children in Palestine. Overwhelmed, the children clutch each other's hands.

Upon their arrival in Palestine, the Teheran Children were besieged by well-wishers, some of whom hoped to identify a lost friend or relative. Here, a young woman believes she has recognized her ten-year-old nephew, but the boy does not remember her.

(Central Zionist Archives)

(Yad Vashem)

The arrival of some of the older girls. They each carry a bundle of whatever possessions they managed to retain throughout their arduous journey.

This cartoon, satirizing the religious organizations' disputes over the Teheran Children, appeared in Palestine's newspaper *Ha'aretz* on November 26, 1943. The banner on the left reads: "Welcome from Teheran." The poster on the right reads: "A glass of milk and soap also for our new children." The bottom caption reads: "Don't cry Sarah. We were rescued from our enemies: we shall also be rescued from those who love us."

Lonek, soon after his arrival in Palestine, about 1943.

Lonek (*first row, far left*) at the Ludwig Tietz school, about 1943. His admission to the technical school when he was fifteen was a passage into adulthood for Lonek.

Lonek, after his discharge from the Israeli army, about 1950.

During their 1992 return trip, Eliott (*left*) and Heimek visited the synagogue in Lvov, which was the first stop for the family when they arrived in 1939 after fleeing Jaroslaw.

Elliott and Heimek take a rest during their "You can't go home again" journey in 1992.

particularly enjoyed the mornings when, after breakfast, the children marched into a field, assembled around the flag, sang songs, and were given their assignments for the day. Although no textbooks were available, a regular academic schedule was instituted. Teachers taught in Polish, Russian, and Hebrew, the official language of the camp; they taught mathematics and history. The children were informed about world events and given an identification with Zionist goals. The counselors encouraged the children's individual talents. Those youngsters with nice handwriting helped the secretaries, girls who enjoyed sewing assisted in repairing clothes, and some children wrote stories and poems while others drew posters.

Eliott recalled the remarkable dedication of the staff with awe: "They were very devoted. Unbelievable what they went through. They deserve all the medals. They were not all adults like thirty or forty years old. Some of them were only eighteen, twenty years. Most of them went in Poland to high school and by the time they finished "College Siberia" in Russia, they already were adults. This is why they were so devoted, because they think of their own skin and how it is to be like us. The counselors were everything to me at those times. They was like my parents, my brother, my family. They know everything; they kept us occupied all the time."

Just as Lonek's life began to improve, he abruptly and without warning, experienced a fearful blow. He suddenly became blind. Both the physical and emotional impact were devastating. Eliott still shuddered as he recalled the events.

CHAPTER XIV

The Darkness

*L*onek's blindness was a sudden and devastating shock. "After I arrive [in Teheran], it was a short time, maybe a week or two, suddenly I start to be blind. I could see nothing. I wonder just how it was and whether sight would come back to me. This was on an afternoon and suddenly I see dark." Eliott grew increasingly incredulous as he recounted this period of his life, questioning what other horrors could possibly have befallen him. "Just like dark and dark. I ask myself what to do. Maybe call somebody to bring me back to the tent. I went back to the tent and they called the nurse and they decided to send me to the hospital. Because they didn't know what happened. I lost my vision."

Because Lonek's ailment was considered too serious to be treated by the camps' volunteer Jewish doctors and nurses, he was placed in a hospital run by Polish Gentiles. Lonek's room was filled with Polish childen. "And there was Christian nurses from the Polish army. I was lucky that they give me a little food. They did me a favor. They put food somewhere on my bed and I used to eat." How did he locate the food on the plate? "You feel something warm or something cold. Finally you are getting used to it. The nurses didn't care about me. They didn't behave very good. They called me 'Jew Boy.' Nobody nice. Nobody. Nobody ever take care of me."

The children in Lonek's room were all Polish. They taunted him with jibes and exploited his helplessness. "I was the only Jew there. Sooner or later they identify me as a Jew. Children are very rough and if they are Polak [Polish] they don't need much. They treat me like a leper. It's like a sickness of them. It's terrible! They put ropes and broomsticks at my feet so I fall down when I walk. They put salt in my food so I can't even eat. Laughing all the time and spitting on me, the Gentiles! Spitting!" To take care of himself, Lonek put his few possessions and a potty close to his bed. He tried to fight loneliness and boredom and longed to feel fresh air on his face. "I was sitting all day on the bed; sitting and that's all. So I went out from my bed, and bed by bed I was going and I ask somebody where is the door. I got familiar how to go outside. I ask somebody if I can sit somewhere." Most of the time Lonek was terrified. He was haunted by the fear of never regaining his sight. When I asked Eliott whether he ever complained to anyone, he replied with an infinitely sad expression as if to say: "Little boys should not be abandoned in such fearful situations." Out loud he confessed what had been his biggest fear: "I just kept quiet because I was scared that they would deport me. Send me back to Russia."

The memory of his parents kept flashing back to him—his last walk with his mother to the orphanage and the picture of his ailing father: "I remember my father only when he was sitting on a bed, a wooden bed—he was laying there and was numb. We didn't know what going on with him, except we saw he got hot fever. My mother always putting some cold water on his forehead to reduce the fever and she gave him something to drink, tea or whatever, water. Those two pictures and my little brother that was running between my legs all the time." And now Lonek was just as helpless as his father; only there was no one to smooth his brow or bring him tea.

Days dragged into weeks. Nobody could explain to Lonek what was happening to him. "I was thinking I would never see nothing. Nobody knew what happened. Nobody." Finally, after some days passed the doctors diagnosed a vitamin deficiency and assured him that he would probably regain his vision. And after about four to six weeks and almost imperceptibly, Lonek's sight did begin to return: "Slowly my vision came back. I saw like you see difference between day and night. Change more and more and more." He became conscious of daybreak and began to perceive what appeared to be shadows. Eliott reconstructed this event with astonishment, almost awe: "The first time I remember I saw, I was so happy, even though I only saw a shadow. Like something unbelievable! It was like being born again." Toward the end of his stay at the hospital and to Lonek's delight, his friend Krauss managed to visit him. Soon after, Lonek was able to return to camp. Later, some other children from his group were also laid low by vitamin deficiencies. But, because by then the doctors had learned through Lonek's experience how to diagnose their affliction, the later sufferers recovered faster. As the first, Lonek had been adrift in unchartered waters.

When Lonek returned to camp, his sight had greatly improved, though it was some time before the doctor removed his eye dressings. At first, the bandages had only slits for openings, which were slowly enlarged to permit more light to enter. Impatient to be normal again, Lonek would cheat sometimes and widen the holes a little farther himself. "I was like in heaven. The whole world was my world. I could see my friend Krauss all the time."

Back in camp, the children's morale was definitely improving. It was evident that the unstinting and self-sacrificial efforts of the counselors were paying off. The counselors' complete devotion to the children's emotional and physical health had transformed this waiting period, in spite of great want, into a positive experience for the children.

At the same time, days were stretching into weeks, and weeks into months, and the children were still in Persia. Children and counselors waited impatiently and apprehensively for their departure to Palestine. Originally the children were supposed to have traveled from Persia to Palestine through Iraq, but to everyone's dismay and acute frustration, the Iraqi government vehemently prohibited the children from traversing its country. No pleading by the Jewish Agency in Palestine or by Jewish officials in Teheran—not even pledging to seal the trains the children were to travel in—softened the Iraqi stance. They remained unyielding. Everyone was at a loss. There were no alternatives. The children simply had to pass through Iraq to get to their destination. In a manner of speaking, the children were walled in. Children and counselors huddled together in their tent city, in their mind's eye looking longingly toward Eretz Israel.

CHAPTER XV

Britain Behind the Scene

While the Allies were fighting for their very survival and millions of displaced people were fleeing, what powers could be recruited, to aid Lonek and almost one thousand Jewish children stranded in Teheran waiting to find a home? These children had become pawns in the Middle Eastern political chess game involving the Arab-Israel conflict and British interests in the Middle East. When aeons ago, Lonek had played happily in front of his father's factory in Jaroslaw, there had been no indication that his life would ricochet between such impersonal forces as the Third Reich's extermination policy, the Russians' insane xenophobia, and Middle Eastern power politics.

The British government wanted to help the Teheran Children. Genuine concern is reflected in the letters, memos, telegrams, and personal notes that passed among the various British government offices.

It is not easy for government officials to extend help. Every step becomes entangled by official procedures, national interests, and international consequences. Government correspondence about the Teheran Children began with a simple letter from the Jewish Agency in Palestine, requesting the British Foreign Office in Whitehall, London, to obtain transit visas through Iraq for Polish Jewish refugees stranded in Teheran, emphasizing the five hundred children [the number assumed at that time] among them. The Jewish Agency had apparently committed a faux pas: The request should have been directed to the Colonial Office, not to the Foreign Office. Some consternation was expressed about this breach of etiquette, but in view of the pathetic condition of the children, the Foreign Office decided to overlook it and forwarded the letter to the Colonial Office. The correspondence that ensued between the different British government departments—the Colonial Office, the Eastern Department, the Foreign Office—indicates clearly that they immediately recognized the difficulty of their task. Complicated issues arose: How could the Iraqi government best be pressured to allow the Jewish children to travel through its territory? Should the Iraqis be approached immediately, or should the request be delayed until visas for the children to Palestine had been procured? Which way would be more persuasive to the Iraqi government? Opinions differed. One official anticipated correctly that the Iraqi government would, consistent with its past record, refuse to cooperate. He wrote: "We are up against the same difficulty as previously—the unwillingness of the Iraqi government to grant transit visas." This kind of opposition was not easily accepted by another official who fumed: "It is a question of perfectly legal immigration into Palestine, approved by us in accordance with our general policy and for the Iraqi Government to withhold transit facilities is surely open to question. I therefore hope . . . [to] press the Baghdad Government to grant the facilities we (and not only the Jews) require."

But the situation in the Middle East, as usual, was complex. The basic issue was the Arab-British dispute over Jewish immigration to Palestine. The Iraqi position on this matter was clear: It would not lift a finger to allow even one Jew to reach Palestine. Not every British official understood the underlying issue. One British official took a rather naïve point of view: "It is surely possible to put the case of children up to the Baghdad Government. There is no possible chance of the young people staying in Iraq and I think the assurance of an earlier train [to Palestine] should overcome all hesitation." Another shrewder British official noted, Iraqi objections were not based on a fear that the Jews might stay in Iraq, but were fueled by the fear of Jewish immigration into Palestine. (In any case, the Jewish Agency had been entirely opposed to sending the children to Iraq and letting them remain there.) A Mr. Walker of the Foreign Office indicated that Iraq's resistance was rooted in its desire to "demonstrate its disapproval of British policy in Palestine." Recognizing the Iraqis' determined opposition, the Eastern Department suggested another route, possibly through Turkey and then by sea to Palestine, which, however, would be very indirect, expensive, and dangerous. As it turned out, the Turkish government also refused passage to the children.

Further complicating the Teheran Children's plight were questions about the extent to which the British should antagonize the Iraqis during wartime by allowing Jews to immigrate to Palestine. Not everyone agreed that the Iraqis' resistance was unreasonable. An official at the British Embassy

with a less sympathetic view toward the Jewish children and a strong identification with British interests commented:

> It is tiresome of the Iraqis not to let the Jewish children
> through but I cannot altogether agree that is is unreasonable of
> them. On the contrary. It is, I think, the Zionists who are being
> unreasonable. They pursue a policy in Palestine which they
> know to be offensive to the Arabs and at the same time expect
> an Arab government to provide them with facilities. As allies,
> the Iraqi government has many obligations towards us, which
> we do our best to see that they fulfill, but I cannot see that
> facilitating Jewish immigration into Palestine is one of them . .
> unless we are prepared to make a big issue of the question and
> use the big stick—which seems to me quite unjustified.

He further expressed the hope—indicating an annoyance with Jewish
insistence—that when this explanation was to be given to the Jewish representative, Professor Namier, "[We] shall not take too apologetic a tone."
Judging from another Foreign Office letter to the Colonial Office, there
seemed to be an additional concern, namely, the danger of antagonizing
the new Iraqi minister, Nuri Pasha. "In view of the Arab feelings about
Palestine we do not feel that we can press hard and make a big issue of
something which would be a favour to us but one which, when it got known,
would gravely compromise Nuri Pasha's position."

The British officials' concern over the Iraqi situation was motivated by
their interest in the children's well-being, as well as by their desire to avoid
being perceived as heartless. Possibly contrite about dismissing Professor
Namier so cavalierly, one of the officials suggested convincing him that
attempts by Britain to bully the Iraqi government would affect Anglo-Iraqi
relations and further alienate Baghdad. Another British communication
read: "We have asked the Embassy at Washington to explain to the State
Department and Rabbi Wise that the question is not as simple as it looks. .
. . Our telegram to Washington will have indicated that the situation has
difficulties of which the Americans are unaware." The British Embassy in
Baghdad also requested the British Foreign Office in Washington to try to
influence the new U.S. Undersecretary of State, Sumner Welles, to pressure the Iraqis. But because the British sensed that the Americans did not
truly understand the complexity of the situations and because Welles was
new at his job, they suggested that "it might be unwise in all the circumstances for the new Minister to gallop too hard at this, his first fence."[1]

In spite of Britain's good intentions, there continued to be an endless series of fences and not too much gallop. The situation was truly complex with so many countries involved and such varied interests at stake.

In the past whenever Lonek's fortune ebbed, just when all hope seemed lost, some turn of events, some *deus ex machina* emerged and snatched him to safety. And again this time, almost as if he were a character in a cautionary tale, some guardian angels arose to lead Lonek and the other orphans to asylum. These kindly angels took the form of dedicated, hardworking, and resourceful women whose enterprising spirit helped to bring about the impossible.

CHAPTER XVI

The Lion-Hearted Women

While the British labored from their vantage point on the other side of the Atlantic, Hadassah, the Women's Zionist Organization of America, picked up the cudgel for the Teheran Children. How fitting that Hadassah would play a central role in delivering the Teheran Children. The organization, based on the tenets laid down by its founder Henrietta Szold, had always been dedicated to Jewish humanitarian causes. Its creed was to translate idealistic purposes and principled aims into practical actions.[1]

Alerted by the Jewish Agency in Palestine, the Hadassah leadership in New York—Tamar de Sola Pool, national president; Gisela Warburg, chairman, National Youth Aliyah Committee (an offshoot of Hadassah); and Denise Tourover, a lawyer on the National Board of Hadassah and its Washington representative—immediately dedicated themselves to evacuating the Teheran Children to Palestine. In their far-reaching plans, the women contrived to involve people of power who might intimidate others less self-assured. So confident were they that their discussions of how to influence the British and American governments to move planes or ships assumed an almost casual tenor. No matter how dark the prospects looked, they continued without hesitation in their unremitting quest to bring the Teheran Children to safety. They were resolute: the Teheran Children would get to Palestine.

The determination of the Hadassah women is evident in a letter written by Gisela Warburg on October 28, 1942, to Myron Taylor, who apparently wielded influence with Under-Secretary of State Sumner Welles. In it, she urged Taylor to present the children's case to the secretary. After summarizing the problem, Warburg continued:

117

We turn to you for assistance in meeting this problem, which we have been unsuccessful in solving thus far. Up to the present the following steps have been taken: We were successful in enlisting the sympathy of the British Ambassador, Lord Halifax, who cabled to the Foreign Office. This office, in turn, made representations through their official representative in Baghdad to Nuri Pasha. Similarly, our own State Department has made representations in Baghdad through our official there. According to information given by Mr. Sumner Welles to Dr. Nahum Goldman of the American Emergency Committee for Zionist Affairs, they have thus far not succeeded in obtaining permission for transit. . . . What could be done at this point you will know best. It has been suggested that a representation by you to the Iraq Minister here and a cable from you to Sir Herbert Emerson of the Intergovernmental Committee on Political Refugees might be determining factors.

The numerous government departments and VIPs mentioned in Gisela Warburg's letter make one's head whirl: the British Foreign Office, the American State Department, the Iraqi government, the Intergovernmental Committee on Political Refugees, the American Emergency Committee for Zionist Affairs, Lord Halifax, Sumner Welles, Dr. Nahum Goldman, Sir Herbert Emerson, and Nuri Pasha. And this was only one letter among a great many! These women wielded no political power nor did they have any resources other than the Jewish women who stood behind them. Yet they sat in their offices spinning schemes that would have daunted even personages with greater resources. It would be impossible to envision how many behind-the-scenes contacts, word-of-mouth inquiries, false leads, unanswered communications, and dead-end phone calls answered by reluctant secretaries and apathetic officials the women must have encountered in their pursuit of getting the children out of Teheran. Anyone who has ever applied for a visa, other than a tourist visa, may have an idea of the indifference or sheer hostility such a request engenders in easily irritated officials. Moreover, Gisela Warburg was not simply searching for one visa—she sought almost one thousand. (The number of children mentioned in the correspondence varied continually.)

Moved by Gisela Warburg's letter, Taylor handed it to Under-Secretary Welles accompanied by a note in which he inquired: "Can this situation be brought by the Department to the attention of the Minister of Iraq in Washington with a view of securing the necessary transit visas from the Iraq Government?"

On October 29, two days after Warburg sent her letter to Taylor, she directed a memorandum to Mrs. Tourover. It was written in the confidential tone of friends who know each other well, share the same concerns, and are used to exchanging ideas. Penned with an even, strong handwriting, Warburg mentioned that in spite of her secretary being away, she did "not want to let the day go by without my daily resume on the Teheran front." Some names mentioned in the memo are still familiar; others are not, but evidently, they were then people of influence, as exemplified in the following memo:

Dear Denise [Tourover]

1.) I met to-day with Mr. Galligher and Mr. Sidel [president] of the Standard Oil of New Jersey. Upshot of conversation:

a.) The American Minister to Iraq has died recently. His successor is about to leave. They suggest we should meet him. I shall call to-night a personal friend of mine who was for many years Consul General in Italy and is now chief of the Division of Foreign Service Personnel in Wash. and ask him whether he can make me meet the new man.

b.) They think the only pressure possible is through lend-lease (as you said from the beginning) and think Barny [Bernard] Baruch is the man.

The Hadassah leaders also attempted to influence the White House through Elinor, wife of the U.S. Secretary of the Treasury Henry Morgenthau, who was Mrs. Roosevelt's friend. After learning that the president himself was interested in the rescue of the Teheran Children, prospects brightened for State Department intervention.

Despite such progress, the Hadassah women explored other alternatives for rescuing the children, including their removal by the Allies by plane. This plan is examined in an undated and unsigned memo scribbled in haste—the kind of note people pass back and forth between each other at a meeting when it is urgent to communicate an idea but there is no opportunity to talk. In the first of a series of jottings, Miss Warburg writes: "Denise: I wonder about something else. The State Department did say that there were no American planes in Persia. But I don't think they really know. I suppose only the War Department knows. Could you find out authentically whether there are any [planes]." Tourover scribbled back: "Even if there were some [American planes] there, I doubt if they would use them on their [the children's] behalf."

Warburg refused to take no for an answer. She scrawled in haste, judging by the rather sloppy writing, under Tourover's response: "They may. . . ." And she passed it back to Tourover., who replied: "I'll look into it—"

The women simply decided in the middle of the war, when all information was restricted by censorship and the Allies had few, if any, planes to spare, to check on the availability of British and American planes for the Teheran Children. Nothing seemed to faze these lion-hearted Hadassah leaders.

Still, uncertain about the availability of planes, the women continued to pressure Iraq by writing to Robert McDaniel , who was acquainted with Ali Jewdat, envoy extraordinary, minister plenipotentiary of Iraq, at the Iraqi legation in Washington. Informed of the women's letter, Jewdat questioned how anyone could possibly be so misguided as to expect the Iraqi government to permit the Teheran Children to pass through its country. Yes, the government was deeply sympathetic to the children, but why must they go to Palestine? And why should the American government meddle in matters not concerning its citizens? As to the possibility of the Iraqi government's resistance spawning bad publicity, they could not care less. Jewdat wrote:

> I am afraid that you have not understood clearly our point of view in regard to the refugee children passing through Iraq from Iran to Palestine.
>
> If it were purely a question of humanity, our government stands ready to do all in its power to help. However, we fear that there is also a political question involved and one contrary to the policy of the Iraqi government and unfavorable to the cause of the United Nations. [!]
>
> We are at a loss to understand why these children can only go to Palestine. There are many other places equally safe, if not safer, from a humanitarian point of view. Iraq even stands ready, worst comes to worst, to receive these children into its own country and to care for them, as of course, it is most improper that innocent children should suffer because of war.
>
> Furthermore, we do not see how the United States Department of State can protest to the Iraqi government since these children are not American citizens. If such a protest is made we greatly fear our government will decline to accept it.
>
> We note from the clipping enclosed in your letter, the unfavorable publicity given Iraq due to this policy and that you say it may be

assumed such publicity will continue unabated until these children are allowed passage across our country. All we can say to that is please mail us clippings of all such publicity and we will send them on to Baghdad. That is all that we can do.

Please believe that we sympathize with your efforts to help these refugee children. If you care to discuss the question further with us and feel the need for more clarification on our stand, we shall be very glad to have you come and see us again.

The letter's tone of evasion—if not hypocrisy—must have been quite insufferable to Hadassah officials. Nevertheless Mrs. de Sola Pool made one last-ditch effort on December 1, 1942, to reverse the Iraqi government's decision, but to no avail. The coup de grâce came in the form of a brief letter from Jewdat. Sounding irritated, he insisted that the matter was closed once and for all. Unlike his previous communication, any invitations for visits to the Royal Iraqi Legation were omitted: "In reply to your letter of December 1st, about the transit through Iraq of several hundred Polish-Jewish children to Palestine, I have to tell you that this Legation has been asked before to deal with this matter. Since this question is connected with the fundamental policy of my government it was referred to Baghdad at that time. Inasmuch as these children are not American citizens I regret there is nothing more that can be done by this Legation."

Other efforts also came to naught. Although the Quakers had provided exemplary assistance to the children arriving on *Kindertransports* in England from the Continent, they were unable to help rescue the Teheran Children. Nor were negotiations conducted by the Jewish Agency successful. Although sufficient planes could not be found to fly the children from Persia, the British offered to provide ships to ferry them through the Mediterranean to Palestine. But because Persia had no outlet to the Mediterranean, the plan would have required the children to travel by road through Turkey to a Mediterranean port. Debates among the camp leaders in Teheran over the safety of Turkish roads became moot when Turkey refused to provide transit visas.[2] In desperation, hare-brained schemes were discussed. The suggestion was raised not to inform the Iraquis that the children were Jewish. Wiser heads countered that such a deception would certainly not escape the Iraqis. A proposal by the Jewish Agency that "the children might be smuggled through Iraq by the British or Polish Army and that the British and the Iraqi governments . . . might look the other way" was also rejected. The idea that the children might be allowed to pass through Iraq if dressed in Boy Scout uniforms, as some Polish children had been, came to nought.[3] One of the more bizarre plans was to dress the children in Polish military uniforms and pass them off as soldiers.[4]

Time dragged on. A memorandum dated December 24, 1942, named "Re All Transport of Refugee Jewish Children in Teheran" and not addressed to anyone in particular, reported no progress with Iraq. The memo also mentioned—without further explanation—that the children were now facing eviction from Persia. It spoke of seven hundred "sorely tried and ravaged children." Probably due to wartime conditions, estimates of the number of Teheran Children varied constantly.

None of these setbacks slowed Hadassah officials either in New York or in Palestine. Undaunted by the continuing discouraging news, the eighty-two-year-old Henrietta Szold continued preparing for the children's arrival in Israel. She never doubted their coming.

Since her early twenties, Henrietta Szold had been dedicated to the education of immigrants, for whom she organized the first night school in Baltimore. Her approach was well ahead of her time. The students were not just taught vocational subjects, such as bookkeeping and dressmaking, but were also helped to advance in such academic subjects as English and mathematics. Moreover, the schools had another purpose besides education: They aided the integration of newcomers into American society. To achieve this goal, Szold discarded archaic authoritarian approaches to education and boldly involved the students in the running and decision making of the school. The day the school opened, over three hundred students registered, and many more were turned away. In fact, the program grew so large and successful that several years later the city of Baltimore assumed its leadership.

Henrietta Szold's interest in education flowered even more in Palestine. Included among her many missions was the revitalization of Jewish schools when they were in a pitiable state. Salaries were erratic, and teachers and children were burdened by poverty and hunger. Because Szold had established an excellent reputation with the British while completing previous projects, she was able to obtain grants from them for educational purposes. Henrietta Szold's ability to innovate, improvise, manage, and remain personally interested in teachers' and children's problems, and apply sound pedagogical knowledge, completely transformed the school system.

In charge of the education of others, Szold constantly carved out new directions and provided new opportunities using such novel measures as the introduction of vocational and technical workshops, special training for disturbed youngsters, and supplying case workers for families with special problems.

Already at an age when others had long retired, Henrietta Szold was ceaselessly involved in the rescue of European children, in their education once they arrived, in the need to raise money, and in the many other labors and requests that poured in hourly and were connected with these enormous tasks. Henrietta Szold was overwhelmed by the demands made on her. Her workday started at seven o'clock A.M., when she arrived with a little paper bag containing her lunch, usually eaten at her desk. At night after dinner, work resumed again, until she returned to her very simple living quarters.

Perhaps Henrietta Szold's greatest contribution was the work that she started at age seventy-four, as she sat in her modest room in Palestine, her clothes packed in preparation for her return to America and possible retirement. It was then that a request reached her from Palestine Jewry to help rescue Jewish children from Hitler's Germany. Without hesitation, Henrietta Szold unpacked her trunks and accepted what she considered to be her duty. As a result, Youth Aliyah came into being.

In connection with her rescue work, Henrietta Szold made three trips to Germany; each one was more wrenching than the last.

> Those who saw her off at the railroad station [on her last trip
> in 1937] said good-bye to a sprightly quick-stepping figure,
> but when she returned her friends were shocked to see the
> bent and shrunken figure looking her 77 years. There was no
> need of words to tell the harrowing experience—the meeting
> in the synagogue with the Gestapo on watch, desperate
> parents hanging on her words, some pleading for rescue of
> their children, some wanting a living word from little ones
> they were never to see again. When she had finished speaking
> [to a Jewish audience in Germany] and answering all the
> questions, the congregation, emotionally all but spent, rose
> and sang under the eyes of the Gestapo "Hatikvah," the hymn
> of the Zionist movement and now Israel's national anthem.[5]

Once more, Henrietta Szold mobilized all her strength, this time to aid the Teheran Children. She began to make all the necessary arrangements for clothing, shelter, and all the myriad details involved in receiving so many children . The dearth of money presented severe problems:

We had to seek places which offered kitchen and dining room accommodations ready-made. Every plate and glass costs fortunes these days. The places secured are not sufficient for the 933 children waiting at Teheran. We are hoping that they will come not all at once, but in age groups, so as to give us a chance to dispose of a number of them before their successors appear. During the past week, luck would have it that I was brought in contact with one of the "exchanges" from Poland, a mother of three children, who succeeded in bringing with her only one of them; the other two had disappeared. . . . From her I heard details so gruesome that I cannot recover my balance. Meanwhile the children waiting at Teheran do not receive a transit visa from the Iraqi Government. So they suffer from the cruel (so I am told) Persian winter. The children at Teheran is the only subject I can think about.[6]

The year was drawing to a gloomy end. A letter written on December 30, 1942 on behalf of Henry Morgenthau finally conceded the failure of American efforts. Specifically, the letter informed Mrs. Tourover that the American resident minister in Baghdad had taken up "the matter [of the Teheran Children] with the Prime Minister of Iraq, presenting it strongly and in detail on humanitarian grounds," but to no avail. The British ambassador to Baghdad had "also pressed the Prime Minister to grant the visas, but, despite the treaty alliances between Great Britain and Iraq, this effort also met with failure." At the time, however, it seemed that both Secretary Morgenthau and Mrs. Morgenthau had done all they possibly could to help in connection with this difficult situation. "I need not tell you that I, also, would be glad to do everything in my power to help in the effort that is being made to rescue the children. We can only hope that eventually the matter may have a happy outcome."

As an afterthought, at the end of the page the writer scribbled: "Best wishes for a happier year in 1943" between the typed page and his signature. The wish sounded wistful and less than convincing—a mournful ending to three months of unstinting efforts, and a gloomy, melancholy ending to 1942.

Lonek knew nothing of all the failed negotiations. The counselors attempted to keep the children informed, but they were equally as isolated from the outside world. Yes, trust in the adults around him made the delay somewhat easier, but whereas under normal circumstances children wait fretfully for their first bicycle or grandma's arrival with birthday presents,

Lonek faced continual suspense about weightier matters. Yes, life was better than in Siberia, but it was still full of privations. Yes, there were caring adults watching over them, but where were his parents? Yes, his life was not immediately threatened, but would the insecurity ever end? Did he have a future? No one could answer his questions.

CHAPTER XVII

A Fortunate Turn of Fortune's Wheel

While the Iraqi and Turkish governments remained adamantly opposed to granting passage to the Teheran Children, an audacious plan was being hatched, apparently initiated by Moshe Shertok, head of the Jewish Agency's Political Department in Palestine, and conveyed to the British government. In postwar years, Shertok recalled: "When I was in London, in 1942–43, I gave up the idea of transporting the children via Iraq, but I did make strenuous efforts to obtain a ship to take them by sea."[1]

The idea of taking the children by sea was an ingenious one, not meant for the fainthearted. As Iran has no outlet to the Mediterranean, a sea route would require the following itinerary: The children would be entrained in Teheran for Ahvaz, roughly a thirty-six-hour journey within Iran, and on arrival, temporarily settled in an English-Polish military camp. As soon as a ship was available, they would travel to the port of Bandar-e Shahpur, located at the northern end of the Persian Gulf. From there, they were slated to travel through the Persian Gulf and the Gulf of Oman. After sailing along the coast of India (now a part of Pakistan), the vessel would anchor for some days in Karachi. Setting sail again, it would turn west and reach Aden, Yemen, by way of the Arabian Sea. Continuing through the Gulf of Aden, the vessel would proceed through the Red Sea to its final destination, Port Said in Egypt. From there the children could travel by train to Palestine.[2] It was a formidable and dangerous trip. Communications and provisions in that part of the world were complicated even at the best of times, but now a war raged. Shortages of almost everything, heavily mined seas, and lurking submarines complicated every move.

Once the plan was decided and the British government had granted permits to the travelers to enter Palestine, there was still a missing link: The lack of available shipping to transport the children. All who had invested in the children—the British and American governments, the Jewish Agency, and, of course, the Hadassah women—immediately began the complicated task of searching for a seaworthy vessel for over one thousand people. The prospect of moving such a large group by sea in wartime was daunting. For those involved and determined the matter was clear-cut: If the children could not be moved by truck, train, or plane, they would have to go by ship.

Arrangements for shipping the Teheran Children were to be handled by the Near East Division of the U.S. State Department and the U.S. Maritime Commission, departments with which Mrs. Tourover remained in constant contact. Through these departments, she was referred to John S. McClay of the British Ministry of War Transport, who worked assiduously to locate available ships. The indefatigable Mrs. Tourover pursued potentially helpful contacts. Her report on November 19 to Miss Warburg reflects the complexity of her task:

> *Our stock is going up in the State Department! Mr. Rostow, Assistant to Secretary of State, to Mr. Dean Acheson called me this afternoon (if he hadn't, I would have called him). . . . Mr. Rostow said he would see what he could do to work from that angle, but in the meantime, he suggested that we try to start the ball moving . . . and suggests that we communicate with General Connelly, the American Embassy, Teheran who is informed re the shipping possibilities and who may be helpful. He suggested that we communicate this to our people in Palestine so that they may act in accordance. I told him I would give the information to my headquarters in New York and that you would decide what is best to do.*

A maritime expert recommended transporting the children in smaller ships rather than one large one. In case of a mine or a submarine depth charge, rescues involving fewer children would more likely be successful. But such thoughts were a luxury. All the participants would consider themselves fortunate just to find any seaworthy vessel. Telegrams describing the worldwide search for ships are still yellowing in the Central Zionist Archives in Jerusalem.[3] A cable by the Jewish Agency to a shipping company in Bombay reads:

```
CABLE WHETHER YOU COULD ASSIST IN CHARTERING
LOCALLY STEAMER FOR TRANSFERRING FROM PERSIAN
GULF TO SUEZ JEWISH REFUGEE CHILDREN STRANDED
TEHERAN NUMBER 1000. PLEASE SPARE NO EFFORT.
STUDYING ALL POSSIBILITIES. CABLE JEWISH AGENCY.
```

After being contacted by the Jewish Agency, the Palestine Transport & Shipping Co. Ltd., in turn, cabled requests for ships to other transport companies in such far-flung places as London, Alexandria, and Basra. The urgency of such communications was indicated by the final words: "a firm proposal hurry."

```
JEWISH AGENCY URGENTLY INTERESTED PASSAGE ABOUT
1000 REFUGEE CHILDREN ONE OR SEVERAL VOYAGES
BENDER SHAPUR SUEZ. PLEASE SUBMIT DETAILED PRO-
POSALS.
```

Finally, a triumphant telegram by Moshe Shertok from London to Eliahu Dobkin, Jewish Agency (possibly sent January 7, 1943) proclaimed:

```
HAVE DEFINITE PROMISE TRANSPORT BE AVAILABLE
EARLY JANUARY SENIOR NAVAL OFFICER INSTRUCTED.
CONTACT OURS TEHERAN STOP. CABLE SIPPORAH.
```

An equally joyous telegram arrived at the New York Hadassah offices on January 6:

```
600 CHILDREN WITH 60 GUARDIANS LEFT YESTERDAY
FOR AHVAZ ON SEAROUTE PALESTINE OTHERS LEAVE IN
FEW DAYS.
                HENRIETTA SZOLD
```

If doubts persisted about the news, reassurance arrived the next day in a letter from the British Embassy in Washington, D.C., confirming that the British had managed to locate ships and had arranged for the transfer of the Teheran Children to Palestine:

British Embassy
Washington, D.C.

January 7th, 1943

Mrs. Tamar de Sola Pool
National President of Hadassah Gisela Warburg
New York City.

Dear Madam,

> *I understand that the British authorities are making the neces-*
> *sary arrangements to enable them [the Children of Teheran] to reach*
> *Palestine shortly. No details can be supplied at present, since all*
> *transportation in that area involves questions of a secret character;*
> *but should further details be forthcoming I shall not fail to inform*
> *you.*

Yours truly,
W. G. Hayter

What immense joy and relief the embassy's letter must have brought! What overriding satisfaction the leading figures in this drama must have felt, that while cannons were still firing, they helped rescue the children and send them to a haven where they might recover. At that moment, no one knew just what the sea route entailed. Just where would the children embark? What were the ports of call? How long would the journey take? And what were the perils of the route? The seas were infested with U-boats and strewn with mines; overhead lurked the threat of strafing planes. But right now, these considerations were put aside. This was simply a glorious moment. The women, with the help of the British, had accomplished the undoable. The children, who had spent seven months in Teheran, were finally headed for Palestine.[4] Some of this elation, as well as wartime uncertainties and the censoring of news, was reflected in a letter on January 9, 1943, from Denise Tourover to Gisela Warburg.

Dear Gisela:

> *We are on the road to having THAT party! . . . To record:*
> *Mr. McClay, Minister of the British War Transport called me*

late Saturday to confirm that the children have been moved. He said that his information was that 800 children were involved. They were moved by sea. He could not give me details, obviously. He indicated that the children had been moved to India; they had had to change boats; they were on what he termed a "good boat" and were well protected. You can fill in the details.

So, we shall have to wait for the remainder of the details, but in this meanwhile, it is good to know that so far so good. When at long last the children will have arrived in Palestine, I shall drink your good health in honest to God and sure-enough champagne. Until then,

Fond regards

At the end of a letter, Mrs. Tourover noted the expenses accrued in Hadassah's rescue efforts. "There is one interesting final word: I find that we paid the bill of the State Department for cables sent on our behalf in this matter in the sum of $57.46, which so far as my records show, was the only expense incurred by us in this matter." It is apparent that everybody involved gave from the heart.

Delight and visions of future celebrations were in order, but sitting on one's laurels was not. What would be needed most on their arrival was money. The children would need everything—housing, food, and clothes—to replace the rags they had been wearing for months. They needed to be medically checked and to be prepared for schooling. And where would the money come from if Hadassah did not raise it? Within the week, on January 14, a cable was on its way to Palestine:

```
NLT SCOLD SIMON
JEWISH AGENCY
JERUSALEM, PALESTINE

RECOMMENDING FULL NATIONAL BOARD MEETING FEB-
RUARY LAUNCHING OF EMERGENCY DRIVE $500,000
ADDITIONAL ADOPTED YOUTH ALIYAH BUDGET

                         HADASSAH ORGANIZATION
```

Delighted, Henrietta Szold replied on November 21 from Jerusalem:

NLT HADASSAH ORGANIZATION 1819 BROADWAY NYK

DELIGHTED GRATEFUL PROPOSAL LAUNCH DRIVE ADDI-
TIONAL FUNDS STOP SIX POLISH CHILDREN ARRIVED
VIA RUSSIA BOMBAY AND 50 FIRST DETACHMENT HUN-
GARIANS STOP DEPARTURE ANNOUNCED SECOND GROUP
72 STOP.

HENRIETTA SZOLD

Besides raising money it was time to thank those who had helped. On February 23, Mrs. de Sola Pool and Miss Warburg sent a letter of gratitude to Mrs. Roosevelt who had apparently endorsed a fund-raising meeting on behalf of the Teheran Children. (As in so many of the missives, the number of the Teheran Children varied again.)

February 18, 1943

Mrs. Roosevelt
The White House
Washington, D.C.

My dear Mrs. Roosevelt:

On behalf of the National Board of Hadassah and the National Youth Aliyah Committee, we wish to express our heartfelt gratitude for your message to our meeting on 14, at which we launched an emergency drive to raise $500,000 toward the cost of maintaining and educating 6,000 children for whom we have certificates of immigration into Palestine. Your sponsorship, your interest, and your understanding of our task to save the child victims of Hitler's persecution is a source of continual and deep encouragement to all of our people.

We know you will rejoice with us in the knowledge that the 835 Polish Jewish refugee children who had been stranded in Teheran, and in whose fate you took such a deep interest, are about to arrive in Haifa. They were sent from Teheran, with the aid of the British Government, to a port in India and then by boat through the Persian Gulf around Arabia through Suez to Haifa. As Miss Dorothy Thompson [newspaper columnist] who was our guest speaker, so beautifully said: "What will be most retained in the minds of today's children—the hatred that sought to destroy, or the love that sought to

131

save?" We have set ourselves the task of exerting every human effort to ensure that there be many children who will remember "the love that sought to save" them.

Very sincerely yours,

Mrs. David de Sola Pool
National President, Hadassah

Gisela Warburg
Chairman, National Youth Aliyah Committee

Copy to Mrs. Tourover

What made these women who wielded no official power on the national scene able to achieve such an extraordinary feat? What made them so determined, so intrepid, so audacious? The answer may be found in part of a letter written on October 29, 1942, by Mrs. Tourover to Miss Warburg, that reflects the women's outrage at injustice and a sense that the strength of women who join together in action can raise mountains and defeat giants.

As the final background, when all the diplomats and others may have failed, I still feel that the voice of the outraged women of Hadassah can make itself felt by one means or another. I am truly incensed that a 2 by 4 government, like Iraq, should set up its will against such a humanitarian effort, when all the governments of the world have refugee committees concerned with the fate of helpless people. . . . It is idle talk for diplomats to tell us it cannot be done, and all else failing I believe that the high-pitched voices of Hadassah women might well tell Mr. Welles and the Iraq Minister and anybody else who may be responsible for the failure to grant visas that our membership, our contributors, to say nothing of the American public who might well be interested, cannot understand how on one hand you can set up mechanisms for solving refugee problems with government assistance, and on the other hand destroy that mechanism.

Now with the task done, what did the three women say to one another? Surely an extraordinary camaraderie must have developed among them, a feeling that their achievement had forged an insoluble bond. Perhaps their emotions matched those of Henry V when he spoke to his little band of men:

From this day to the ending of the world,
But we in it shall be remembered;
We few, we happy few, we band of brothers.

Just substitute *sisters*.

CHAPTER XVIII

Finally – An Exit

Once more, the children were about to move. For Lonek, this was nothing new. By now, he had crossed countless miles of unfamiliar farmlands, bleak landscapes, and lonely steppes. The journey from Jaroslaw to Lvov had been relatively short, accomplished by horse and cart and interrupted by hiding on two different farms. The next trek had taken him by cattle car through vast areas, penetrating the heart of Russia through the Ural Mountains to Siberia. After regaining his freedom, Lonek, aboard another cattle train, had journeyed to the south of Russia to a warmer region, crossing Kazakhstan into Uzbekistan to Tashkent. Tourists today traveling by modern planes, more convenient trains, and accessing comfortable accommodations would still shudder at the prospect of such a passage. But Lonek had by no means finished his journey. One almost equal in distance and danger still loomed ahead of him.

Nevertheless, Lonek was eager to set off. The frustration and uncertainty of the daily wait for news of departure tore at him, and from all their ordeals, the children had learned never to trust the future. Eliott remembered the constant uncertainty: "In Teheran we were so frustrated many times, because every day was a different rumor. 'We are going tomorrow!' 'Tomorrow we are not going.' Came September and October, every time was talking we can go to Iraq or Turkey and every time something came and changed everything. So we stopped believing in those rumors." The children's mentors tried assiduously to keep up their spirits. "The counselors always gave us maps. They wrote out the journey; how we'll go and from where we'll go. They inform us very often to make us occupied."

Suddenly, the rumors became reality. The children were to depart in two groups, one on January 2, and the other on January 6, 1943. After immigration permits for Palestine had been obtained from the British Mandatory authorities in Iran, the children and their escorts were informed that the path was open for them to leave Iran for Karachi. The first stop was Ahvaz, a British-Polish military camp located not too far from Bandar-e Shahpur, a port on the Persian Gulf from where the children were to embark on the *Dunera*.[1]

The fragile emotional and physical state of the travelers presented grave problems to the staff. During their seven months at the Teheran Jewish Children's Home, the children had begun to adjust. As difficult as conditions had been, the camp had offered the children stability, that is, a regular routine and an ordered life. They saw the same faces every morning and looked forward to some happy moments during the day. They had become familiar with what they could expect of the people around them, and in turn what was expected of them. Their associations with the quasi-families formed between them and their trusted counselors also contributed to their sense of security. The realization that they were to leave behind everything familiar suddenly aroused many of the old fears and dreads that they had at least partially overcome.

The youngsters responded to the impending departure in different ways. Some lost their appetite and others gorged themselves, finding consolation in food. Some became irritable, quarrelsome, and oppositional, and others turned more clingy, tearful, and anxious. Some who had hoped that lost parents, brothers, and sisters would catch up with them before departure realized that their dreams had been unrealistic. Throughout the nights, before the children's departure the counselors moved among the tents, comforting crying and sobbing children.

During the final morning in Teheran, the youngsters packed their pathetic bundles of torn and tattered possessions. They held on to every foul-smelling rag, ripped pair of shoes, or frayed photograph, refusing to let go of the little that was theirs, even for a minute. Suggestions that the bundles be sent on separate trucks triggered wails of despair. The idea of letting the little ones travel separately with sheltering adults came to naught because the older children resisted being parted from younger friends and relatives, and it became impossible to load the children onto the trucks in any organized fashion.[2]

Slowly the journey began. For the next thirty-six hours, a cavalcade of military trucks carrying over one thousand people, including over eight hundred children, began snaking over mountainous roads. Tarpaulin covered the trucks to prevent the children from being frightened by the sight of the sheer precipices along the route. The driver cautioned the children not to cluster on either side of the rickety vehicle, thereby sending it over the edge of the cliffs. At frequent intervals, the children were asked to disembark and continue on foot for short distances while the bus negotiated particularly steep curves. The trucks rumbled along very slowly, moving, stopping, looking, proceeding, and stopping again.

As if their shepherding responsibilities were not enough for the counselors, they now experienced new travails. A notice arrived from the Polish authorities who continued to be in charge of the civilians accompanying Anders' army. Seven of the counselors were commanded to enlist in the Polish army. This request filled the young men's hearts with terror. Responding to it would require them to abandon the Teheran Children, as well as their hopes of reaching the Promised Land, while doomed to membership in the very anti-Semitic Polish army. Six of the men immediately resolved to disappear underground. With some help, they were smuggled onto a train, for a thirty-six-hour ride to Baghdad. To avoid questioning from Polish and Iraqi soldiers who regularly searched the trains for deserters, they masqueraded as deaf mutes! They remained in Baghdad for six weeks,[3] and with the assistance of local Jews, obtained British uniforms. In the guise of carefree British soldiers headed for leave in Palestine, they finally crossed the Palestinian border.

One other drafted counselor refused to leave the children. Twenty-seven years old, a former prisoner in Siberia himself, David Laor had informally assumed the duties of camp director. More knowledgeable about the youngsters than anyone else, he felt that his expertise was essential at this critical time. Shoeless, owning only a shirt and a beltless pair of slacks, he was able—for a price—to hide in a hospital. It was Zippora Shertok who finally happily informed him of the good news that he had been upgraded to the status of a Polish officer, given a uniform and was now officially in charge of transporting the children from Teheran to Palestine.[4] Eliott recalled watching David attend to an endless round of responsibilities. Among them was the recruitment of other adults to travel with the group to take the departed counselors' places. Another crisis had been overcome, but each one took its toll.

The children and the staff were delighted when they first spied the ship awaiting them at Bandar-e Shahpur. On January 11, 1945, roughly one thousand people, children and adults, boarded the British *Dunera* for a two-week journey to Karachi.[5]

While the children prepared for their journey to Karachi, the transatlantic wires had began to hum again in anticipation. A cable dated February 12, 1943, from London to Youth Aliyah in Jerusalem, warned of the coming arrival of a boatload of passengers who needed everything from shoes to underwear to clothes suitable for the Indian climate.

```
EIGHT HUNDRED DESTITUTE ORPHANS AND FOUR HUN-
DRED AND FIFTY ADULTS IN KARACHI.... ESSENTIAL
WE PROVIDE CLOTHING LOCALLY.
```

The cable writer also urged Youth Aliyah to alert the Bombay Jewish community to raise funds for the children. A quick reply from the Jewish Relief Association in Bombay dated February 18 assured that the community was organizing itself immediately to do as much as possible while they remained in Karachi. A report touchingly describes the readying of kosher food packages as well as such "goodies" as fruits, sweets, and cakes.[6] In true maternal fashion, the "mother" of the Teheran Children, Henrietta Szold, not only anticipated the children's stay in India but looked to their ultimate arrival in Palestine, which would be considerably colder in winter than Karachi. She cabled to Bombay: "Purchase warm underwear for refugee children"[7]

CHAPTER XIX

The Last Lap

Once on board, almost everyone became eager to leave. As Eliott recalled: "We was glad. We was sick and tired of sitting. Is better to move. So we went on the ship."

The condition of the ship was another story. Due to the overflow of passengers—adult Polish Jewish refugees were also onboard—there were not enough life preservers. For much of the day, the children were instructed to remain below deck, where the heat was oppressive. The constant swaying of the boat caused severe seasickness. The children vomited over themselves, and, because of the crowded quarters, sometimes on others. Without facilities for washing and changes of clothes, the youngsters' clothes soon became filthy and beset by lice. The available food was most unappetizing, not too surprising during a brutal war.[1] Eliott recalled the discomfort: "The beds were from rope [hammocks] and the ship got tilted and we got sick. Only at night did they let us go on the top."

On January 21, when Lonek and his friends docked in Karachi they looked like an army of little beggars. The officers of the Bombay Jewish Relief Association who met the boat were appalled by their condition and wired the Jewish Agency in Jerusalem:

CHILDREN COMPLETELY DESTITUTE DESOLATE CONDITION NEEDING BADLY CLOTHES SHOES VITAMINS STOP HAVE COLLECTED STERLING ONE THOUSAND URGENTLY REQUIRE AT LEAST FURTHER THREE THOUSAND COMMUNICATE HENRIETTA SZOLD CABLE REMITTANCE URGENT.

138

Lonek soon realized that he and the other members of his transport were not the only destitute individuals in Karachi. The moment the boat docked, an army of skeletal men clambered up the side of the ship. They were gaunt, undernourished, and covered by, what seemed to Lonek, rags. He slowly discerned what the men were after: the scraps of leftover food that the crew had daily tossed onto the corner of the deck and that had decayed.[2] Eliott recalls his shock at the sight: " People, half-naked with towels on [*dhotis*], they climb up with a rope to get whatever is left on the ship—the garbage! And the captain and the British soldiers that was there, they gave them something. The food was rotten."

During his long journey, Lonek had lived in many exotic places and viewed many amazing sights. Yet, when he disembarked in Karachi, he was overwhelmed by the multitude of new impressions and sharp contrasts the city presented. The mixture of the exquisite and alluring with the grotesque and abhorrent, not unusual for India, astounded Lonek. In the marketplace, he was startled to see graceful women wrapped in captivating saris making their way through crowds of deformed beggars. "There was a lot of very poor people. And the men with the head wrapped around [turbans]. And people washing themselves in the street. Big trucks with water and they have a shower on the side." Eliott was now doubling over with mirth: "I remember I was going to the city, I saw the first time the snake. The snake charmer whistled to a snake! I was so shaky when the snake jump up. Was so amazing! And I saw somebody walking with a monkey on his shoulder. And there were monkeys holding hands like children. And when a cow goes by, everybody goes on the side to let it pass."

Lonek was fascinated by the stately Indian soldiers, royal in their bearing, who guarded the British army camp outside Karachi where the youngsters were quartered. Nevertheless, as far as the children were concerned, the soldiers "were speaking funny." Actually they spoke English (with which the children were not acquainted). In turn, the Indian soldiers must have been perplexed by the truckloads of youngsters of all ages, arriving suddenly, seemingly out of nowhere in the middle of a world war. Their languages were as strange to the soldiers as English was to the children. It is unlikely that either Polish and Yiddish had ever been heard around the army camp before.

Lonek relished the new camp. Surrounded by large fields, it was sectioned off by ropes into numbered units—each housed a small group of children of comparable ages. The units were connected by pathways lined with white painted rocks to indicate where the children were allowed to walk. The careful organization gave Lonek a sense of security. Eliott's voice swelled with pride and happiness as he recalled: "They took us to this camp from the ship. This was, I don't know how far away from the water, but we didn't see the ocean after we left the ship. So it must be inland somewhere. It was a *rich* camp! It was more order, more nicer, more organized. They put us four or five in a tent which has already cots with mosquito nets. Very nice and neat. We get a big white hat. It's a special hat [tropical helmet] in white. And this was donated by Jewish people. A guy came and asked the measurements of all the children, and they give us shoes and white shorts and white shirts. Was a counselor in charge of each unit. Was also the soldiers with the turbans to help us. What a different story! We was very happy there. But all night, hyenas were yelling. It was terrible. Was so scared. They are like dogs and they yelling all night. They put fire against them in front of the tent. The soldiers make big roads of fire to prevent them to come close."

Despite his close friendship with Krauss and other youngsters, Lonek continued to yearn for his parents. He did not cry as much anymore, but "I never lost my memory from my parents. I thought of them all the time, all the time. The memory still haunting me today." Lonek had a family photograph given him the day his mother had deposited him at the orphanage. "I kept it in my socks. The shoes I wouldn't take off. They was screaming on me: 'Take off your socks.'" But for a long time he would not. The children were urged to write to their parents once a week. "The counselors make us write to occupy us. It was like a therapy, I believe. And everyone compared letters and changed his letter to what the other person was writing. And to make my parents not worry, we wrote about food and clothes. We wrote we got soap, we got chocolate, we got dates and pita bread. The main story on those letters that I wrote to them: 'Do you have enough food? Do you have enough clothes? And how is my brother?' These are all the three questions I always ask." None of Lonek's letters ever reached his parents, neither did he ever hear from them. But at least writing helped the children create imaginary parental connections.

Like the rest of the children, Lonek remained preoccupied with the fear of food shortages. He sewed a little bag for himself that he hung around his neck. He described its purpose: "Every time I have a little food I put it inside in case tomorrow I would be hungry and so that I have something to eat. I didn't trust the world that tomorrow I will again have the food that I have today. And often the food spoiled, was stinking sometimes because we keep it for days and it was rotten. But was very painful to throw out food because after being so used to not having, even spoiled food is good." Up to the present day, Eliott confessed, when he goes shopping he buys three or four packages or everything; in case of war, he will have provisions. Laughingly, he concluded that he could probably supply the whole neighborhood. Lonek particularly enjoyed the morning parade when the children assembled around the flagpole to sing songs and receive their assignments. The counselors made do with minimal equipment. For instance, lacking suitable clothing, the younger children had gym lessons in their underwear.

Lonek admired and respected the counselors. But in spite of his warm feelings for them, he never spoke to them about his worries and personal concerns, homesickness, loneliness, and fear of losing contact with his parents. I had encountered the same phenomenon when interviewing the former *Kinder* (children) who had been sent to England on *Kindertransports* by their parents. Very few ever unburdened themselves to their teachers or foster parents. I asked Eliott why he withheld his personal feelings from his counselors. "I felt a wall separating us," he explained. "I was a child and they was big. And we have nothing in common. After all, they had the authority over us. They had a little distance from us. If they will be too friendly, we wouldn't listen to them. If they said: 'Go to bed!' We wouldn't go to bed. Or: 'Take a shower!' We wouldn't take a shower." When I remarked that he used to confide in his mother, who also had authority over him, he replied: "Because my parents—I grew up with them. With them, the counselors, I didn't grow up. It's a big difference I believe." And then he added mischievously: "You are the doctor. You should know!"

When Eliott was a boy, even benevolent parents and other adults were considered too remote to serve as confidants. Nor, in those years, did adults explore children's feelings. On the whole, adults assumed that if youngsters were treated kindly and provided with all the necessities, their emotional life would take care of itself. Besides, there were neither sufficient time nor resources to dwell excessively on any one child's problems. As one former *Kind*, who arrived in England on a children transport, remarked: "As far as discussing my specific problems or feelings with anyone other than a friend of mine, it never entered my head. And certainly none of the staff ever volunteered for such a discussion. Why my problems? There were lots of other boys who no doubt had problems. And even had a member of the staff voiced an interest in my problems, I doubt if I would have been willing to be more than polite in return. Somehow this notion of confiding did not fit the environment. After all, psychologists were still a rarity then."[3] Among the Jewish population in Poland, they had been nonexistent.

Once the children arrived in Karachi, they were more optimistic that they would ultimately reach their destination—Palestine. They were excited at the prospect of reboarding for the last lap of the sea journey through the Red Sea. Yet some of the old anxieties remained, particularly the fear of accidental separation from their siblings or friends.[4]

The plan was for the children to disembark in Egypt; the Egyptian government had cooperated closely with the British Mandatory by granting visas to the children. Then they would travel by train through Egypt to Palestine. On February 6, 1943, the children boarded the SS *Noralea*, which offered no better conditions than the *Dunera*. The ship stopped in Aden, Yemen, but hopes for respite on land from the overcrowding, heat, and odors were dashed when all passengers were instructed to remain on board. This was particularly difficult for the girls and women who were instructed to remain below deck out of fear that so many females displaying their faces and bare arms might arouse antagonism in a Muslim country.

When the ship pulled up anchor after its brief stay in Yemen, the children's excitement rose when they realized that they were setting off for the very last leg of the sea journey. Perhaps the children would have been less excited if they had known that the waters they were about to ply were heavily mined, and no minesweepers were available to clear their path. Instead, the ship followed the wake of small boats that looked for bobbing mines—hardly providing a foolproof defense. The fact that the mines had been laid by the Allies, made them no less menacing. Enemy planes posed other threats. In addition, the captain suspected that they were being pursued by a German submarine.

Together with the head counselor, the captain decided not to inform the rest of the staff of such dangers. No additional precautions could be taken, and so alarming the passengers further would have been pointless. It was very difficult to conceal the reality. The children became distressed by the sounding of alarms that followed frequent sightings of enemy ships. Sometimes the children were directed to go below deck, where hermetically sealed departments would protect them from flooding waters following a hit. On other occasions, the captain summoned the frightened youngsters on deck, pretending that he was simply holding an emergency drill, but the children had previously confronted too many hazardous situations not to recognize peril very quickly when it was at hand.[5]

In fact, Eliott was clearly aware of the danger: "The captain was so nervous, he didn't sleep all night. He aggravate himself and said he didn't believe that he was still alive. He kept us all on the bottom of the ship because the airplanes was flying above. And was a story that a U-boat was all the time looking for us to blow us up. [Because of the mines], we try to go very slowly, maybe ten times the time it would be normally. We was traveling like walking on the water. The ship was going and looking, going and looking. Most of the time they keep us below deck."

Slowly and with great caution, the ship steamed through the Suez Canal, and, finally, on February 17, it docked at Port Said, Egypt. This glorious moment was celebrated by the children, counselors, and crew. The captain, delighted that he had safely delivered such a precious cargo, insisted that the ship's successful two-week journey was a miracle that could only be explained by the Jewish children's presence.[6]

When the Teheran Children looked down from shipboard onto the pier, they were suddenly gripped by fear at the sight of rows of soldiers facing them. Past experience had taught them that military uniforms could mean anything from mere threat to deportation . However, these soldiers seemed different. The youngsters noticed their benign expressions and warm, welcoming smiles. Then suddenly the soldiers began to pelt the children with small parcels. They were tossing their meager rations wrapped with little notes reading: "Blessed be the ones who come. You shall never be a refugee again."[7]

Such generosity quickly convinced the children that these soldiers were different from any they had encountered before. And indeed they were—belonging to either the Jewish Brigade serving with the British Army's engineering corps or the Haganah. Together with officials of the Jewish Agency and Youth Aliyah, they had been anticipating the children's arrival with eagerness, joy, and incredulity. To them, it seemed that the impossible had happened: A thousand Jewish children had been snatched from the grave and had managed to survive.[8]

The passengers of the *Noralea* descended into small boats that had come to meet them. Disembarkation was in good order: The line was led by infants carried down the ladders by their caretakers. As soon as the small boats returned from delivering the little ones, the elderly passengers on board climbed down. Next came the children carrying their ragged bundles and whatever precious possessions they still owned. They were accompanied by their counselors who led them in song: "We ascend and sing, above death and ruins" Last came the rest of the adults.[9]

One Haganah soldier, Meir Bar-Ray-Hai stood on the shore that day with some of his comrades, watching the children disembark. The men had spent the previous night raiding their canteen for all kinds of delectables, wrapping them into inviting packages, and marking them with: "And the children will return to their homeland" (Jer. 31:17). Meir recalled: "Those were the days when the news of the Holocaust first began to reach us. Then and only then did we begin to grasp the enormity of the tragedy of European Jewry. Only then did we, who had originally volunteered for war against Hitler, begin to grasp and appreciate our rendezvous with destiny—to help rehabilitate the survivors of the destruction. This meeting at Suez was the first of a series of meetings by the soldiers from Eretz Yisrael with the spared remnant, whose welfare became the life mission of my colleagues." When the children responded to the soldiers' welcome by singing, "We are all children of Mother," Meir was stirred to the quick, "knowing that it was we who represented Mother, we who were privileged to welcome . . . with open arms in place of Mother, who is no more or is still a prisoner in Russia."[10]

Eliott recalled, his eyes misting over: "They [the soldiers] were very, very friendly to us. They spoke to us in Yiddish, Hebrew, and Polish. They brought harmonicas and they was playing for us and singing with us. They told us stories. They cheer us up. We didn't know exactly who they was, but later we find out they were Jewish soldiers from the corps of engineers who were working with the British. They wore uniforms marked with "Palestine" and a little star. They were like fathers to us. For them was a miracle that we survive because the war was almost over. The Germans try to eliminate all the Jewish people from Europe. They don't leave nothing. Children and wives and everything. At least the Jews in Palestine have one piece left. Who knows, would they ever see other survivors? In the middle of whole Europe burning, we was the survivors."

The next morning, after raising the blue-and-white Jewish flag and singing "Hatikvah," the children climbed onto the train bound for their final destination: Palestine.

CHAPTER XX

Welcome Home

With mounting excitement, the children, scrambled onto and overflowed the trains that would ferry them to the Promised Land. At last count, there were 6 infants, 214 children between the ages of one and ten years (119 boys and 95 girls), and 638 youngsters between the ages of eleven and twenty years (334 boys and 304 girls).[1] A number of adults who had been part of the Anders' amnesty, and who had sailed with the children, now joined them on the train journey.

Fourteen-year-old Lonek, lacking a seat on the train, found an empty space on the luggage rack above and secured himself by tying his belt to it. Too excited to sleep, he looked out from his perch onto the passing countryside. He was transfixed. Eliott described the crossing into Palestine with a rapturous expression as if he were viewing a spectacular sunrise, still spellbound by that glorious moment of relief. He recalled that seeing the green trees laden with fruit convinced him that he was approaching paradise. "In the morning I saw the desert. Usually you don't see nothing in the desert. It is the naked desert. Suddenly we saw that everything was blooming. Was a big difference to us! This I remember!"

The warm greeting given the Teheran Children in Suez foreshadowed an even more enthusiastic welcome in Rehovoth and Hadera, in Palestine. Not only were officials of the Jewish Agency and the British Mandatory present, but so too were hundreds of waving, shouting people lining the platform as far as the eye could see. Word had spread like wildfire from town to town, from one neighbor to the next. Throngs of eager people ran to the train station to participate in the unfolding miracle. Nearly a thousand children saved! A miracle! An unforeseen wonder! Almost everyone in the crowd had lost a daughter, a son, a niece, a nephew, a grandchild, or the child of a friend. The few fortunates who had not suffered such deprivation knew one or more neighbors who had. After years of disconsolate news, at long last there was a happy event The reception committee consisted of officials of organizations, representatives of the Jewish Agency, rabbis, relatives, later to be president of Israel Dr. Chaim Weizmann, and, of course, the "mother" of the children, Henrietta Szold.[2] It was the moment she had worked and planned for to the smallest detail. The older children greeted her with songs and flowers. Henrietta Szold wrote in a letter: "The whole country seems to have gone plumb crazy."

Hoping against hope, some members of the crowd clung to the faint possibility of finding a lost relative on the train; that some long lost figure given up for dead would suddenly appear; and a familiar face might emerge from the train, stretch out a hand and say: "But you were wrong! I am alive!" Others merely hoped to find someone who could offer a shred of information about some kin who had disappeared into the void And indeed, a few—but only a few—of the onlookers were so rewarded. For example, one woman on the train unexpectedly and ecstatically spied her husband standing on the platform; they had not seen each other since they had been separated in Russia; an Israeli kibbutznik greeted his brother, the only survivor of parents, grandparents, aunts, uncles, nephew, and sister; and a girl reunited with a former friend.

The children leaned out of the train windows, their little blue-and-white flags fluttering gaily. At every station, the surging crowds had given them what little presents they could muster—delicacies such as oranges, chocolates, and cookies. The women in particular embraced, hugged, and kissed the children, wanting to soothe, cuddle, feed, cheer, and reassure the newcomers.[3] Some train compartments were filled with little babies and toddlers under four years old. They had forgotten, or perhaps had never known, how to smile, chatter, or play. Quiet and restrained, tearless and subdued, they sat quietly without even whimpering. They had learned that to survive, they had to be mere shadows.

The children were overwhelmed. As recently as a year ago, they had been cast away as prisoners and pariahs. Now suddenly they were hailed as virtual gifts from heaven. From a struggling band of children held together by the efforts of their leaders, they suddenly became a triumphant procession, a symbol of life over death.

Eliott reported in a tone of awe as tears coursed down his cheeks: "So everybody was for them like some miracle that we survived. It is very hard to describe. Because it was like a big fire and suddenly you find in this big fire a little jewel after the whole house was burned. In those times was already sinking the whole Europe. So they treat us as something unbelievable. In every station where we went hundreds of mothers was hugging us, with cake, with chocolate, with flags, with all the goodies what they could bring. Just kissing us, almost choke us from love. Some people gave us Israeli flags. I felt like I was on the top of a mountain. We must be something very important to get treated like princes. Every station people ask about our names. Because everybody knew that childrens are coming and they was thinking maybe they will find a relative. The first question was 'What is your name and from what city you are and where were you and where are your parents?' Some children even found their parents." We was so happy. They were crying, everybody was crying. Tears—they could fill up the Jordan River! From happiness, you know. After so many years going around half of the world finally to come to somebody that wants to help me, wants to give me goodies, and ask my name. It was something like going back to your family, going back to your parents. And I began to dream. Maybe I will find my mother. Maybe I am not alone."

In the evening, the children, exhausted but exhilarated, arrived at the Atlit Refugee Camp, which had been prepared for them with loving care. They could not believe their eyes at the luxuries awaiting them. Beds covered with spotless white sheets, inviting warm blankets, and soft pillows decorated with WELCOME HOME signs met their fatigued gazes. Smiling women in neat aprons awaited them with glasses of fresh milk and hot showers. Little girls were given dolls. New clothes were available for all the children. Counselors from Aliyat Hanoar, the homes for refugee children founded by Henrietta Szold, were ready to draw on their long experience and help the youngsters with yet another chapter of their lives. The children, unfamiliar with pampering, delighted at whatever was offered. Ordinary necessities of life appeared like extravagances.

Eliott recalled the reception: "At Atlit, there is like a camp where foreigners come to register. We were met by doctors, nurses, and ambulances. Was plenty of food and we couldn't believe it. They make two little mountains of oranges and we couldn't understand so much oranges. We never saw such a thing. And everybody was hiding their oranges under their shirt and running and hiding them under their bed. And everybody got sick from eating so many oranges. And we got new beds with white sheets. The first time I slept in a long time with nice sheets. And the blanket was very clean, nice and fresh."

The cozy setup was no coincidence. Henrietta Szold had planned it in detail, and had scrounged and begged for money for every plate and glass, which seemed to cost a fortune when measured against the funds available.[4]

Lonek was safe at last. The incredible journey that had taken him from Poland to Russia, to Siberia, to Tashkent, to Persia, to India, to Egypt, and finally to Palestine was over. When Lonek went to bed that night, he reflected that he had left Poland in the autumn of 1939, Tashkent in the summer of 1942, and finally reached Palestine in February 1943. It had taken almost four years to find a place where he belonged. In retrospect, it was almost impossible to recount all the strange coincidences and fortuitous circumstances that had made his survival possible. What if the farmer whom his father had sent to fetch the rest of his family from Jaroslaw had accepted his father's bribe and then reneged on his side of the bargain? What if the family had not found a sanctuary with their loyal nanny? What if Lonek and his family had been physically too weak to survive the cruel Siberian winter? What if they lacked the resourcefulness to devise all kinds of measures to gather additional food to add to their meager rations? And what if the most unbelievable, almost miraculous event of all had not occurred—what if the paranoid, ruthless dictator who thought nothing of eradicating millions of kulaks, imaginary enemies, and "Jewish traitors" had shut the portals of the gulag? Would not Lonek have died like millions of others, unheard, unseen, unmourned by the rest of the world? Could not Lonek's long journey easily have been terminated by a mine or a torpedo before he ever reached his destination? It is impossible to calculate the dangers weathered and the disasters avoided.

Not that Lonek, upon settling in Palestine, would be able to assume a "normal" existence. That kind of fate was not in the cards for any Jew escaping the Nazi terror, whether as a former ghetto or concentration camp survivor, as one who had lived hidden during the war years, or even as an escapee. There were too many personal losses, too many encounters with bestial cruelty, unimaginable before the Hitler era, too many upheavals, too much time lost, and too much agony and pain to resume a "normal" life.

No matter what the problems and difficulties Lonek would encounter in the future, they would be drastically dissimilar from the ones that had preceded his arrival in Palestine. All would be different, for Lonek knew that he belonged; he was no longer an outcast, and he had become a citizen with the security of being guarded by the laws of the land—laws that were predictable, fair, and equitable. In the face of injustice, disaster, calamity, he was now protected by safeguards. Only refugees can fully understand the horror of being without that security. It has been said that "home is a notion that only nations of the homeless fully appreciate and only the uprooted comprehend."[5]

As a former escapee wrote about her time under the Nazi regime:

> The number of people who vanished and were never heard
> from mounted daily. With every passing day the human
> tragedy around us multiplied. The number of people we knew
> equaled the number of tragedies we witnessed. The taking
> away of all possessions counted as nothing. We had to give up
> our money, homes, jobs, life work, honors, professions. It
> meant nothing. In those days we realized what it means to
> live without the protection of the law. Human beings can
> adapt to fearful situations. They can live through war and fire
> and still think life worthwhile. To live without the protection
> of the law is worse. Nothing is left but the naked fear of the
> hunted.[6]

It is this aspect of life that Lonek left behind. Although he would always remember losses suffered, his shattered security and hopeless attempt to substitute for lost family, life at last would also offer a forward-looking direction. He would no longer be preoccupied with survival, trying to hold his own, with schemes of weathering the day, the week, the month. Lonek was no longer either hated or merely tolerated or at the mercy of a government that suffered his presence. He was now an active member of a community. From now on, Lonek no longer needed to hide food on his person. He knew that tomorrow would again provide food.

CHAPTER XXI

What Now?

The children remained briefly at the Atlit Refugee Camp for medical and administrative reasons. But due to Henrietta Szold's pedagogical orientation, they were not merely arbitrarily assigned to more permanent settlements. Rather they were each individually interviewed about their personal preferences, which were then considered when final choices were made for them.

Eliott recalled standing on line waiting to be questioned. "They found different people to question us from where we come, where we want to go, and if we want to go to a kibbutz. The children between themselves already started to talk. You understand, children, they know. So one child came out and we asked him what they asked you? So everybody knew what they asked." The children could choose between joining a kibbutz, a school, or a family that might even adopt them. Lonek, like many of the children, resisted placement in a kibbutz. "It reminded me very badly of Russia when we were in Uzbekistan, which was similar to kibbutz—a collective farm." Many of the children were horrified at anything that even remotely recalled any part of their lives in Russia and thus rejected placement at a kibbutz out of hand. No amount of explanation about the fundamental differences and purposes of a kibbutz and a collective farm was convincing. Visits to a kibbutz mollified some of the children, but many remained adamantly opposed.

Lonek did not even want to live with a family, let alone be adopted by one. For one thing, he was uneasy about the unknown. "I didn't know what would be with a family." In addition, Lonek did not want to sacrifice the profound emotional support he had gained from living with Krauss and the other children. There was also another reason for Lonek's resistance to placement with a family—distrust of people's motivation. Over the years, he had been exposed to too much venality to rely blindly on others, even in a benign setting. As he talked about the families who volunteered to take in children, Eliott described what he believed might have been their purpose: "They have farms and they want to have cheap labor, so they figure maybe they raise the children and later in the future they [the children] will help them."

Somewhat taken aback by Eliott ascribing such a mercenary design to what might seem a selfless act to others, I asked, "Do you think you might be somewhat cynical? Perhaps they wanted to have the children because they loved them, not just for labor."

Eliott agreed, but on terms different from the ones I had intended. "They didn't suffer from raising the children from infant. This way they have already [a family] made. They see the product. They could chose a boy or a girl."

I wanted to determine whether Eliott could accept a more altruistic reason: "Couldn't it also be because they were really humanitarian? Is there a small possibility?"

Possibly to pacify me, Eliott now modified his initial proposition. I had learned from his ambivalence about his mother's actions that Eliott tended to swing between distrust and subsequent regret for that distrust. "Maybe they had love for somebody and they feel they can split a little bit from love to the other children. Could be. There are hundreds of possibilities. I am sorry if I was wrong."

"Life has made you cynical," I said. "I don't blame you. You have good cause."

After we both laughed at the ironies of life, Eliott replied, "After you went so much through hell, you see the whole thing on the dark side. You don't see the good. Sometimes behind me there was a dark side that I was thinking this way. But the years passed, and more and more I started to think from the other side." I always felt that when I pointed out the possibility of a more positive interpretation of an event, Eliott seemed relieved. He apparently wanted to think that life was not always as threatening as past experience had taught him.

There was another issue affecting the children's placement—the insistence of the Orthodox and more religiously liberal communities that the children be assigned to families or institutions that reflect the degree of religiosity previously practiced in their parents' homes. As a result, Lonek's choice of location was also dictated by sensitive political issues, and as on so many other occasions, Lonek's life was determined in large part by political currents rather than personal choices.

The various religious communities each wanted to claim the children as their own. Henrietta Szold was eager to keep religious strife out of educational decisions. At one point, she commented, "I am religious and Jewish myself, but I do not believe in the rule of priests. Schoolchildren must not be drawn into religious strife.[1]

However, Henrietta Szold did not get her wish. Even before the children's arrival, the Orthodox community had begun to pressure her in person and by letter to place all the children under their care. They argued that all Polish children, had their parents lived, would have been brought up in Orthodoxy and thus should be educated only by the Orthodox community. For instance, a telegram sent by Rabbi Meyer Berlin from South Africa on December 20, 1942—before the children had even left Teheran—accused Henrietta Szold of planning to place all the children into nonreligious homes. The writer expressed outrage at her actions, demanding that the children's education be placed under Chief Rabbi Herzog and emphasizing that the Polish government was still involved in the children's upkeep. Excerpts from the cable read:

```
NLT MIZRACHI ORGANIZATION
P.O. BOX 7197, JOHANNESBURG

FOR YOUR INFORMATION EXPECTED ABOUT NINE HUN-
DRED CHILDREN REFUGEES FROM TEHERAN SEEMS ...
THESE NEWCOMERS WILL COME MOSTLY INSTITUTIONS
LEFT WING ... WITHOUT DISTINCTION ... GREAT AS-
TONISHMENT AND DEMAND INTRODUCE THEIR SPIRI-
TUAL EDUCATION UNDER AUSPICES CHIEF RABBI HERZOG
STOP MIZRACHI CHAMPIONS THIS DEMAND ... GREATEST
PART UPKEEPING COVERED POLISH GOVERNMENT.[2]
```

The conflict rose to such a pitch that, as Henrietta Szold wrote: "Someone applied to the Polish Government-in-Exile and urged its interference for the purpose of assuring religious education under the authority of the Chief Rabbi." She was so appalled by such a step that in a letter to Tamar de Sola Pool she wrote: "Even to you I do not care to give a complete record of this incident, how it happened, how it was brought to me and what it implies." She then described the demands made by the Polish government to educate the children as Polish citizens: "So far as implications are concerned, [there is] only one. The Polish government is said to have demanded, in view of its promised monthly payment for each child for the duration of the war, and as a result the interference petitioned for, that the children be taught the Polish language and Polish history, in view of the fact that the Polish government considers them as potential future Polish citizens. I am most desirous of forgetting the incident."[3]

She was not able to do so as organizations and individuals from the Orthodox community continued to accuse her of bias. Even the various Orthodox factions debated which one of them was most representative of the Polish Jewish children. Henrietta Szold described her relief when once she received a fairer hearing: "Three representative members of the 'left' organizations came to see me two days ago and showed a clear and not unsympathetic attitude towards the demands of the religious groups. Primarily, they encouraged me by revealing their confidence in my honesty of purpose and in my judgment even on so delicate a question as the religious question."

The criticism must have stung because Henrietta Szold felt the need to justify herself to her correspondent:

> *Presuming an equal confidence in my honesty and judgment on your part, as well as in my desire for fairness and justice, I am not going to go into the details of the methods I intend to employ in order to give each child the education, religious and otherwise, its parents presumably would have him receive in Palestine. I shall make mistakes I am sure, but I am taking every precaution intellect and heart can suggest that the mistakes be confined to the smallest number possible when those who deal with the question are frail human beings, myself, of course, included.[4]*

The controversy grew sufficiently intense for Henrietta Szold to appeal to the press and the public on March 14, 1943. Explaining that she needed the assistance of both in settling the children, she laid out her plans for placing the children according to a number of factors. One of these was "the most sacred task . . . that connects the individual child to the form of education his parents would have desired for him. . . . The Bureau of the Youth Aliyah, therefore, pleads with the press and the public to refrain from giving publicity to all sorts of rumors and reports, most of which have been found to lack all basis, and in particular to refrain from exercising undue influence upon the children whose future happiness is at stake unless their status, physical and psychic can be determined." She emphasized that if Youth Aliyah was to be allowed to proceed with "plans laid out in the course of many months of preparation, it will be able to give a good account of itself."

Even in the most worthwhile projects infighting invariably raises its contentious head. In a lengthy private letter to Tamar de Sola Pool, Henrietta Szold unburdened herself about her problems with the Polish Jewish community: "It has been said more or less openly that persons who have conducted the Youth Aliyah for German children are presumably not equipped for the task of adjusting Polish children to Palestinian life. " Even though Henrietta Szold gave the Polish Jewish groups an opportunity to speak with her and express their concerns, they, in turn, attempted to circumvent her. "The feeling seems to have made itself dominant that the Youth Aliyah, which served its purpose in bringing over 9,000 young people and children, and had brought them from 15 different countries [such as Austria, Czechoslovakia, Bulgaria, Romania, Italy, Yugoslavia, Latvia], not excluding Poland itself to the number of over 200, could not be permitted to run along the grooves adapted to its purposes by time, experience and I think I may say, success."[5]

Responding to the objections of the Orthodox community nearly exhausted her. She wrote:

> *The excitement among the Polish Jews as such did not reach, neither in intensity nor in its extent, that which pervaded the religious circles. The Agudat Yisrael and the Mizrachi sent delegations to me and wrote countless letters. The religious committee which has been associated with the Youth Aliyah Bureau, the chief Rabbi, individuals throughout the length and breadth of the land have kept me busy with interviews and correspondence to the full measure of my strength. I may say, I think, that I yielded to their demands in every jot and tittle that could be approved by my conscience, religious and pedagogic. Alas, I did not assuage them but succeeded in arousing the acrid opposition of the radical elements who have been the firmest supporters of the Youth Aliyah ideal and who feared complete exclusion from the great Mitzvah (good deed) embodied in the care of the Teheran group.*[6]

The newspaper *Ha'aretz* summarized the final decision made by the Committee for Religious Youth at the Youth Aliyah Department headed by Henrietta Szold:

1. The education the children will receive will be in accordance with the lifestyle to which they were accustomed in their parents' homes. In marginal cases which Miss Szold will determine, the children will be handed over to religious institutions.

2. Children fourteen years old or older will decide themselves the education they wish.

3. The placing of the children and control over the various institutions in which they are will remain the responsibility of the Youth Aliyah Department . . .

4. The best educators from the religious kibbutzim and other religious institutions were enlisted to take care of the children from the very first days of their arrival. About 750 of them who came were placed in eleven religious institutions. Seventy instructors of different levels of Orthodoxy were enlisted to take care of them.

The children's level of religious observance was determined through individual interviews. Eliott recalled his: "The rabbi was there with the black hat. He asked: "Did your parents light the light?" [light candles on Sabbath]. I said my parents were not religious. They light it because it's tradition. I told them my father observe the holidays, maybe, and this is all. He sent me to school on Saturday. So came over another guy who was from the left [less Orthodox]. He said: 'Your father sent you to school Saturday. So you were not religious.' Was about four or five on the committee. And the man that was talking to me, he was very persuading. A young fellow, you know. He didn't go with a yarmulkah, he go with a hat, the same hat I was wearing. He was looking like my type. They fight over every child. Was unbelievable."

I was struck by Eliott's practicality. He had based his choice on the similarity between his own clothes and those of the interviewer. He intuitively realized they were "the same type." I commented to Eliott that I thought he had frequently made shrewd emotional decisions; not only in this case, but in many others, such as when he formed the "family" with Krauss. Eliott was always touched by compliments: "Thank you for your encouragement. Don't forget something. When you are in a situation like this, when I travel the ten countries, you are getting very much older than your age. You are getting more observing. You look on somebody's eyes and you know what is behind them or behind his mind. You see the guy that talk to you, you see if he wants to get you, if he is trying to take things. You are judging because you have only a few minutes to judge the guy. Later you cannot come back: 'I change my mind. You take me back.' You understand? You are getting much older than your age. You are thinking different."

Finally, placements ended on a most gratifying note for Henrietta Szold and Lonek. A few children were fortunate enough to find relatives and acquaintances who wanted to care for them. The rest were placed in a variety of institutions whose diversity reflected Henrietta's unbiased attitude: 298 were sent to Labor Zionist kibbutzim, 288 were placed in Orthodox religious institutions, 38 joined Agudat Israel—an ultrareligious movement, and 36 were accepted in traditional middle-of-the-road settlements.[7]

Conscientious, as usual, Henrietta checked the results of her work herself and wrote: "I spent the week rushing hither and thither and succeeded practically in completing the survey of the Teheran children in their permanent placements. On the whole I am pleased with what I have seen of them. They are apparently making good progress towards normality. They study with vim. Most of them have already acquired enough Hebrew to carry on a conversation. . . . What pleases me most is that they are beginning to frolic, to be children. They will snatch back a little of the heritage of youth that the Hitler war robbed them of."[8]

Lonek obtained in part what he wanted. He was placed in a school, not a kibbutz or a private home. The school, however, was somewhat more Orthodox than his background would have indicated. Nevertheless, in many essentials it suited him well.

CHAPTER XXII

A Decisive Meeting

Another warm welcome awaited Lonek when he, together with some other of the Teheran Children, arrived on April 16, 1943, at Kfar Hanoar Hadati, a religious village school located less than ten miles from Haifa.[1] The local population awaited the newcomers with traditional welcoming gifts of bread and salt, and even more delectably, with ripe bananas and little gifts prepared by the local children.

Eliott remembered the school affectionately: "It was like a camp. In the morning one of us is on duty to wake up the whole regiment. You have to do your bed, clean your room, wash, sweep and then we went to play for fifteen, twenty minutes. Each day a few children help set up the breakfast. It looked to me like a big dining room. After I came back about four years ago, looked to me so little. There was about twelve tables. For breakfast we got jam in a little jar, bread as much as we want and half an egg. Sugar we didn't have. We had tea."

One of the school's purposes was to help German refugee children, who had begun to arrive since the early 1930s, to readjust. As a result, in spite of the primitive facilities, the staff was sophisticated in its psychological approach. Based on Henrietta Szold's philosophy, great weight was placed on academic pursuits, as well as Zionist goals. Cooperation, independence, and resourcefulness were its trademarks.[2] The children helped cultivate the land, planting potatoes, grapes, and apples. Eliott recalls, "Half the day you learn, half the day you work. In the morning we went to regular school. Each age group have a different class."

"How did the children manage since they had actually missed several years of schooling?" I inquired.

"They gave us a little help. They tutored us to bring us up to the level,

157

but we were always behind. But they always try to upgrade us. In summer, we were studying in order to pick up. They gave special evening classes to teach us Hebrew, and the counselors gave us lectures. And finally we pick up. After lunch we was assigned to different tasks: One was assigned to maintenance; another was assigned to agriculture, working with cabbage, for example; another was to take care of the vinegar or the fruit trees; another group was working with the chickens and another with the cows."

At one point, Lonek worked on the farm and rose at five every morning to milk cows. The new, healthy life appealed to him: "The milk was very warm and to take a sip is like to take a sip of champagne. I can still taste it in my mouth. It was a relief for the cow to give a big bucket of milk. Sometimes the cow gets very mad on you. You sometimes pull too hard— you are thinking about something else. Maybe the cow had a bad time. They kicked the bucket, all of it spill on the floor." The counselors understood such mishaps and never scolded the children.

The youngsters were also encouraged to participate in sports. "We played soccer and handball. Sometimes in summer we took trips to different parts of Palestine. Was very nice."

With the influx of refugees from the Continent, extraordinary people were available to serve on the staff. When Eliott spoke of his school years in Palestine, his voice was filled with admiration and gratefulness. After so many years of deprivation, he had arrived at a place where everyone's task was to restore the children to emotional health. He could barely express in words what this dedication meant to him: "They have excellent teachers, most of them volunteers. The whole boarding school was from Germany. Everybody was a doctor, a professor somewhere in Europe. The director, Dr. Ochs, was a very nice man. He dedicated his life. He was a doctor of history and philosophy in Germany. His wife was the head nurse. She had two daughters. Everyone was like his own children. His wife, the same thing. I remember my toe was swollen. They gave me the ticket to go to a swimming pool in Haifa! The salt water will help. The money was spent on me to go with the bus. Each counselor was dedicated, unbelievable. They were with us almost like twenty-four hours. They were in a different building near us. They didn't have a life of their own. They have always to be in the camp in case someone get sick or something happen to somebody."

Dr. Ochs was religious, but not fanatically so. Morning prayers lasted for about a half hour, and Lonek, in spite of not being religious, joined in the prayers. Eliott explained philosophically: "I did not have a choice. If everybody jump in the pool, you would not stay at the side. You have to jump too."

The counselors noticed that Lonek was mechanically very adept and encouraged him. "I was very handy. If the mattress was torn open, I sew it by hand or I fill it. Or the bed was broken, or the door, I fix it. So they teach me and I always like to learn. If I see somebody else doing something, I try it myself. And they were very happy for another helping hand. The maintenance department was always fighting to have me." Soon he was given the job of local handyman and was called in whenever something needed to be built or repaired. The staff praised Lonek's resourcefulness and bolstered his self-confidence. Eliott appeared extremely moved by his caretakers' thoughtfulness. As a rule, he was touched to the point of tearfulness whenever he recalled a kindness shown to him by anyone.

"Sweet memories when you are young and you meet the first girl. Was one girl, Rifka Gottlieb. I remember until now. We talked secretly as children. I remember the first date we have and the romance. I remember a little hill there and we met between the wood and you know, like I put my fingers in her hair. We kiss but I did not know what to do with her. She didn't know exactly what we were doing together. Some child saw us going out of the wood. 'The lovers,' they call us. 'The lovers are coming.' And Rifka got so red."

Seven or eight years later, Lonek, looking handsome and feeling proud in his army officer's uniform, accidentally encountered Rifka at a bus station. It was a breathlessly brief meeting as Rifka could not afford to miss the bus, which was taking her to nurses' training school. She called to him to meet her that evening at eight o'clock in front of the Tamar, a local cinema. Lonek, heart pounding, arrived on time. But as hours dragged by, he realized that Rifka was not coming. He felt crushed. "I remember the first date we had and the romance. We were very close, you understand, we were at that age. I was thinking maybe something happen to her. When she didn't come, was like somebody stabbed me." There were dozens of possible reasons for her failure to keep the date. Perhaps she had to work late, and without either his telephone number or address, she could not contact him. Lonek could have located the nursing school, but the fear of rejection was too great. Laughing sheepishly, as if he were still puzzled about himself, he commented, "Many times I have a car, I want to drive to see her. I don't know for some reason I didn't do it. It's silly. I was thinking about it. It's very silly, you understand. I wanted to leave the same memory as was before."

To Lonek's immense pleasure, sometime after his arrival two of his cousins who had long ago emigrated from Poland to Palestine came to visit him after glimpsing his name on a list of the new immigrant children in a local newspaper. "One of my cousins, Joseph, was warm to me like Africa. He was always saying: 'Maybe I can bring you back to Haifa. I can more see you then.'" Joseph also wanted to remove the boy because he objected to the school's academics. Therefore, Joseph wrote to the "mother" of the Teheran Children, Henrietta Szold. He knew of her progressive educational leanings and her unfailing interest in the Teheran Children. He listed the following complaints:

1. There are not enough instructors to educate the children.
2. There is no permanent school room for the children; teaching is carried out in the children's rooms, the children sit on their beds. This is not serious.
3. Children are not put in the proper classes according to their level.
4. There are no fixed hours for learning, but only for work. Children work two to seven hours a day in agriculture. This is hard work for children, especially for small children who are sent to work together with the bigger ones, weak and strong children together. All are required the same productivity.

Eliott explained his cousin's point of view: "He wants more for me not to be a farmer like all children was then but to go to technical college, where I will get more educated. He already have a good opinion about me that everybody wants me to be the handyman. He spoke to the counselor and they told him to send me to some technical school." Easily said, but who would pay for it? Moreover, a transfer was discouraged by the director of Lonek's school, who feared that Lonek would become irreligious, eat nonkosher food, and turn into a "Gentile" if he moved to Haifa. Joseph persisted in trying to find a solution. He was convinced that Lonek was a gifted boy who showed remarkable mechanical talent. Although Joseph assumed that his letter, arriving among hundreds of other requests, would be overlooked, he did receive a response: Henrietta Szold would travel from Jerusalem to personally meet Lonek and decide the merits of the case herself.

Had Henrietta Szold referred Joseph's letter to a trusted aide, no one could have blamed her. In most other offices, a letter from an unknown, lowly supplicant might sit with the incoming mail for months. Not in Henrietta Szold's letter bin. Joseph's appeal mobilized her into action almost immediately.

Henrietta Szold's reply put the school, children, and faculty in an up-roar of excitement. No one could believe that she would actually make a personal visit just to see Lonek. The lady was no youngster! To think that she would undertake such a trek! And all for Lonek! Eliott's excitement rose as he described the occasion. "All the time she postponed her com-ing from Jerusalem. Back and forth and she postponed. And then she came to see me. It was for her terrible to spend a hot summer seven or eight hours coming from Jerusalem. Now it takes about two hours. In that time, it was a voyage. I was an orphan boy. She was the head of the youth in Palestine—the head position. She can close up [institutions]. Everybody was shaking. Like a king is coming. Somebody big. She came with an old taxi, a black taxi from Jerusalem. I imagine she was in her sixties or seventies. She had gray hair and a very nice voice. She came to see and she spoke with me. I feel like a lord, on top of the world, a celeb-rity. Everybody knew. Everyone was talking. 'She came to see Lonek!' The director made a meeting together for the three of us and to take a walk as we talk. But she said to the director: 'I am sorry you have to leave. I talk with Lonek and then we all talk together.' [How shrewd of her to want to speak with Lonek without the presence of another adult!] After the walk, she called the director. We sat together. She said: 'I will send Lonek to a school for testing in Haifa. If he is okay, I will send him to study, if no, we wouldn't waste time.' She decided that if I will be talented, she will get me the money to go to technical college."

The director's fears about Lonek's religious future probably were not com-pelling to Henrietta Szold who had commented: "School children must not be drawn into religious strife."

Ludwig Tietz, the technical high school selected for Lonek, boasted high academic standards and an excellent educational staff, consisting mostly of German refugees. Until the testing could be arranged, the an-ticipation and strain mounted daily for Lonek. When the day arrived, Lonek was sent off with the children's and the staff's blessing. "The pres-sure in the morning! To go to the test it was half day traveling. They give me the fare and I had to wait on the bus. In the morning, I was so anx-ious"—and now Eliott's voice was thick with tension—"I was shaking half an hour. The woman who gave me the test, she knew. She sat me down and made me relax. She said: 'Relax. Take it easy. Just be yourself. It's a very simple test.' I was a child shaking. It was a hundred or some-thing degrees. I remember I was sweating. No air conditioning. You sit-ting there under pressure. Testing was for about three afternoons. It was a simple test, but you know, I was getting nervous." Eliott's voice duplicated his former nervous state: "I get tears in my eyes even now! And when I came back on the bus, my friends in my room asking: 'So what did you do? How was it?'" Eliott added conspiratorially and with a chuckle, "And later five or six children went to the same test, and they cheated a little, because of my memory."

"After a week I received a letter from Henrietta Szold with a statement that I am capable to go to school. She take the funds and send me there. I put the letter on the wall and everybody was looking." By now Eliott was simultaneously laughing and crying with relief. His words came pouring out: "You know, from about two hundred and fifty children maybe twenty or twenty-five went there. I was very pleased. I wanted to get more educated. I wanted to learn more." Sounding as elated as if he had just received the letter of admission, Eliott added, "Not only I was pleased. All the children. Everybody was screaming: 'He's got the scholarship. Finally he go to school.' Everybody was happy with me, like a celebration. I always owe to my cousin my future. He gave me a new hand in life!" So moved that he could no longer sit, Eliott rose. "I go and get a tissue box. I don't hope to cry anymore." I commented that I hoped in the future his eyes would brim with tears because of too much laughter. He replied: "Now I can laugh at the whole thing."

Soon after his acceptance, Lonek moved to the Kibbutz Yagur, located between Haifa and Nazareth so that he could study at Ludwig Tietz. His admission at fifteen meant that Lonek was progressing into young adulthood. He was now facing a new period in his life, a span of years that would be turbulent and adventurous, but quite congruent with the turbulent and adventurous years the young state of Israel was facing, as it moved toward independence.

CHAPTER XXIII

There Is Something About a Soldier

The cataclysmic events raging in Europe had spun Lonek from place to place like a grain of sand in a tornado. Rather than coming to rest in a bucolic landscape as expected, he landed directly in an earthquake. The *Yishuv*, the Jewish community within Palestine, was faced with overwhelming problems, though it had very few resources with which to solve them.

World War II was in progress, and the Yishuv was only too conscious of the peril European Jews were facing. In fact, the German army came dangerously near Palestine when the German general Rommel, known as the "Desert Fox" for his cunning and skill, brought his formidable forces to North Africa, thereby highlighting Hitler's far-reaching power.

The murder of millions of Jews in Europe underscored the need for a homeland where all persecuted Jews could find refuge. Too many Jews were dying because other countries' borders were closed to them. The Yishuv considered unrestricted immigration one of its fundamental principles. Most of the Arab population were vehemently opposed to allowing further Jewish immigration. Compromise on the issue of unlimited immigration was impossible. As a result, the Arabs and Jews became bitter enemies.

Additional dangers arose from the deteriorating relationship between the Palestinian Jews and the British. At one time, the relationship had been excellent. In 1917, the British government, to the great rejoicing of the Jewish population, issued the Balfour Declaration, which stated, "His Majesty's government viewed with favour the establishment in Palestine of a national home for the Jewish people." On April 24, 1920, the British, as one of the first and strongest supporters of the creation of a Jewish homeland, were given a mandate by the League of Nations, which meant that they were to establish a responsible government in Palestine. Specifically, the British were to secure "peace and security" in Palestine and "facilitate the establishment of a Jewish national home."[1]

But over time, British interests changed. In 1939, as danger from the Continent loomed, Prime Minister Neville Chamberlain concluded that the Yishuv would remain Britain's ally against the Nazi menace no matter what the British stance was on immigration. It was apparent, however, that continued British support of a Jewish homeland might sway the Arabs to align with the Germans. In 1939, the British government issued the infamous White Paper, which fixed the Jewish population in Palestine at current levels and recommended the creation of a Palestinian state in which the Arab population would outnumber the Jewish population.

The White Paper devastated Jewish hopes of establishing a homeland. Therefore, it pitted the Jews against Britain—a tragedy because Britain, at enormous sacrifice and with conspicuous bravery, was fighting the common German enemy.[2] Britain had opened its gates to thousands of refugees and in addition had accepted transports of ten-thousand Jewish children whose parents had given up hope of escaping the Nazis. Although it was perhaps a drop in the bucket in view of the millions of Jews lost, it was more than other nations had done. David Ben-Gurion (later to become Israel's first prime minister) met this dilemma by stating, "We shall fight the war as if there were no White Paper. And we shall fight the White Paper as if there were no war."[3]

The Yishuv was thus torn. Although allied to the British in pursuing victory over the Nazis, it also wanted to end the Mandatory so that an independent state for the Jews could be created. In addition, the Jews faced the constant risk of attacks from the local Arab population and hostilities from the millions of surrounding Arabs who opposed the creation of a Jewish state.

By 1920, the Arab-Jewish conflict had been brought into high relief; Arabs constantly attacked Jewish settlements. At the same time, Jewish immigrants—survivors of European pogroms—were growing increasingly wary of their exclusive reliance for protection on the British. Too many Jewish immigrants had experienced pogroms in Europe to risk relying on anyone but themselves. Moreover, they realized that when the British someday left Palestine, they would—without their own army—be fully exposed to the Arabs' intransigent hatred and overt determination to annihilate their Jewish neighbors.

Under the circumstances, the Yishuv deemed it essential to create a citizen army, the Haganah,[4] subject to civilian control under the authority of the Jewish Agency that coordinated all Zionist activities in Palestine and abroad. (Once independence was achieved, its executive committee became Israel's first government.) Ben-Gurion issued a clandestine appeal to the Jewish population to join the Haganah. Because the Arabs outnumbered the Jews three to one, the Haganah functioned as a civic guard and watched over Jewish lands.

At first, the Haganah was mostly a defensive force. Slowly, it gained tactical experience, became more active than reactive, and was capable of consolidating areas already in its possession. Eventually, it developed into a formidable fighting force.

It fulfilled many functions both legal and illegal, including stealing and smuggling weapons, conducting rescue work on the Continent, and manning ships. With great foresight, the leaders of the Haganah planned new settlements in areas that were to outline and guard the future borders of Israel.[5] These settlements were frequently erected secretly. If appropriate locations were found, walls, barracks, and watchtowers were constructed in concealed locations and installed in the dead of night. For example, in a single night, eleven settlements were installed by Golda Meir, then head of the Jewish Agency's Political Department.[6]

Equally important was the Haganah's work in resisting the mighty force of the British by aiding and abetting the entrance of illegal immigrants. Shaul Avigur was head of the illegal immigration organization of the Haganah. Having survived pogroms in his native Russia, he was passionately dedicated to resistance and survival. He managed in secrecy, and with minimal funds, to collect a fleet of ships and boats to ferry refugees from the Continent to Palestine. When these vessels released their unlawful human cargo on isolated beaches under the darkness of night, members of the Haganah guided them to safety. Similarly, when ships foundered on beaches or sandbanks, members of the Haganah hastily helped the refugees disembark before British patrols located them. At times, measures became desperate. When the British rounded up eighteen hundred refugees for deportation on the *Patria*, the Haganah slipped them explosives to destroy the ship's engines. The result was unforeseen disaster. Two hundred and sixty refugees drowned. Yet, in spite of such tragic setbacks, in the final analysis, the British Coast Guard was unable to prevent thousands of other refugees from finding refuge in the Yishuv.[7]

A new arrival described his reception by Haganah members as he waded ashore in the dark of night after disembarking from a vessel that had successfully evaded the British Coast Guards: "Out of the dark appeared two men on horseback, armed with rifles, the ammunition belt slung around their shoulders and talking Hebrew. We couldn't believe our eyes and ears, but they were hurrying us to march further inland, to wade through deep sand dunes to a place to rest and to assemble. We fell down on the spot, exhausted, emptied our boots and organized ourselves. We stayed at this place till all of our transport came ashore. But then the horsemen went into action and led us on a terrible forced march over dunes of moving sands, our feet sinking deep into them with every step. All the time the horsemen rode around us like cowboys leading a herd of cattle, urging "*schneller, schneller* [faster]!" After an hour or so they let us rest for a few minutes. We felt very weak, having had nothing to eat for almost three days. We were thirsty and awfully tired. But the two horsemen aroused us and we had to struggle for another hour, till we came to a little eucalyptus grove. There we fell down like dead. The horsemen left us, but not before calling to all of us: "Shalom!"[8]

The world's conscience was aroused by photographs of the decrepit transport *Exodus* being pursued by a British destroyer. How ironic that a ship that had formerly fought Hitler's forces was now battling the dilapidated *Exodus* and dragging off its cargo of Jewish women and children for deportation to Germany. United Press International described the mournful scene: "British troops today landed 1400 screaming, kicking and weeping Jewish refugees from the Transport Ocean Vigour using physical force to compel recalcitrants to set foot on German soil. Truncheons were employed sparingly."[9]

Resentment against the Mandatory crested when England added insult to injury. In 1945, after the end of World War II and after the fall of Churchill's government, Foreign Secretary Ernest Bevin released a statement that must have left the Jewish population gasping. He warned them that Hitler's victims should not try "to push themselves to the head of the queue" for special attention, as such action might provoke anti-Semitism. A better path for the Jews might be to aid in the reconstruction of Europe. A seemingly grotesque thought that the European Jews who fled to Palestine should assist in the rebuilding of Germany! In addition, Bevin also refused President Truman's recommendation to allow one hundred thousand European Jews to enter Palestine.[10]

In Palestine, as in Europe, the Jews were targets, but they were indomitable targets. The perils confronting them from near and far drew them into a close, familylike circle that deemed each member's survival of paramount importance. Lonek joined this circle out of appreciation for his rescue and welcome, and out of a sense of loyalty and patriotism instilled in him at the local schools he had attended.

Thus motivated, seventeen-year-old Lonek dropped out of the technical school after studying for only two years and momentously decided to join the Haganah, one of the Jewish defense forces, renowned for its bravery and resourcefulness. Eliott dryly described the day he volunteered: "It was near Haifa. Was a theater place and near the theater place, they [induction center] have a place. I didn't have to volunteer. Nobody call me. I came early in the morning, stayed there for half day because there were big lines of people. They ask me how old I am. I lie a little bit. I say I am eighteen, instead of seventeen. Okay. They took my name and they gave me a card that I have to go to another place. There I will get orders." It was accomplished—Lonek was in the Haganah.

He stopped by his cousin Joseph's office located in downtown Haifa to proudly announce the great news. His cousin was appalled at Lonek's decision to volunteer and queried him angrily: "Are you crazy? You went to volunteer? Who asked you? This is terrible what you did!" Eliott related, "I said to myself: 'How could he say like this? He is like a traitor.' I went out. I didn't spoke to him anymore." In later years, when Eliott looked back he became more sympathetic to his cousin's point of view: "He was right. He thought of my parents. Because God forbid I would die or get killed, they wouldn't know where I am. Lots of volunteers got shot. They only had broomsticks. They didn't have rifles in those times. All those Arab countries fight against a little tiny quarter million people. My cousin was worried. He was thinking not as a good Zionist, he was thinking more as a parent. But for years I was so mad at him that I didn't want to talk to him or see him." Casualty rates bore out Joseph's concern. Before Israel gained its independence, 6,000 Jews out of a population of 650,000 lost their lives. Proportionally, this would be comparable to 2.5 million American soldiers dying in battle.

In spite of the Haganah commitment to fortifying its strength, there was little time and few facilities or opportunities to train new recruits such as Lonek. When I asked Eliott how long his basic training had lasted, he answered matter of factly: "I didn't train at all. They never trained me. When I was at Kfar Hanoar Hadati at fourteen, fifteen, they always teach us how to fire with rifles and how to throw hand grenades. We learn Morse Code—how to communicate. Day and night, sometimes for weeks we went training. Every year in autumn we got training for about a month. In the army they didn't teach us nothing. In the army we went already like made soldiers. In those times, the army was not standing on their two legs. It was standing maybe on one foot, maybe one toe even."

Eliott became increasingly disturbed as he spoke, "A lot of people killed like flies. Specially people they come from Europe, from Russia. Most of the people was there a day or two in Israel. They pick them up. Somebody was eighteen or twenty, and they ask him if he can shoot. Everybody start to be a hero. Everybody [thought] they was a general. Everybody thought they fought the whole German army. So they gave them a rifle and said: 'If you fight the German army, you can fight the Arabs.' And most of them got killed like flies. It was terrible, terrible. It's hard to describe this."

Lonek was aware that one offshoot of the Haganah received particularly intensive training: the Palmach units. Originally trained by the British to resist the German advance through Tobruk in Libya, these highly experienced combat troops were invariably assigned to areas of great danger, involving exceptionally daring and frequently secret missions. One Palmach unit, for instance, consisted of blond, blue-eyed, and very Aryan-looking soldiers who infiltrated and carried out missions behind German lines. Another unit consisted of dark-complexioned volunteers from neighboring Arab countries who were well versed in various Arab dialects, customs, and mannerisms. These volunteers were dedicated to ferreting out military secrets from the Arabs.[11]

Although average soldiers rarely encountered Palmach units, Lonek did encounter them once, though he realized it only later. While spending time on a kibbutz, he noticed a number of men in Arab garments. "Sometimes when I was in the kibbutz I saw them. Most of them was from the Middle East. You couldn't recognize they were Jews. They didn't speak one word in Hebrew. They only spoke Arabic. Sometimes they even speak against the Jews. It was for them to show that they are really Arabs. I said, 'What are Arabs doing here?' And somebody told me, 'It's not your business.' They didn't want to tell me, you understand.

"This was one division of the Palmach; others were different. One was like a fox division. They used to go to places at night. Let's say, for example, the Arabs, we knew from intelligence, were planning to attack this or that kibbutz. Before the Arabs attack, the Palmach units ambush them. Or let's say, from the next house an attack comes at night from the Arabs. They send the Palmach to the area. This was very high combat people. Very well trained. Like the Green Berets, or maybe more. They are very famous."

Lonek felt a great sense of pride and patriotism serving in the army, and not all of his army life was hard. He was young and handsome in his uniform and full of adventure: "I was very happy. Was like excitement. You meet a lot of different people. You get different views." He was particularly gratified at being selected by the army for an important mission and felt exhilarated by being a small but important cog in a weighty enterprise. I invited him to tell me the story.

CHAPTER XXIV

A Tale of Two Tanks

*E*liott recalled with wonder in his voice: "I don't believe it even. Today looks like a miracle. I was standing in line. They ask if somebody wants to volunteer to make mechanical work. I didn't talk. I was shy, maybe. My buddy next to me said—pointing at me—'Here is one volunteer. He knows what he is doing.' So they took me out. I remember like today." Apparently, Lonek's reputation for mechanical wizardry had qualified him for his next assignment: help build a tank unit for the Yishuv.

The stark reality was that the Yishuv suffered from an appalling lack of arms. Under the Mandatory, the Yishuv was not a sovereign state and therefore was unable to purchase weapons on the international arms market. As a result, the Yishuv did not possess even a single tank. By contrast, as sovereign states, Syria, Lebanon, and other Arab countries could purchase weapons freely. Therefore, their armies were well equipped.[1]

The Yishuv's crucial need for weapons called for innovative, ingenious, and even drastic methods. Secretly, Jewish workshops produced copies of Sten submachine guns and manufactured primitive flamethrowers. Out of desperation, they also invented the "Davidka" mortar, affectionately named after its inventor. Although it did not fire accurately, it spewed forth nails and pieces of metal with such a thunderous boom that it terrorized the Arabs. Discarded machinery useful for manufacturing was also imported from the United States. In addition, members of the Haganah and volunteers stole as many weapons as possible from British army depots, disguised them as ordinary machinery, and shipped them to Palestine, frequently by way of France. Thousands of rifles, submachine guns, machine guns, ammunition, and explosives were also packed in Italy, registered as destined for Ethiopia, but then smuggled into Palestine by way of Hungary and Yugoslavia.

Even after the Palestinian Jews gained independence, the scarcity of arms presented a desperate problem to the Israeli army. How desperate can best be gauged by an incident that involved David Ben-Gurion. After Israel finally came into being, Arab invasions loomed from every border. Ben-Gurion was informed that weapons were available from Czechoslovakia, but, and this was a very big but, a guarantee of $6 million was required for their shipment to Israel. Such a large sum of money was simply unavailable. What should be done? Ben-Gurion silently weighed his options. Then he replied: "Give them [the Czechs] a deferred check. If we win the war, we'll have the means to honor it. And if we lose—" He did not complete the sentence but the implication was clear. Fortunately for the state of Israel, the government was ultimately able to honor its debt.[2]

Faced with Arab tanks, the Yishuv resorted to desperate measures to acquire their own tanks. Eliott describes how it was done: "They bribed some British guards and stole two British tanks from the English. They disassembled them in Zichron Yaakov near Haifa. And they hide them in straw used for cows. Later they bring the tanks to us and we assembled them in Zichron Yaakov, a village near where the airport is today. And this was the first regiment from tanks."

I was thunderstruck. "Wait a minute. You mean you went up to tanks that were in pieces and assembled them. How did you do it?" Perhaps inspired by his father's fashioning of eating and cleaning utensils from bits and pieces found on the tracks during stops on the Siberian railroad, Eliott opined that if a problem is at hand, particularly one of a mechanical nature, you just go and solve it. That was all there was to it. Eliott described how he, and other selected men, met clandestinely to solve the mechanical puzzle. He had never even been close to a tank before: "I knew nothing about it. We was a group of seven, eight people and we assembled the tanks. They show us pictures. They have catalogs from somewhere. You figure this way, that way. So you put together."

"It's a good thing the tanks weren't put together so they ran backwards by mistake," I exclaimed.

"No, no," he replied, laughing. "This was the two tanks that fought for Israel in the War of Independence." With a mixture of pride and modesty, Eliott added, "I make a lot of good things for Israel because of my education. Lot of good things. I assembled the first two tanks in Israel."

In quick order, and in view of a lack of other candidates, Lonek became an expert in tank maintenance. He was assigned to the 82nd Division, the ammunition supply section. His job was highly problematic. Not only was the army too new and inexperienced to be knowledgeable about its mis-

sion, but ammunition and different parts arrived daily from various countries. Eliott remembered this period well: "Nobody knew how to set up.
Sometimes I receive ammunition that didn't fit one to the other. They was
saying to me: 'This is what you need.' And I said: 'What do you mean? For
the guns on the tanks it doesn't fit. I need different ammunition!' They
said: 'Ah, we make a mistake.'"

While the Jews were engaged in bloody encounters with the Arabs,
they also struggled to rid themselves of the British Mandatory. The urgency for independence became clearer every day. Neither the United
Nations nor the British nor the United States took up the cudgels for the
endangered Yishuv. The Yishuv was left to ensure its own survival. This
could be accomplished only if they had their own state and could make
their own decisions.

Pressured by the urgency of the situation, the United Nations developed a partition plan that would allocate part of Palestine for an independent Jewish state. But noting the strength of the Arabs and the desperate
struggle of the Jews, the UN support of partition began to waver, convinced that independence would bring hopeless chaos and defeat, even
extermination of the Jews. On March 19, 1948, the United States with-
drew its support for partition and favored a UN trusteeship for Palestine
until Jews and Arabs could reach an agreement. By pressuring the Yishuv
to delay their quest for independence, the United States was actually re-
versing its own position. In the United Nations, arguments went back and
forth between those who endorsed partition and those who favored a UN
trusteeship. A decision had to be made by six o'clock on May 14 when the
British Mandate ended.[3]

The British had little desire to continue the Mandatory because they
were beset by their own problems. The country had won a war but lost an
empire. Still reeling from the devastation of the war, it needed to rebuild.
Its people were weary and drained. The Mandatory had been considered
by some as "a high vision with no precedent in law or history, and it had
known some years of radiance. But it had long declined into what Win-
ston Churchill had called a squalid war." On September 26, 1947, British
Colonial Secretary Arthur Creech Jones had announced to the UN General Assembly that if no end to the hostilities between Arabs and Jews
were in sight, England would withdraw from Palestine.[4]

Ben-Gurion objected strenuously to a trusteeship or to any delay to
independence. True, the Jewish forces seemed on the verge of being overwhelmed by the Arabs arrayed against them, but he was convinced that
the opportunity for independence must be seized and that the Yishuv was

capable of whatever was necessary to achieve so worthy a goal. A debate raged between Ben-Gurion and other members of the Provisional People's Council of the Yishuv (set up until Israel's independence would allow for a more permanent government) about the advisability of postponing independence. Ben-Gurion's view prevailed. In spite of possible dangers, the Jews would wait no longer for independence. They had waited too long already.

On May 14, the Jewish population followed with bated breath as the United Nations debated. Slowly during the day, proponents of trusteeship lost heart. As the hands of the clock crept toward four, five, and finally six o'clock, the world awaited the United Nations' final decision. At four o'clock precisely, two hours before the official hour, Ben-Gurion rose dramatically in the Knesset, and, not waiting for the decision of the United Nations, read Israel's Declaration of Independence.

Exactly at 6:15 P.M., and to the Jews' relief, the U.S. representative in the General Assembly, Ambassador Warren Austin, announced U.S. recognition of the Provisional Government of the new State of Israel. Ben-Gurion immediately announced the birth of the State of Israel. On May 14/15, 1948, at 00.11, 6.11 P.M. Washington time, Sir Alan Cunningham, the British high commissioner, boarded a British destroyer and left Israel. On May 15, President Truman recognized the government of Israel. Three days later, Moscow followed. Agreement between these two governments was unprecedented. Nevertheless, most of the world remained skeptical, convinced that Israel would fall to the Arabs in no time at all.

Some hopeful and naïve souls assumed that, at long last, the Yishuv's troubles were over. They expected the Jews to run the country in peace once the British left; but the Arabs had other ideas. They immediately formed the Army of Liberation, under the direction of the Arab League, and remained committed to swiftly erasing the newborn state of Israel. The Secretary-General of the Arab League, Azzam Pasha, described openly and triumphantly the manner in which the Arabs were going to fight. "This will be a war of extermination and a momentous massacre which will be spoken of like the Mongol massacres and the Crusades."[5] The new Israeli borders were to be ignored. The Arabs stated quite clearly: "Any line drawn by the United Nations will be nothing but a line of blood and fire."[6]

Although bloody attacks from the Arabs had preceded Israel's independence, even bloodier, longer, and more frustrating ones followed. Practically from the instant of Israel's birth, the Arabs took the offensive. On May 15, 1948, Tel Aviv was bombed by the Egyptians, who had been so confident of ultimate triumph that they had printed celebratory stamps even before Israel became a state. High-level Arab officers eagerly identified which houses in Tel Aviv they planned to seize for their own personal use. In quick succession, the Arab League invaded Israel from all sides. All the Arab nations were far better equipped than Israel, which possessed only an army, without a navy or air force. But the greatest threat came from Jordan, whose army, was composed of crack troops trained by the British.

Both before and after independence, Lonek participated in the battle for Israel's very existence. His identification with Israel was profound. As he described the events of this period to me, his voice dropped low, and he confided that he suffered two great disappointments in the army: one during the battle of Latrun and the other in connection with the *Altalena*.

CHAPTER XXV

The Uncertainties of Battle

Of all the places contested during the War of Independence, the most intensely tied to Jewish history was Jerusalem. After entering the Old City of Jerusalem on May 19, 1948, the Arabs took Latrun—a vital point along the road connecting Jerusalem with Tel Aviv. The threat of losing western Jerusalem, where the majority of Jews lived, particularly horrified the Israelis. Recalling the desecration of dead Jewish soldiers and massacres of civilians by the Arabs, Ben-Gurion issued orders to uproot the Arab forces at all costs. Without Israeli access to the Jerusalem–Tel Aviv road, Jerusalem would not survive the lack of supplies and inevitably would fall to the enemy.[1]

Planned for May 24, "Operation Maccabi" was designed to dislodge the Arabs from the strongholds around the villages of Beit Machsir and Latrun. Two battalions, were to attack Latrun. One of these consisted of soldiers whose background was European World War II, who were unfamiliar with the Israeli terrain. Opposing them was the fierce Arab Legion. For several days, the Jewish troops attempted to take the area, and succeeded on occasion, only to be quickly thrown back again.

Eliott recalled his participation in the June 8 battle for Latrun: "There was a little hill. We were standing with our tanks at the bottom. Not a big hill. A stretch maybe seven, eight hundred feet. From the bottom, people went up the hill to capture the hill. On the other side was standing the Jordanians, the Legionnaires. They were the best fighters in the Middle East. Other fighters, the Arabs, if they hear a shot, they run away. But those, the Legionnaires, were really the fighters. They were British trained, very well trained. They fought hard. Hundreds of Jewish soldiers go up the hill, fall down, and another hundred go up. They were falling like wheat on the field when there comes a big storm. It is hard to describe this. It was terrible, terrible."

The two hastily assembled, precious tanks, the only tanks, were also deployed in the battle. Each tank was manned by three people: the driver, the radio operator, and the gunner. Strangely enough, the drivers were not Jewish. Eliott suspected that they were the soldiers who had originally stolen the tanks from the British. "I believe they got good pay," reflected Eliott. "But they hated the British more than the pay. They were Irish, I believe. They spoke very funny English. When they saw the English, the Irish would look up and start to curse them. They say: 'The bloody bastards!' By the way, [the Irish] they married Jewish girls!"

Speaking about the battle seemed to upset Eliott. I had noticed that at moments of acute emotion, it was easier for him to respond to questions than to continue his own descriptions.

"And you were there at Latrun?"

"I was there with the tank. We were down at the bottom of the hill. The two tanks."

"And what were you supposed to do with the tanks?"

"We were supposed to shoot. But the tanks didn't do much to the Legionnaires."

"Why? How come?"

"Because we didn't have a range against the hill. The tanks could not fire over the hill. We were afraid to go up because if we went up we were afraid the tanks would get hit. Because," at this point Eliott shrugged his shoulders with an expression of wonderment and pity, "the two tanks were the whole tank army. If we lost them, we would sacrifice everything."

"So you had to conserve the tanks and could not go up the hill. It must have been terrible. How did you feel sitting there and seeing all those people get killed?"

"Terrible, terrible! I cry. I cry. I hide myself near my tank, behind my tank, and I was crying."

"Were you the gunner?"

"No, I was with the ammunition. I was on the bottom of the hill outside the tank. My job was to supply the ammunition."

"What happened finally?"

The Arab Legion didn't proceed up the mountain and we didn't go either. They didn't run after us. We didn't let them come down on our side of the hill. Support for the army came from outside. And we stopped the whole thing. In those times came a cease-fire."

A young commander, wounded in the stomach and leg, was ordered to withdraw with his men. A number of them had been killed, and many of the survivors were bloody and severely wounded. Trapped in a ravine, their water and rations exhausted, they were forced to drink fouled water. But the commander possessed one invaluable strength: the total trust of his men. They followed him from their precarious position, retreating through burning fields that scorched their legs and bodies. The commander later recalled: "During those bitter hours of that terrible day on the battlefield of Latrun, I swore to myself that in all future encounters between ourselves and the Arabs, we must always emerge victorious."[2] The commander later became known as General Ariel Sharon, one of Israel's foremost generals.

Some time after the battle, the Haganah, under harrowing conditions, constructed a road south of Latrun, referred to as the "Burma Road." It was renamed "Kvish Hagevurah" or the "Road of Heroism." When Jewish convoys finally burst into Jerusalem to the rejoicing, but deprived and exhausted Jewish population, one of the lead trucks carried the appropriate sign: "If I forget thee, O Jerusalem, may my right hand forget its cunning." Despite victory in Jerusalem, Israel did not recapture Latrun until the Six Day War in 1967.[3]

After Latrun, Lonek was posted in the south in the desert against Egyptian troops. By this time, King Farouk of Egypt had joined the Arab invasion of Israel much the same way as Mussolini had joined Hitler—with more greed than heart. Eliott recalled, "Was a very famous battle. The Egyptians got maybe fifty or sixty tanks against the two Israeli tanks." But, apparently, the Haganah had learned something from Field Marshal Rommel, who had decorated jeeps so that they appeared to be tanks. "We outsmarted them. We took jeeps and made tanks with cartons. We made believe we have hundreds of tanks. Making like in a movie. It's unbelievable. And then the two tanks got stuck in the field."

Both Eliott and I looked dumbfounded and appalled. "What do you mean, they got stuck in the field?"

"One of the Arab hits got the cannon. We couldn't operate it anymore. A tank without a cannon is not worth much. And the other got hit in the engine. Couldn't go."

"So what happened? Tell me!"

"They sent a guy. He said he was a big general in the Russian army. He was a volunteer, and he knew how to hook the two tanks with a chain: the one that is missing an eye can pull the one that is missing the leg. One that didn't have the cannon can pull the one where the engine didn't work. That was the deal. So the general was staying there a few hours. He was screaming away, he was afraid. He was a big general, but when it came to hooking up those two tanks he was like a baby. He was scared to death because they were shooting. So he wait until after dark and then they move the tank.

"It was a little bit dark." Eliott looked out of the window and was suddenly deep in thought. He repeated: "It was a little bit dark. An afternoon like this one."

"And did he fix it?"

"Yes, he fix it and finally they move the tanks out—the blind man with the two legs."

The troops had to maneuver the invalid tank and the camouflaged jeeps. Their ability to innovate and manage an almost bizarre situation amid fierce enemy fire would seem comical had it not been so tragic.

Thanks, in part, to such resourceful schemes, the Haganah outfought the Egyptians and were on their way to victory. They were just about to seize the hill. Eliott still recalls that moment of elation. But on the brink of triumph, the men received the most stunning news: A cease-fire was proclaimed that froze their current position just short of victory. Instead of grasping the hard-fought-for hill, the men had to stop the fight. Lonek was devastated. "We were on a hill near Gaza. A lot of people got killed on this hill. Maybe a few hundred. Finally we win. We got everything what we wanted. Then came this big general, an old man with a beard. He was not religious, but he was going with a beard. And he said he didn't want to upset us. We have to back off. It's a cease-fire! He was sorry, but we depend on the United States with money, with ammunition. Was so upset about the United States. We said, "Why? All this for nothing?" We were on the top and they was on the bottom. They had the ammunition, they had the tanks. They were fighting fire like rain. And finally we got them. We make holes and we dig ourselves in and we got them. Then we have to back off. That was the second cease-fire. It came from the people there in Washington and Jerusalem or Tel Aviv. And that's it. We can do nothing. Was very frustrating. They let the Egyptians go, but the ammunition they have to leave there. The Egyptians destroyed most of their tanks, but the weapons we got—rifles and ammunition. Was a famous Egyptian general who surrender. Later he became president of Egypt. It was a terrible disappointment."

Eliott continued his heartbreaking tale. "Next, they told me to unload my ammunition and to pick up wounded people on the battlefield. It was an armored car, like a tractor. We pick up one wounded here and one there." By now Eliott was holding back tears. "We put them inside the car. One on top of the other. I pick up about twenty people and I brought them near Rehovot. On the road we got so scared. One was crying, 'Water!' and one was crying, 'Pain!' One was crying, 'My leg is hurting me!' Of those twenty, I believe ten were dead when I brought them to the doctor. Lucky the doctors and the nurses were waiting in Rehovot. They say, 'This is a miracle that some survived!' Because it was a ride of maybe four or five hours. Seemed to me like days we were going and finally we got them there."

The tragedy of the soldiers' deaths was intensified by the futility of the battle. After finishing the story, Eliott looked disheartened and fell silent. His downcast appearance reminded me that he had another tale to tell of a disappointment that, as so many others in his life, was due to political rather than to personal causes.

CHAPTER XXVI

Resisting Orders

*L*onek's second disappointment involved a long-standing and tragic schism between two Israeli military factions—the Irgun and the Haganah. These two fighting forces originally split over how to deal with the British during the Mandatory. The Haganah, headed by Ben-Gurion, searched for a peaceful solution with the British, who, after all, had been instrumental in ridding the world of Hitler and his cohorts. The Irgun, a more militant defense force, advocated more violent measures. Menachem Begin, like Lonek, had arrived from Poland by way of Siberia in 1943. Skeptical of peaceful approaches, he went underground, and led the Irgun in sabotaging British installations, such as railroad tracks, telephone lines, and government buildings.[1]

In spite of their different philosophies, the Haganah and Irgun had the same goals: to rid Palestine of the British Mandate, to form the independent state of Israel, and to allow unrestricted Jewish immigration. To these ends, the military factions cooperated in sabotaging the British. For instance, on one night they sabotaged the railroads in 180 separate locations; on another night, they attacked three British air bases; and again at another time, the Haganah destroyed all bridges connecting Palestine with neighboring countries.

After World War II, Irgun resentment of the Mandatory deepened and the clashes with the British became increasingly fierce and bloody. When, for example, the Irgun liberated a British prison holding some of its members, three British subjects were killed. For this, three Irgun members were sentenced to death. They refused to appeal their sentence as they did not recognize the legality of the Mandatory. One of the condemned uttered the following words: "In blood and fire Judea fell. In blood and fire shall

Judea arise." And singing the "Hatikvah," the men went to their deaths. In retaliation nineteen days later, two kidnapped British sergeants were hanged by the Irgun.[2]

The Irgun also blew up the King David Hotel in Jerusalem, killing ninety-five people, mostly British. Condemning terrorist activities, the Haganah thereafter broke with the Irgun. The rupture between the two organizations deepened even further after the Arabs attacked the Etzion Bloc, a constellation of Jewish settlements situated to defend Jerusalem. Although thirty-five members of the Palmach and Chel Sadeh (garrison troops) attempted to rescue the settlers, the soldiers were ambushed, and their bodies badly mutilated by the Arabs. In response, the Irgun attacked the Arab village of Deir Yassin, and, in the battle, many Arab civilians were killed. The degree of justification for this attack, involving the loss of so many civilian lives, is still hotly debated today.[3]

The Arab retaliation was no less cruel. On April 14, the Arabs waylaid a Jewish convoy en route to besieged Jerusalem and then shot its passengers as they tried to escape the burning vehicles. Seventy-seven of the 105 riders—doctors, nurses, and teachers—perished.[4] Nevertheless, in addition to the Haganah, the Jewish Agency and other organizations expressed deep disapproval of the Irgun's methods, which violated the articles of war.[5] Ben-Gurion was so deeply shocked by Begin's philosophy that, for many years, he refused to refer to him by name. Even in the Knesset, he alluded to him only as "the man sitting next to Knesset member Bader."[6] The schism between the Irgun and the Haganah deepened still further after the Haganah became Israel's official army. Ben-Gurion was convinced that a sovereign state could possess only one army under one supreme commander. An independent army, such as the Irgun, led by Begin whom he considered a terrorist, threatened the security of the state and might trigger civil war.

While Eliott and I discussed these desperate circumstances, I suddenly realized that he had failed to mention his second disappointment in the army. When I reminded him, he responded by describing his job: "Most of the time I was not really along the front because I was in charge of the ammunition for the 82nd Division. Remember, this is the first tank division of the Israeli army. It was also the regiment of the regular soldiers of the 82nd Division. Was a few hundred people. I was a sergeant. Then I was a lieutenant. I teach them about ammunition. Big responsibility. And then," he added with a deep sigh and an expression of acute embarrassment, "I made a boo-boo. This is a sad story."

Eliott's tale of woe was rooted in the schism between the Irgun and the Haganah. As the leader of the Irgun and a fervent patriot, Begin believed that his army should provide volunteers and arms to Israel. To this end, he raised money wherever he could—even from as far away as Shanghai. With the considerable funds he collected, he purchased a ship, the *Altalena*, and filled it with arms. The bill of lading was like manna from heaven: 5,500 rifles, 300 machine guns, 300 Bren light machine guns, and 150 heavy machine guns.

Begin was unwilling to deliver all these weapons to the Haganah, and insisted on keeping some for the Irgun forces fighting in Jerusalem. The *Altalena* continued to idle about one hundred feet off shore in the Tel Aviv harbor as the fate of its cargo was being determined. Ben-Gurion ordered Begin to relinquish the arms. Begin refused. Ben-Gurion, backed against the wall by Begin, responded with an act some considered a courageous necessity, and others an outrage. He ordered Palmach units to open fire on the *Altalena*. As the ship's ammunition cargo exploded, Begin, standing at the rail of the beached ship, witnessed sixteen of the volunteers who had come to fight for Israel killed, twenty injured, and the destruction of the arms, so painfully collected. The Jewish population ringed by enemies was wrenched by the sight of Jew fighting Jew.[7]

To Lonek, the incident carried a very personal meaning. Eliott, his voice quivering, recollected how the events affected him: "This was a very sad story. They bought a ship with ammunition. Begin's party. A lot of people sell their jewelry and watches, whatever they have, giving their last penny so they could buy ammunition. We don't have nothing because no other country was sending us any. Finally comes ammunition. This ship that everybody was hoping for was an old tanker from World War II. The Irgun bought some ammunition from Czechoslovakia. Rifles and machine guns. The ship was filled with volunteers and on Ben-Gurion's order, they blow up the ship.

"I was in Natanya. This is between Tel Aviv and Haifa, and I was in charge of a group of soldiers. They told me I have to take them to fight. Rabin was in charge of the operation to blow up the ship. The people aboard the ship was Jewish. The Haganah was afraid the Irgun would take over the government. So the Haganah shoot against the ship. And people got killed. The fight was all for nothing, for no reason. We needed this ammunition so badly. Every bullet was important because sometimes we run out of bullets. We didn't have machine guns, we didn't have the apparatus. "And, his voice dropped to a whisper, "they told me I have to take these soldiers to fight brother against brother and I didn't want to."

It is always a formidable decision for a soldier to resist an order. The potential consequences can be severe, even deadly. For Lonek, the loyalty to country conflicted with loyalty to family. He felt indebted to both. He realized that by firing at the *Altalena*, he might fire on his cousin Joseph, an Irgun member who was his whole family in Israel. "I refused to go because of my cousin. I mentioned to you my cousin that took me to the school. He was in the Irgun. And I was afraid." Lonek felt compelled to disobey orders.

The response from Lonek's superiors was swift: "They took away my belt, my shoes and everything. They threw me in jail for disobeying orders." Although Lonek's decorations were removed and he was reduced in rank, he was still devastated by the fraternal strife. "The whole thing was very upsetting. A sad story in the Jewish history. We were fighting each other and the Arabs were laughing. A very sad story. Even now I cry for the memories."

Then, he suddenly brightened again, because the next notification he received from the army, when he was released from jail, produced unmitigated joy—a cable informed him of his parents' arrival in Israel.

CHAPTER XXVII

Reunion

Since his departure from Tashkent, Lonek had remained in the dark about his parents. But after the war ended, the Red Cross located them and the family was able to correspond. Many years later, Eliott learned what his letters meant to his family while he was separated from them. Contentedly smiling, he told me how welcome his communications had been. "My brother told me that they always, when they receive a letter from me, were so happy. He was running under the skirt of my mother and ask her: 'What he is writing? What he is writing?' And she always told him what I wrote and he memorized this."

In 1949, when Lonek was still in the army, he received a telegram informing him of his parents' arrival in Israel. It had been ten years since the family had left Jaroslaw and over seven years since Lonek had last seen his parents.

Lonek's family had endured quite an odyssey. After Lonek joined the orphanage, the family lived on a collective farm near Tashkent. Because the Germans had not penetrated this area during the war, many factories were built or moved there. There was, however, such a dearth of experienced labor that officials visited Lonek's father's collective farm to recruit anyone able to run a small shoe factory of about two hundred workers. Although Lonek's father had no idea how to produce shoes, he volunteered. By chance, a Jewish shoemaker lived on the collective farm, and the two decided to become a team. They agreed that, as the administrator of the factory, Lonek's father would hire the shoemaker. In return, the shoemaker would surreptitiously instruct Lonek's father how to produce shoes. "My father knew he would be very important and get a high wage in the factory. He was very intelligent and knew how to manage people. He had the experience. So he was faking that he knows how to run a shoe factory. The shoemaker taught my father what to do. Where to start—from the top or the bottom of the shoe." Every time a problem arose in the factory, the shoemaker would investigate, explaining that he had been sent by Lonek's father. The shoemaker then told Lonek's father in Yiddish how to fix it, and Lonek's father, pretending to be in charge, repeated the orders to the workers in Russian.

At this point in the story, Eliott doubled up with hilarious laughter. "The trouble was they make too many left shoes." The factory had accidentally turned out hundreds of left shoes, and no right ones. "So they bribe the supervisor of the factory. They told him they made a mistake. So the supervisor said, 'Nothing happened.' My father said, 'We have a solution. We sell the shoes on the black market.'" At that time, shoes were in enormous demand. His father assumed correctly that people would simply buy two lefts and then repair one of them to fit the right foot. The plan worked. "But later they found a way not to make too many left shoes."

Lonek's father's position made it possible for the family to obtain a better apartment and additional food and clothing. However, when the war ended in 1945, the family still wanted to leave Russia. Eliott commented with some satisfaction: "They went back to Poland, but they didn't want to stay more in Poland. They want to go to Israel because they knew I was there." Lonek's parents and Heimek traveled through the devastated Polish countryside to reach the West German border. As Jaroslaw was not on the route to West Germany, they did not stop there. They remained in Poland for only a few days, staying in an abandoned house. The Polish people treated them with condescension, hostility, and suspicion. Needless to say, they did not reclaim their seized possessions.

It was dangerous to cross the border illegally from the eastern to the western German zone. The family solicited help from Ha-Bricha, an organization dedicated to helping Jews who had survived the Holocaust to reach Israel from Eastern Europe. Eliott explained, "They tried to smuggle themselves from Poland to Germany. There were special guides that knew how. You pay them per head and they take you over the border at night. They went to a river because it was not so well patrolled. And the Russians catch them and put them in jail. For some reason, bad luck, the Russians caught fifty, sixty people, and they jail them for a few months. What they went through! There you go to jail you disappear like a fly. Today you're a name and tomorrow you are nothing. This happened to them three times. How do you say, if the first time you can't succeed, you start the second time."

The first time they were caught, Lonek's family was snatched from a freight train and landed in jail. As an adult, Heimek still remembered that in jail, to his surprise, he was handed some white bread, a delicacy that he had never seen before. The second escape returned the family to jail. As repeat offenders, they were treated more harshly—even separated and threatened with deportation back to Siberia. In spite of these discouraging setbacks, Lonek's parents remained unwavering in their resolve to join Lonek.

During the third try, Lonek's family was again apprehended by Russian soldiers, but a Jewish soldier took pity and released them. Soon after, they were able to contact Ha-Bricha and with the help of a Jewish guide, Lonek's family crossed into the West on foot. Eliott commented about his family's repeated attempts: "My father never gave up! Never!"

Once in the West, the family entrained for Berlin. From there, the Americans transported them to an American camp near Munich, where they had to wait for permission to enter Israel. Although Lonek's parents were put on a priority list of immigrants who had children in Israel, time dragged on endlessly. Lonek's parents found work and Heimek went to school. Finally, after two years the family was granted permission to leave. They had no idea what circumstances would face them in Israel. Drawing on their past experience, they assumed that conditions would be harsh. With the money they had earned in Germany, they bought a tent in case there was no housing, a water pump in case there was no water, and some metalwork equipment in case Lonek or his father needed tools to enter a trade.[1] The family was loaded on a truck and driven to France, and from there, they made their way to Israel.

The moment Lonek's parents arrived in Israel, the army notified Lonek at his station in the southern Negev. He immediately borrowed a car and drove to Tel Aviv to meet them. Lonek, the twenty-year-old soldier, had hoped, waited, and fantasized this moment many times, and when it arrived, it was a profound disappointment. "I took an armored car to see them. I loaded a lot of things. On the way over, I was so excited, I was so anxious. I drove, I believe the whole night, because the road was very bad. And I got the glasses, some dishes, pots, and some clothes, and I had it on a box on my shoulder. I was a big guy already. My father, for him, I was a little child, so we fight each other as to who will carry the box. The whole thing dropped and fell on the floor."

Both parents and son would have to adjust to the considerable changes they had undergone since they had seen each other last, roughly seven years ago. "I was very . . . I was so upset. I didn't . . ." As usual when Eliott was agitated or dismayed, he had difficulty formulating his thoughts quickly. "Many times I said to myself, 'This is my parents? This couldn't be my parents!' I saw them differently. My father was gray, my mother almost gray. My mother had been like Ingrid Bergman. Suddenly she had become fatter, more round, heavier. When I left them, they were young. People change in those times. I feel very strange, very strange. Even the talking was funny. They talk half Yiddish, half Polish. Is funny because I spoke Hebrew. They didn't. I got a lot of hopes, but is like a balloon. You blow it up, and then it get so big and you put a pin in it and the whole thing is gone." Now Eliott's voice sank to a whisper: "I said to myself I have a dream of them. I was dreaming. I still saw them as a little boy. And they from lot of trouble, they change. I was measuring all the teachers that I had in school against my father. Sometimes I look, I say this teacher must be like my father. Suddenly I saw a different person. This is a big disappointment."

Eliott's reaction was familiar. I had heard the same sense of disillusion expressed by former *Kinder* who had been reunited with their parents after many years. In contrast, parents were much less likely to have such reservations. True to form, Lonek's parents were thrilled to see him, kept hugging and kissing him, and reacted to Lonek as if they had just discovered the greatest treasure on earth—which he was to them.

Lonek's parents, having lived under various oppressive regimes, had developed a different approach to life. "The way they dressed, the way they talked, the way they think. Everything is different. Everything for them was you should keep quiet, you should not make noise. For instance, they move into a room half the size of this one [the study we were in]. I said, 'Why couldn't you get a different room?' But they were happy. They are in Israel. They didn't want much. And I wanted themy to have more. I wanted to give more. I want them to have everything.

"Later, slowly I start more to realize: 'This is your parents. You cannot change it. You take it or leave it.' Very simple. So I try to compromise—to get it in my head: This is it. They seem hopeless. So I asked the army to send me to Haifa near my parents. Because of my background, they transfer me where they make parts for the army. They gave me some position helping the headman there. He didn't understand nothing about parts—I was more like an adviser to him. I was sleeping at home and I got salary from the army and began to support my parents." Lonek was in charge of ammunition of the 82nd Division, a posting that kept him away from the front.

Lonek adjusted to living in close quarters with his family. "We were sleeping, me, my brother, and my parents, in one room. Took me a little time to get used to them. I want to be with them. Every day waiting to be with them and to help. And later I took my father working for me as a civilian in the army." Only Lonek's boss knew that the civilian was Lonek's father. The latter was a difficult employee. Due to stresses of his life, he had become a compulsive chain-smoker. This habit presented dangers in an ammunition depot! Eliott recalled, "My boss gave me full support and said, 'I see your father cannot hold out. Send him outside into the fresh air to smoke.'" With this help his father managed to keep his job. "My mother was at home. She never worked. Plenty enough she had to take care now of four people She was waking up four o'clock, preparing food, washing. She didn't have a washing machine, everything by hand, scrubbing the floors. It was hard. She was a hard worker."

When Lonek completed his army service, his father lost his job. The latter reflected that he had once been a businessman, and he could be that again. Thus, he decided to open a small store, with the bulk of the trade, as in prewar days, consisting of brushes. He was now on more familiar ground, more secure, and as a result was able to cut down on smoking. His position began to resemble his life of former years: "Everybody liked in the mornings to take a schmooze with my father. He was very friendly with people. They asked his advice. He made money. He started to be more himself. He came back to himself."

Lonek's fortunes were also rising. He was called for an interview at the Henry J. Kaiser Co., which built American cars in Israel. Competing for the job with five or six people, he waited anxiously to hear whether he had been selected. The company interviewed the candidates again and again, calling them back with unnerving repetition. Finally Lonek was summoned by a visiting American, who said, "This [meaning Lonek] is the guy we are looking for." Lonek had no idea what this phrase meant, so he courteously mumbled, "Excuse me," went outside to look for someone who spoke sufficient English to explain to him that he had been offered the job, then nonchalantly returned to the conference room and accepted.

Eliott reminisced, "So I got mechanical training. I was in charge of an assembly line of cars. And they gave me a car from the factory. I want to bring you a picture from the car. I was very happy. I got a big salary." For a while, Lonek lived in splendor. He was given the use of a company car, unusual for those times when only VIPs such as generals or essential people such as physicians owned cars. It was a great magnet for girls, and whenever there was a party, he was in charge of chauffeuring them to their destination. He earned a kingly salary. His father was proud of him, and all his neighbors were in awe. However, with the introduction of other cars, the Kaiser disappeared from the map, and so did Lonek's job.

Undaunted, Lonek acquired a job as foreman in a company that manufactured, among other products, bombs for the army. It was a venture to be kept secret from the civilian population. When questioned, he was to reply that he was producing milk cans. Although it paid well, the job lost its luster after the powers-that-be visited because the plant had fallen way behind its quota. "One day, the big generals from the army came. The boss introduced me. He started to scream at me in front of the generals. 'I told you long ago that you should have started the work.' The generals had already given the boss money, but he spent it on different things. He hadn't even bought the materiel, yet. I don't know what he steal, that's not my business. But after the visit, I went to his office. I said, 'You son of a gun, what are you screaming on me? You know you didn't even buy the materiel. What's the matter with you? You crazy or what?' But the boss gave me a very smart answer: 'What do you want? I should scream on myself in front of the generals?' This was certainly indisputable logic, but Lonek had had enough. He said, "I don't want the screaming, and I don't want your job, and I am getting out."

As a result of these less than promising experiences, Lonek went into business for himself, designing and manufacturing drill presses suitable for various types of machinery. Without much capital to invest, he squeezed his equipment into an embarrassingly small space and conducted his business by mail order. When army representatives wanted to visit his shop before placing an order with him, he improvised by saying that the workshop could not be viewed at this time because it was being moved and currently was in transit. Although the army was not fooled, they were so impressed with Lonek's ability to produce such sophisticated and complicated machinery all by himself and in such small quarters, they placed an order anyway.

Eventually, Lonek married and had a son. By 1963, he and his wife decided to join her parents in the United States. Lonek sold his shop to raise money to pay off his debts and buy tickets to the United States. He sadly parted from his parents, who remained in Israel. In New York, Lonek continued to live with his wife, son, and second child, a daughter. He opened a workshop for designing machinery and acquired a number of patents in his name both here and in Israel.

That is where we must leave Lonek, because by now he had become Eliott. The years of his voyages were far behind him. The children who had been part of this odyssey had made their contributions to Israel. They had fought in its wars; indeed, forty-five men and women had given their lives in battle. Those who survived became part of every conceivable aspect of Israeli life. They became educators, entered the fields of art, architecture, diplomacy, industry, law, medicine, religion, and trade, and had contributed to the kibbutz life.[2]

Yet none of their achievements could match the astounding odyssey that they had endured. They walked through prison doors that remarkably opened for them, defied near starvation, crossed precipitous mountain roads, sailed over dangerous waters, and traversed strange and exotic lands, finally to be greeted and welcomed by a citizenry who recognized them as symbols of survival and as fitting counterpoints to the tragedy of the many murdered Polish Jewish children.

CHAPTER XXVIII

Lonek and Eliott

Had Eliott grown up in a stable country, surrounded by parents and grandparents who could have constructed a solid base for him, he could have carefully planned and made deliberate choices about his life. Such luxuries were denied to him, as well as to millions of Jews who were cast into an inferno of agony by Hitler's anti-Semitism and lust for world conquest, and by Stalin's brutality and paranoia. Ferocious political storms wrested all control from these Jews over their lives.

The Polish Jews were among the most grievously stricken. The simultaneous invasion of German troops into Poland and the commencement of World War II isolated and trapped them. The survival of individuals almost always hinged on some fortuitous event that counteracted the cruel blows of fate. In fact, survivors' tales invariably pivot on some random event, some lucky coincidence. These include a friend's or stranger's unexpected assistance, a bureaucrat's willingness to overlook an official dictum, or, in more global lifesaving circumstances, Stalin allowing the Polish exiles to depart Russia.

Of course, such strokes of good fortune, such almost unbelievable happenstances, are met with incredulity and joy. But though welcome, luck does not necessarily counteract anxiety, fear, and apprehension. In fact, it can accomplish the opposite. Luck, by definition, is a chance event. Because it cannot be anticipated or controlled, it cannot empower. If one survives merely due to a chance event, one remains a wretched subject of fortune.

Luck and misfortune for refugees such as Lonek were often too interwoven ever to be untangled. Even the location of Lonek's family home defied simple classification as either lucky or unlucky. To be sure, the family was cursed just to be living in Poland in 1939, a time and place that could hardly be more dangerous for Jews. By the same token, Lonek and his family unlike many even less fortunate Polish Jews lived relatively close to Russian-occupied Poland. The family was fortuitously motivated to flee there by the devastating deportation of Lonek's father by the Germans. Without this very disguised blessing, Lonek and his family might have missed the brief period for escape that remained after the German invasion.

Later, what initially seemed like a lifesaving event to be under the "protection" of the Russians turned into a hellish nightmare when the family was forcefully removed from what appeared to be the relative safety of Lvov to Siberia. Once more, however, a misfortune disguised the fortunate: The family's deportation to Siberia saved them from being killed in Lvov by the departing Russians or falling into the hands of the murderous, invading Germans. What seemed the greatest debacle of all, the early disastrous defeats of the Western allies, prompted Stalin to permit the evacuation of the Poles, Jewish and non-Jewish alike, which led to Lonek's ultimate deliverance to Israel.

During those long months, the prisoners had no way of gauging that their disastrous circumstances contained the seeds of a better tomorrow. Their future seemed devoid of hope. A deep depression settled over them. As a rule, despondency triggers apathy, which makes even the smallest task seem insurmountable. But the prisoners were not able to cater to their melancholy. They were called upon to muster all their resourcefulness and all their ingenuity every hour of every day.

Lonek's family continually had to battle against the vagaries of fate. Passivity was out of the question. Foresight and courage were called for and became an integral part of the family's struggle for survival from the moment the Germans invaded Poland, and Lonek's father noticed the eastward direction of his German prison transport. Rather than accept the inevitability of imprisonment in a remote eastern camp, he jumped off the train into the darkness, dodging German bullets. In part, his reunion with his family can be credited to his forethought in secreting the funds that enabled them to bribe unwilling rescuers into retrieving the family from their hometown. Once in Russian-occupied Poland, the family shrewdly refused to apply for Russian passports, possession of which might have prevented them from ever leaving Russia. Probably among the family's many heroic struggles, Lonek's mother's decision to place her son in an orphanage ranks among the highest. As she testified later, it was a decision about which she agonized daily for many years. Yet, it must also be remembered that thousands of others who made equally astute decisions succumbed all the same.

Once Lonek's family arrived in Siberia, they faced the grim prospect of permanent imprisonment. In spite of the hopeless conditions and with impressive resourcefulness, they began the task of survival. They prepared themselves for a devastating winter as best they could. Lonek's father fashioned furniture, and Lonek foraged for food that his mother conserved for the time when the forests would be covered with snow. Less foresight could have destroyed them all. When the family later arrived in the south of Russia, they resorted to black-market dealings in spite of the grave risks involved. With great ingenuity and without money, in spite of lack of funds, they managed to secure some items for trading. Those "subversive" acts prevented immediate starvation, and it was immense good fortune that prevented the authorities from discovering the family's "unlawful" deeds.

Coping skills not only were essential for daily survival, but also for maintaining self-esteem. For example, in addition to struggling to meet their minimal needs for food and water en route to Siberia, Lonek's family clung to keeping a morsel of dignity by cleaning out the befouled railroad car whenever possible. Such seemingly small accomplishments went a long way toward helping these victims preserve their dignity.

When Lonek arrived in the United States, some years had passed since his early ordeal, and he soon metamorphozed into Eliott. Yet a great deal of Lonek still remained inside Eliott. From the early years onward, Lonek had observed his father's inventiveness and enterprise and his mother's intrepid spirit. He realized that determination and skill were needed for survival. Lonek had exhibited these traits all along: through Siberia, through Tashkent, during his boarding school years, and while in the army. Whether it was catching fish, collecting nuts, fixing whatever was broken at his boarding school, or helping to build tanks from a manual, Lonek managed to solve problems. This same resourcefulness characterized his adult professional life. In fact, problem solving was his metier. For example, Eliott overcame the unpredictability of working with difficult people by building his own business. As an engineer, Eliott used machinery as a problem-solving tool. Eliott explained, "People come to me with ideas. They want this or that kind of machinery. If you make a sweater in the factory, the sewing is from inside the sweater. After the sewing is completed, somebody has to turn the sweater the right side outward. So I made a machine that turns the sweater from inside to outside automatically."

Lonek's ingenuity helped him on many occasions and through many hard years. The ability to prevail under duress instilled in him, as it did in other escapees, a sense of accomplishment and self-worth.[1] He enjoyed being organized, controlled, and in charge of a situation. Yet emotions that stemmed from the past were never far from the surface. It is the fate of refugees and survivors never to be entirely free of past events. As another escapee commented, "It is remarkable how quickly one becomes a refugee and how eternally one remains one."[2] Not that the past was always with him. Eliott enjoyed his daily life and his work. During our sessions, he joked, laughed, and found pleasure in discussing events, personalities, and politics. But he, like most survivors and escapees, ran on "two tracks."

"One track consists of the escapees' daily self, their work, their interactions with peers and family, the track which makes for daily living and can be quite joyful. And then there is the track loaded with memories of terror, sadness and losses which belongs to another [happily former] life. It is the existence of this second track which makes the survivors feel different from other people. That second track is not necessarily deeply buried, nor need the survivor be unaware of it. It can be put aside for even very long periods of time. Yet it emerges, frequently unexpectedly, in situations when the stimulus is so powerful that compartmentalizing is no longer possible.[3]

"Memories may be strong at one moment and weak the next. They may go underground for years only to be reawakened by an encounter, a memento, a place, a word, a sound. And even if [the survivor] tiptoes carefully to avoid all reminders, at some unexpected moment, at some unexpected place the ghost of the past will rise again."[4]

Many incidents and memories could resurrect Eliott's second track. Examples abound. When I questioned Eliott whether the surges of fear he experienced when he was hiding from the Germans at Sosa's home ever return, he answered, "Sure. When, for example, I was now in Germany, when I hear the train or the announcement or loudspeaker, it remind me from the past. When you hear the German language speaking so loud, some memories come back like mad."

At another time, Eliott wanted to call the Internal Revenue Service (IRS) because of a long-delayed refund. He dialed the number, and as the electronic voice explained various options, he became increasingly nervous. He began to relive the emotions he had experienced when his family had to deal with the brutal and irrational Russian bureaucracy. Finally an IRS voice with a slight southern accent which sounded strange to him, picked up the receiver. Flooded by anxiety, Eliott mumbled, "I am sorry, but I don't feel well," and hung up. He made several attempts to call, but each time, overwhelmed by dread, hung up. Finally he asked his accountant to make the call.

Just hearing about the suffering of others, particularly children, reduced Eliott to tears. "Is terrible. Is terrible!" he would say. Recollecting past events, he seemed to feel about them almost as acutely as if they were current. In a flash, he could change from cheerful laughter to pained empathy.

Eliott's greatest regret was in missing so many years of protected childhood, deprived for so long of the personal love only parents can provide. He commented, "What for it was? For nothing, for nothing."

Eliott never ceased struggling against past ghosts. He had indeed been wounded, but never defeated. At times, he coped with the flood of painful memories by repressing them. He remarked, "Sometimes when you think it over and are getting depressed, you start to hold back. You don't want to have the memories. You repress them in order to forget and be more happy for yourself. When you sit with your children, they are smiling and you feel inside miserable, you cannot say it, because you have to be happy with them and try to forget even the worst thing that happened in your life."

Like so many escapees, Eliott viewed the world with cynicism. Not surprisingly, these victims describe their *Weltanschauung*, their view of life, with words like "pessimistic, "cynical, "cautious," and "disillusioned."[5] As one escapee remarked, "My view of people was formed by the Hitler period, the most significant single influence during my formative years." Another noted, "Events were bound to change my tendencies and to create a more hardened, more cynical outlook on life. Events had a lasting effect on me, making me to a certain degree more distrustful and cautious of people." That was also true for Eliott who harbored a strong dose of skepticism. He had good reasons to have qualms about the basic goodness of humankind and to feel distrustful about people's motivations.

Yet, at times Eliott was uneasy about his cynicism. He yearned to be positive and trusting and to believe that the world was not too bad a place. But maintaining a positive outlook was difficult for Eliott. He would attain it, relinquish it, and then try again to shed his worries and suspicions. His ambivalent perspective was, for example, reflected in his indecision over whether his mother had placed him in an orphanage for selfish or altruistic reasons and when he attributed largely pernicious motivation to parents offering to adopt newly arrived children in Israel. Despite his skepticism, Eliott eagerly seized my alternative interpretations of people's actions.

It is paradoxical, though quite explainable, that, though many escapees possess a darker view of the world, they also search for close individual contact. Those uprooted persons who have lost family and friends, tend to yearn for new attachments to reconstitute, in some small measure, the warmth of the human contact that has vanished.[6] Life's circumstances had provided Eliott with a mosaic of events that consisted of the worst and the best. His experiences were similar to those of a particular child who had been sent by her parents to England on a *Kindertransport*. Her laconic comment was, "I learned at the age of eight that not everyone is nice. I have no illusions about people's capacity for prejudice and irrationality. At the same time, there have always been people ready to help. It is other people who made it possible for me to survive."[7] The emotional mix of cynicism relieved by the desire of close human contact color many escapees' life view.

In Eliott's case, the readiness for friendship was quite apparent. In our relationship, he soon assumed the role of a friend. After our interviews, he often remained for a while to chat about sundry subjects. During periods when I was writing rather than interviewing him, he would stay in touch by telephone. When he was aware of illness in my family, he regularly called and inquired. In spite of a certain formality, his demeanor reflected warm fellowship.

Eliott's skepticism was laced with a good deal of humor—a down-to-earth wit that twitted the follies of mankind. He frequently made and always responded to jokes. Recollections of droll situations from the past could still make him double up with laughter. His perspective on life's events lent his thoughts and observations an original cast. The ironies of life often struck him. One day I offered him some goodies, some of which were not entirely fat free.

I said, "Try this. It's good."
He refused and shook his head. "If this was fifty years ago, I could eat it."
"That's right. Then you needed it."
He laughed, and took a piece, and said, "Yes, now it's too late."

Because as a child, circumstances had many times forced Eliott to remain entirely dependent on strangers, other people's opinions of him mattered a great deal. When I complimented him on his ingenious, independent, and pragmatic decisions, he beamed with pleasure and exclaimed, "Thank you, thank you for encouraging." He longed to be cared about and feared rejection. This sensitivity might account for his hesitancy to contact his first girlfriend Rifka, even years after their chance encounter, when the two might have reminisced as old friends. Eliott responded to the smallest kindness with great delight. For instance, even though he ate very sparingly due to health reasons, he was extraordinarily grateful for the little snacks or treats I offered during our sessions. When reminiscing about kindnesses he had received even years ago, his eyes often misted over.

Eliott was also nourished by memories of how close his family was during his early childhood. The solicitude shown to him by some strangers during the hard years also remained a shining beacon in his memory. For example, the young peasant girl who had taken care of him as a child and whose father had protected him and his hunted family in Poland remained for him symbols of kindness and loving warmth. A very special corner in his heart was also reserved for the Krauss "family" whose members had consoled and loved each other en route to Palestine. In addition, he maintained a strong affection for the teachers and counselors who had dedicated themselves to the young immigrants. Certainly one of the most outstanding experiences in his life was his participation as one of the Tehran Children, which took him through so many countries and adventures. Eliott often marveled at the large number of people and governments who pooled their efforts to rescue him and the other Tehran Children. It was a reminder to him that decent humanity still existed to those who were part of this extraordinary undertaking.

Eliott wished to forget many aspects of his past, yet he also yearned to revisit both the places of his joyous childhood and even the places of persecution. Since he had known these places, his life had so drastically changed that at times he wondered whether they had even really existed. Could it all really have happened?

The urge to return after many years is almost a rite of passage for escapees. An escapee's description of his emotions when he walked through the long-remembered streets and reached his former home also typified Eliott's emotions:

> The hallway with its curlicue metalwork was unchanged and the staircase still had its ornate handrail. As we slowly walked up one floor to the apartment where I was born, I smelled the familiar musty odor and I was home again. A strange nameplate was on the door, but in my mind I could hear the voices of my sisters and brothers and of my mother and saw myself as a little boy coming back from playing in the courtyard, dirty, hungry and happy to come back to the secure shelter of home. . . . We retraced the route to my elementary school, as well as to my high school. On the way memories of happy and not so happy moments returned. The smell of

disinfectant in the high school was as I remembered it. . . .
The tall linden trees still lined the cobblestoned street. As
soon as we entered the park, memories of walking there on
Sundays hand in hand with my father returned.

Inevitably these soothing memories were mixed with the acute pain of
the past. The man's memories continued:

The next visit was to the joint grave of my grandparents and
my brother. The Jewish section of [Jewish cemetery] was an
unbelievable sight. Big mausoleums fronting both sides of
tree-lined avenues had been desecrated and were partially
collapsed; gravestones were overturned; weeds had grown so
tall that we could hardly get through much less read the
directional markers.[8]

Another returnee also reported mixed sentiments when she passed an
ice-cream parlor she had cheerfully frequented as a child with her school-
mates: "There were the same mirrors, the same small tables and white chairs.
Nothing at all had changed. The establishment had survived the Nazis
and the Russians. Most of the children who noisily crowded in each day
after school let out are either scattered or dead."[9]

The lure to see what had been affected Eliott as it had so many others.
In addition, he had always promised Heimek a trip to the places that he
had been too young to remember. The two met in Vienna; Heimek arrived
from Israel and Eliott from America. After journeying to Jaroslaw, they
photographed their former home, the town square, their mother's shop,
and other fondly remembered places. Because the familiar communist paranoia still existed, a sullen policeman with a bureaucratic mentality threatened to arrest the brothers for snapping pictures until Eliott proudly provided
him with evidence of his U.S. citizenship. The men traveled to Lvov, where
Eliott not only located the apartment where the family had found refuge,
but even remembered the color of the door that led to their former room.
Standing in a tedious line to buy sour-tasting bread, Eliott reminded Heimek
what a triumphant feast such a treasured morsel would have been while
they lived under the Russian occupation.

When Eliott looked back, he reflected that when the Germans first
invaded Poland, his survival had been in part due to his parents' being less
religious than their Jewish neighbors. Unlike most Jewish children who
attended Yiddish-speaking schools, Lonek attended a Polish school where

he learned fluent Polish, which enabled him to pass as a non-Jewish Pole during his flight from Jaroslaw.

Time and life experiences did not substantially affect Eliott's religious views. This stability of orientation seems to be generally true for escapees. When a group of them were questioned about whether life-threatening events had altered their faith, most of those who had been very religious said that they had continued unshaken in their faith, whereas those who had little adherence to religion remained uninvolved.[10] Eliott remained basically a skeptic. Yet, like most escapees,[11] Eliott's identification with Jewish culture and Jewish people increased, apparently out of a desire to belong and to have a sense of solidarity and security. He would have liked to believe, but he found it difficult. He commented, "It doesn't help to believe. That's what I feel now. If it can help why not? But it doesn't help me." Another time he added, "I believe if there was a God, he wouldn't have the whole thing happen. He wouldn't let six million innocent people die." Yet on the High Holidays he did go to temple, partly out of tradition. He pointed out, "When I go to the shul I feel I am with a group. We sitting together. Everybody has something in common. We can affiliate with somebody. Without tradition, we wouldn't be together." When I asked him at another time whether he believed in a personal God, he replied, "Sometimes yes. It's like somebody holding a hand above my head and saying, 'We will survive. Don't worry about it.'"

When I ventured further and inquired, "Do you pray?" he replied, "On the Holidays, yes." Then he added with a very soft voice, "For my health."

During our last session, Eliott spoke about the state of equilibrium he had reached. He recalled that fate had tossed him about mercilessly, but he had held on in the very small canoe he had been paddling and finally he had reached a relatively calm shore. He had decided not to worry, to enjoy life to the fullest. He had come to terms with his past, he said, and was laying it to rest. He also told me that a heart attack he suffered some time ago had left him totally stunned. He had not believed that this could happen to him, and subsequently resolved that he would work less and enjoy life more.

I once commented to him, "When you think of how many Jewish children died in Poland and Russia, it seems to me you won the greatest lottery of all times." He replied, "What I went through I am lucky to be alive. I appreciate every day. I never have so much appreciation in my life as now after my heart attack. I am twenty some years in this country. I never went to a doctor. I didn't have the time, I was always busy. In the morning I didn't have the time to eat breakfast, I was rushing. Make a sandwich and go to work. Didn't even have time to go to a restaurant to eat. Now no more rushing. I am finished rushing. Even in my business now I don't rush. I got an example. A guy owes me a three thousand dollar check. Twice it already bounced. The guy promised to give me money this morning. I said I have time in the afternoon. I am not rushing. My life is more important than the money, than everything. Now I appreciate the light, the trees, the leaves. In my life now I have only time. All the adventure is past. Red light, green light! I enjoy life. I wake up. I thank God I see the light."

He was not sanguine about his health and observed a strict regimen. "I do anything not to have another heart attack. I walk every day about four miles; I don't eat piggy and I stay away from fat. Let others do whatever they want to do. I have my own life. They happy, I am happy too."

Yet uncertainty about his future occasionally crept into our conversations obliquely. In one of our sessions he wanted to point out something on a map printed in very small type when he noticed that he had forgotten his glasses. The following conversation took place:

"Oh, I don't have my glasses." Eliott sounded upset.
"It's all right. You can show it to me next time."
"Okay. Next time I give it to you. It makes me so mad that I forgot my glasses."
"Don't worry. We'll see each other again."
"I know it," Eliott said. (pause) "I hope so. I hope so."

But life played a last trick on Eliott and I did not see him again. He had been told that he had blocked arteries. In fact, a consortium of seven cardiologists at a well-known hospital recommended bypass surgery. One doctor, Dr. H., an Israeli physician, opposed this consensus. "I recommend you take pills," he said to Eliott. The chief doctor of the consortium was vehemently opposed to Dr. H.'s recommendation. Eliott reconstructed his conversation with the chief of the department: "The head of the doctors said, 'I don't care what Dr. H. says. I am the professor. With this heart you will die.' And I said: 'I listen to Dr. H. I take my chances.'"

I deeply wish he hadn't. In October 1995 while I was on vacation, Eliott had a heart attack and died instantly. Ironically, in spite of all his efforts to stay healthy, he was snatched away just when he was in a position to enjoy life with greater tranquillity. To me, it was a profound shock.

Eliott very much wanted to have his life story recorded. Prior to his death, I had only completed the first two chapters of this book, but I wanted to surprise him with a more polished, edited product before I showed them to him. I am deeply distressed that he never saw his story in print, but I do know that he was very pleased that it was a work in progress.

I frequently think of Eliott, and it is always with great respect, admiration, and affection. He was a valiant man, who unflinchingly battled against overwhelming odds and never gave up the struggle. Yet his story is not his alone. In many ways, he represents the myriads of Jews who were hurled by political forces into the most cataclysmic of circumstances.

Eliott's journey had been accompanied by enormous good fortune. Between the group that lived and the group that was annihilated there was only one large difference: luck. Some lived because they had turned right while death loomed on the left. At other times, those who turned left prevailed, and those who turned right perished. Lonek and his family had, by cunning and by chance, always taken the correct turn. But all of them, those who lived and those who succumbed, endured as long as they could by mustering every last ounce of strength, stubborn persistence, and boundless resourcefulness. Of this stalwart and intrepid group, Eliott had been a worthy member.

REFERENCES

THIS BOOK: HOW AND WHY

1. Dorit Bader Whiteman, *The Uprooted—A Hitler Legacy: Voices of Those Who Escaped Before the Final Solution* (New York: Plenum Press, 1993).

2. Irena Grudziska-Gross and Jan Tomasz Gross, ed. and comp. *Hoover Archival Documentaries: War through Children's Eyes* (Stanford, Calif.: Stanford University Press, 1981).

3. Jan T. Gross, *Revolution from Abroad: The Soviet Conquest of Poland's Western Ukraine and Western Belorussia* (Princeton: Princeton University Press, 1988).

CHAPTER I
The Whip Descends

1. *Encyclopaedia Judaica*, "Jaroslaw's History," vol. 9 (Jerusalem: Keter, 1972), 1288–89.

2. E. Thomas Wood and Stanislaw M. Jankowski, *Karski: How One Man Tried to Stop the Holocaust* (New York: John Wiley, 1994), 3–8.

3. Ibid., 5–7.

4. Henryk Grynberg, *Kinder Zions, Dokumentarische Erzählung* (Leipzig: Reclam Verlag, 1994), 14–25.

CHAPTER II
The Cart Rolls East

1. *Hoover Institution on War, Revolution and Peace*, 218 Bulletin Section PAT in Jerusalem 1.7.42; 4.

2. Henryk Grynberg, *Kinder Zions, Dokumentarische Erzählung* (Leipzig: Reclam Verlag, 1994), 25.

3. Ibid., 24.

4. Ibid., 31.

5. *Hoover Institution on War, Revolution, and Peace,* Protokul Nr. 83; HIA-MID Box 197; Protokuxy Palestynskie 7/43.

6. Henryk Grynberg, *Kinder Zions,* 39.

7. Ibid., 31.

8. Ibid., 32.

9. Ibid.

10. Ibid., 40.

CHAPTER IV

From Chaos to Chaos

1. Jan T. Gross, *Revolution from Abroad* (Princeton: Princeton University Press, 1988), 22.

2. Ibid.

3. Ibid., 23.

4. E. Thomas Wood and Stanislaw M. Jankowski, *Karski: How One Man Tried to Stop the Holocaust* (New York: John Wiley, 1994), 14.

5. Jan T. Gross, *Revolution from Abroad,* 23.

6. Irena Grudzin´ska-Gross and Jan T. Gross, *Hoover Archival Documentaries: War Through Children's Eyes* (Stanford, Calif.: Hoover Institution Press, 1981), 122.

7. Ibid., 181.

8. Ibid., 154.

9. Ibid., 184.

10. Ibid., 6.

11. Ibid., 103.

12. Ibid., 7.

13. Ibid., 7–9.

14. Jan T. Gross, *Revolution from Abroad*, 22.

15. Norman Davies and Antony Polonsky, *Jews in Eastern Poland and the USSR, 1939–46*, (New York: St. Martin's, 1991), 16–17.

16. Ibid., 18.

17. Irena Grudzin´ska-Gross and Jan T. Gross, *Hoover Archival Documentaries*, 132.

18. Ibid., 139.

19. Ibid., 169.

20. Ibid., 177.

21. Jan T. Gross, *Revolution from Abroad*, 32–35.

22. Irena Grudzin´ska-Gross and Jan T. Gross, *Hoover Archival Documentaries*, 15.

23. Jan T. Gross, *Revolution from Abroad*, 18–20.

24. Ibid., 37.

25. Irena Grudzin´ska-Gross and Jan T. Gross, *Hoover Archival Documentaries*, 150.

26. Ibid., 79.

27. Ibid., 174, 178.

28. Ibid., 84.

29. Ibid., 159.

30. Ibid., 50.

31. Ibid., 90–91

32. Jan T. Gross, *Revolution from Abroad*, 52.

33. Ibid., 35–36.

CHAPTER V

References

A Failed Haven

1. *Hoover Institution on War, Revolution and Peace*, Testimony of Shimonaz Turner, Protokul Nr. 83; HIA-MID Box 197; Protokuxy Palestynskie 7/43.

2. Norman Davies and Antony Polonsky, *Jews in Eastern Poland and the USSR, 1939–46* (New York: St. Martin's, 1991) 111.

3. Irena Grudzin´ska-Gross and Jan T. Gross, *Hoover Archival Documentaries: War Through Children's Eyes* (Stanford, Calif.: Hoover Institution Press, 1981), 11.

4. Ibid., 205.

5. Ibid., 109.

6. Jan T. Gross, *Revolution from Abroad: The Soviet Conquest of Poland's Western Ukraine and Western Belorussia* (Princeton: Princeton University Press, 1988), 223.

7. Irena Grudzin´ska-Gross and Jan T. Gross, *Hoover Archival Documentaries*, 16.

8. Jan T. Gross, *Revolution from Abroad*, 147.

9. Irena Grudzin´ska-Gross and Jan T. Gross, *Hoover Archival Documentaries*, 72, 84, 134.

10. Jan T. Gross, *Revolution from Abroad*, 53–56.

11. Davies and Polonsky, *Jews in Eastern Poland and the USSR, 1939–46*, 19–20.

12. *Hoover Institution on War, Revolution and Peace*, Testimony of Godali Niewadomsky, Protokul Nr. 156; HIA-MID Box 197; Protokuxy Palestynskie 7/43.

13. Irena Grudzin´ska-Gross and Jan T. Gross, *Hoover Archival Documentaries*, 99.

14. Ibid., 33.

15. Ibid., 92.

16. Ibid., 91.

17. Ibid., 102.

18. Ibid., 133.

19. Ibid., 195.

20. Ibid., 129.

21. Ibid., 112.

22. Ibid., 138.

23. Ibid., 235.

24. Ibid., 230.

25. Davies and Polonsky, *Jews in Eastern Poland and the USSR, 1939–46*, 30.

26. Jan T. Gross, *Revolution from Abroad*, 147.

27. Davies and Polonsky, *Jews in Eastern Poland and the USSR, 1939–46*, 10.

28. Ibid., 72.

29. Ibid., 128.

30. Jan T. Gross, *Revolution from Abroad*, 149.

CHAPTER VI

The Knock on the Door

1. Jan T. Gross, *Revolution from Abroad: The Soviet Conquest of Poland'S Western Ukraine and Western Belorussia* (Princeton: Princeton University Press, 1988), 71–87, 199.

2. Irena Grudzin´ska-Gross and Jan T. Gross, *Hoover Archival Documentaries: War Through Children's Eyes* (Stanford, Calif., Hoover Institution Press, 1981) 22.

3. Ibid., 22.

4. Ibid., 179.

5. Ibid., 155.

6. Ibid., 179.

7. Ibid., 185.

8. Yecheskel Leitner, *Operation Torah Rescue: The Escape of the Mirrer Yeshiva from War-torn Poland to Shanghai, China* (Jerusalem: Feldheim, 1987), 45.

9. Gross, *Revolution from Abroad*, 206.

10. Ibid., 11–12.

11. Irena Grudzin´ska-Gross and Jan T. Gross, *Hoover Archival Documentaries*, 159.

12. Ibid., 138.

13. Ibid., 104.

14. Ibid., 204.

15. Ibid., 203.

16. Ibid., 127.

17. Ibid., 73.

18. *Hoover Institution on War, Revolution and Peace*, Testimony of Godali Niewadomski, Protokul Nr. 156; HIA-MID Box 197; Protokuxy Palestynskie 7/43.

19. Gross, *Revolution from Abroad*, 298.

20. Ibid., 298–300.

21. Ibid., 179–180.

22. Ibid., 146.

23. Ibid., 253.

CHAPTER VII

The Icy Void

1. Jan T. Gross, *Revolution from Abroad: The Soviet Conquest of Poland's Western Ukraine and Western Belorussia* (Princeton: Princeton University Press, 1988), 196.

2. Irena Grudzin´ska-Gross and Jan T. Gross, *Hoover Archival Documen-*

taries. War Through Children's Eyes (Stanford, Calif.: Hoover Institution Press, 1981), 109.

3. Ibid., 79.

4. Ibid., 109.

5. Ibid., 79.

6. Ibid., 169.

7. *Hoover Institution on War, Revolution and Peace*, Testimony of Godali Niewadomski, Protokul Nr. 156; HIA-MID Box 197; Protokuxy Palestynskie 7/43.

8. Gross, *Revolution from Abroad*, 217–18.

9. Ibid., 236–39.

10. Ibid., 75.

11. Ibid., 105.

12. Ibid., 222.

13. *Hoover Institution on War, Revolution and Peace*, Testimony of Godali Niewadomski.

14. Irena Grudzin´ska-Gross and Jan T. Gross, *Hoover Archival Documentaries*, 156.

15. Ibid., 121.

16. Ibid., 19.

17. Ibid., 103.

18. Ibid., 134.

19. Ibid., 223.

20. Ibid., 74.

21. Ibid., 51.

22. Ibid., 106.

23. Ibid., 110.

24. Ibid., 145.

25. Ibid., 144.

26. Ibid., 103.

27. Ibid., 76.

28. Ibid., 236.

29. Ibid., 173.

30. Ibid., 182.

31. Ibid., 77.

32. Ibid., 34.

33. Ibid., 81.

34. Ibid., 111.

35. Private communication from Chaim Jaroslawitz.

36. *Hoover Institution on War, Revolution and Peace*, Testimony of Godali Niewadomski.

CHAPTER VIII

The Gates Open

1. Yisrael Gutman and Shmuel Krakowski, *Unequal Victims: Poles and Jews During World War Two* (New York: Holocaust Library, 1986), 310.

2. Jan T. Gross, *Revolution from Abroad: The Soviet Conquest of Poland's Western Ukraine and Western Belorussia* (Princeton: Princeton University Press, 1988), 229.

3. Irena Grudzin´ska-Gross and Jan T. Gross, *Hoover Archival Documentaries: War Through Children's Eyes* (Stanford, Calif.: Hoover Institution Press, 1981), 203.

4. Ibid., 220.

5. Ibid., 233.

6. Ibid., 199.

7. Henryk Grynberg, *Kinder Zions, Dokumentarische Erzählung* (Leipzig:Reclam Verlag, 1994), 136–140.

8. Irena Grudzin´ska-Gross and Jan T. Gross, *Hoover Archival Documentaries*, 85.

9. Ibid., 51.

10. Ibid., 166.

11. Ibid., 158.

12. Ibid., 213.

13. Gross, *Revolution from Abroad*, 43.

14. E. Thomas Wood and Stanislaw M. Jankowski, *Karski: How One Man Tried to Stop the Holocaust* (New York: John Wiley: 1994), 21.

15. Norman Davies and Antony Polonsky, *Jews in Eastern Poland and the USSR, 1939–46* (New York: St. Martin's, 1991), 390–396.

16. Grynberg, *Kinder Zions*, 142–143.

CHAPTER IX
Tashkent

1. *Hoover Institution on War, Revolution and Peace*, Shimonaz Turner, Protokul Nr. 83; HIA-MID Box 197; Protokuxy Palestynskie 7/43.

2. Ibid.

3. *Hoover Institution on War, Revolution and Peace*, 218 Bulletin Section PAT Jerusalem 7/1/42; 4.

4. Norman Davies and Antony Polonsky, *Jews in Eastern Poland and the USSR, 1939–46* (New York: St. Martin's, 1991), 147–148.

5. Private communication from Chaim Jaroslawitz.

6. Ibid.

CHAPTER XI

General Anders' Army and Lonek

1. Norman Davies and Antony Polonsky, *Jews in Eastern Poland and the USSR, 1939–46* (New York: St. Martin's, 1991), 361.

2. John Coutouvidis and Jaime Reynolds, *Poland 1939–1947* (New York: Holmes & Meier, 1986), 80.

3. Józef Garlinski, *Poland in the Second World War* (New York: Hippocrene, 1985), 154.

4. Yisrael Gutman and Shmuel Krakowski, *Unequal Victims: Poles and Jews During World War Two* (New York: Holocaust Library, 1986), 314.

5. Ibid., 327.

6. Ibid., 311.

7. Ibid., 336.

8. Ibid., 334.

9. Ibid., 346.

10. Ibid., 344.

CHAPTER XII

Bereft

1. Henryk Grynberg, *Kinder Zions, Dokumentarische Erzählung* (Leipzig: Reclam Verlag, 1994), 171.

2. *Hoover Institution on War, Revolution and Peace*, Testimony of Godali Niewadomski, Protokul Nr. 156; HIA-MID Box 197; Protokuxy Palestynskie 7/43.

3. Grynberg, *Kinder Zions*, 165.

4. Ibid., 162.

5. Ibid., 164.

6. Ibid., 163.

7. Ibid., 167.

8. Ibid., 166.

9. Ibid., 172.

10. *Encyclopedia of the Holocaust*, (New York: Macmillan, 1990), vol. 4, 1454.

11. Grynberg, *Kinder Zions*, 169.

12. Azriel Eisenberg, *The Lost Generation: Children in the Holocaust* (New York: Pilgrim Press, 1982), 268.

13. Grynberg, *Kinder Zions*, 168–72.

14. Ibid., 171.

15. Ibid., 171, 173.

16. Ibid., 177.

17. Ibid., 172.

18. Ibid., 176.

19. Ibid., 174.

20. Ibid., 180.

21. Józef Garlinski, *Poland in the Second World War* (New York: Hippocrene, 1985), 173–74.

22. Ibid., 152.

23. Grynberg, *Kinder Zions*, 177.

24. Zeev Schuss, My *Glorious Journey*, Files of the Association of Teheran Children, 5.

25. Devora Omer, *The Teheran Operation: The Rescue of Jewish Children from the Nazis* (Washington, D.C.: B'nai B'rith Books, 1991), 177.

CHAPTER XIII

A Rubicon Crossed

1. American Jewish Archives; Collection Ms. Coll 36; Box number D56; Folder number 9.

2. Zeev Schuss, *My Glorious Journey*, Files of the Association of Teheran Children, 6.

3. Devora Omer, *The Teheran Operation: The Rescue of Jewish Children from the Nazis* (Washington, D.C.: B'nai B'rith Books, 1991), 152.

4. Schuss, *My Glorious Journey*, Files of the Association of Teheran Children, 6.

5. Mrs. Zipporah Shertok's letter; Central Zionist Archives, Archive of the Youth Aliyah Department, Jerusalem: File No. S75/4852.

6. Azriel Eisenberg, *The Lost Generation: Children in the Holocaust*, (New York: Pilgrim Press, 1982) 268-269.

7. Report addressed to the Youth Aliyah Office in Jerusalem: 1/4/1943. Archives of the Youth Aliyah Department; Central Zionist Archives, Jerusalem: File No. S75/1847.

8. Eisenberg, *The Lost Generation*, 270.

9. Omer, *The Teheran Operation*, 149.

10. Azriel Eisenberg, *The Lost Generation*, 270.

11. Ibid., 271.

12. Omer, *The Teheran Operation*, 166.

13. Eisenberg, *The Lost Generation*, 270.

14. Omer, *The Teheran Operation*, 162.

CHAPTER XV

Britain Behind the Scene

1. All the information in this chapter is based on memos, telegrams, cables, and letters in the files of Hadassah, the Women's Zionist Organization of America, Inc.

CHAPTER XVI

The Lion-Hearted Women

1. The bulk of the material in this chapter comes from notes, memos, letters, telegrams, and cables in the files of Hadassah, the Women's Zionist Organization of America.

2. Azriel Eisenberg, *The Lost Generation: Children in the Holocaust* (New York: Pilgrim Press, 1982), 272.

3. Henrietta Szold and Youth Aliyah, *Family Letters 1934–1944*; edited by Alexandra Lee Lewin; Box 6a.

4. Devora Omer, *The Teheran Operation: The Rescue of Jewish Children from the Nazis* (Washington, D.C.: B'nai B'rith Books, 1991), 192.

5. *Henrietta Szold: 1860–1945*, Tamar de Sola Pool; reprinted from *Great Jewish Personalities in Modern Times*, Simon Noveck ed.; (Washington, D.C.: B'nai B'rith Dept. of Adult Jewish Education, 1960), 27–28.

6. Henrietta Szold and Youth Aliyah, *Family Letters 1934–1944*; edited by Alexandra Lee Lewin (New York: Herzl Press, 1986), 90.

CHAPTER XVII

A Fortunate Turn of Fortune's Wheel

1. Azriel Eisenberg, *The Lost Generation: Children in the Holocaust* (New York: Pilgrim Press, 1982), 272.

2. Unless otherwise indicated, the information in this chapter is gleaned from memos, letters, telegrams, and cables found in the files of Hadassah, the Women's Zionist Organization of America.

3. Central Zionist Archives, Jerusalem; S6/3348.

4. Devora Omer, *The Teheran Operation: The Rescue of Jewish Children from the Nazis* (Washington, D.C.: B'nai B'rith Books, 1991), 246.

CHAPTER XVIII

Finally – An Exit

1. Azriel Eisenberg, *The Lost Generation: Children in the Holocaust* (New York: Pilgrim Press, 1982), 272. The ship's name is given as the *SS Donora* in Devora Omer, *The Teheran Operation: The Rescue of Jewish Children from the Nazis* (Washington, D.C.: B'nai B'rith Books, 1991). In a communication from Michelle Ment of the Association of Teheran Children and their instructors, she refers to the British troop ship *Donora*. It is likely that the ship was the *HMT Dunera*, a troop ship used by the British to transport 2,542 Jewish refugees to Australia for internment during World War II. See Dorit B. Whiteman, *The Uprooted—A Hitler Legacy: Voices of Those Who Escaped Before the "Final Solution"* (New York: Plenum, 1993), 318.

2. Omer, *The Teheran Operation*, 210–12.

3. Ibid., 207–09.

4. Azriel Eisenberg, *The Lost Generation*, 273.

5. Ibid., 272.

6. Copy of telegram by Michaelis to Youth Aliyah, Jerusalem; Archives of the Youth Aliyah Department, Central Zionist Archives: S75/1831.

7. Ibid. Cable from Henrietta Szold.

CHAPTER XIX

The Last Lap

1. Devora Omer, *The Teheran Operation: The Rescue of Jewish Children from the Nazis* (Washington, D.C.: B'nai B'rith Books, 1991), 219–24.

2. Ibid., 226.

3. Dorit Bader Whiteman, *The Uprooted—A Hitler Legacy: Voices of Those Who Escaped before the "Final Solution"* (New York: Plenum, 1993), 224.

4. Omer, *The Teheran Operation*, 244.

5. Ibid., 242–45.

6. Ibid., 245.

7. Private telephone communication with Anita Warburg, Gisela Warburg's sister.

8. Azriel Eisenberg, *The Lost Generation: Children in the Holocaust* (New York: Pilgrim Press, 1982), 273.

9. Omer, *The Teheran Operation*, 246.

10. Eisenberg, *The Lost Generation*, 273.

CHAPTER XX

Welcome Home

1. Yad Vashem 13/2/43.

2. Devora Omer, *The Teheran Operation: The Rescue of Jewish Children from the Nazis* (Washington, D.C.: B'nai B'rith Books, 1991), 255.

3. Azriel Eisenberg, *The Lost Generation: Children in the Holocaust* (New York: Pilgrim Press, 1982), 274.

4. *Henrietta Szold and Youth Aliyah, Family Letters 1934–1944*; edited by Alexandra Lee Lewin (New York: Hezl Press, 1986), 90.

5. Lillian Schlissel, Byrd Gibbens, and Elizabeth Hampsten, *Far From Home: Families of the Westward Journey* (New York: Schocken, 1989), 231: Quote from Wallace Stegner, *Angle of Response*.

6. Lily Bader, *One Life Is Not Enough*, unpublished autobiography.

CHAPTER XXI

What Now?

1. *Henrietta Szold: 1860–1945*, Tamar de Sola Pool; reprinted from *Great Jewish Personalities in Modern Times*, Simon Noveck, ed. (Washington, D.C. B'nai B'rith Dept. of Adult Education, 1960), 21.

2. Hadassah Documents.

3. Ibid.

4. Ibid.

5. Ibid.

6. Ibid.

7. *Henrietta Szold and Youth Aliyah, Family Letters 1934–1944*, Alexandra Lee Lewin ed., 93.

8. Hadassah Documents, Letter YA/3114.

CHAPTER XXII

A Decisive Meeting

1. Archive of the Youth Aliyah Department, File S75/1858.

2. *Henrietta Szold: 1860–1945*, Tamar de Sola Pool; reprinted from *Great Jewish Personalities in Modern Times*, Simon Noveck, ed., (Washington, D.C.: B'nai B'rith Dept. of Adult Education, 1960).

CHAPTER XXIII

There Is Something About a Soldier

1. Abba Eban, *My Country, The Story of Modern Israel* (New York: Random House, 1972), 30.

2. A. J. Barker, *Arab-Israeli Wars* (New York: Hippocrene, 1980), 12.

3. Eban, *My Country*, 39.

4. Ibid., 37.

5. Uri Dan, *To the Promised Land: The Birth of Israel* (New York: Doubleday, 1988), 38.

6. Ibid., 39–40.

7. Ibid., 47–52.

8. Meir Neeman, private communication.

9. Dan, *To the Promised Land*, 104.

10. Eban, *My Country*, 42.

11. Trevor N. Dupuy, *Elusive Victory, The Arab-Israeli Wars 1947–1974* (Dubuque, Iowa: Kendall/Hunt, 1992), 159–60.

CHAPTER XXIV

A Tale of Two Tanks

1. A. J. Barker, *Arab-Israeli Wars* (New York: Hippocrene, 1980), 13.

2. Uri Dan, *To the Promised Land: The Birth of Israel* (New York: Doubleday, 1988), 139

3. Abba Eban, *My Country, The Story of Modern Israel* (New York: Random House, 1972), 40.

4. Ibid., 22.

5. Ibid., 12.

6. Ibid., 47.

CHAPTER XXV

The Uncertainties of Battle

1. Trevor N. Dupuy, *Elusive Victory, The Arab-Israeli Wars 1947–1974* (Dubuque, Iowa: Kendall/Hunt, 1992), 38–39, 63–66, 75–58.

2. Uri Dan, *To the Promised Land: The Birth of Israel* (New York: Doubleday, 1988), 168–169.

3. Ibid., 198–200.

CHAPTER XXVI

Resisting Orders

1. Uri Dan, *To the Promised Land: The Birth of Israel* (New York: Doubleday, 1988), 26–27.

2. Ibid., 114–19.

3. Trevor N. Dupuy, *Elusive Victory, The Arab-Israeli Wars 1947–1974* (Dubuque, Iowa: Kendall/Hunt, 1992), 34–35, 159–60.

4. Ibid., 36.

5. Dan, *To the Promised Land*, 63–64.

6. Ibid., 44.

7. Ibid., 221–24.

Chapter XXVII
Reunion

1. Chaim Jaroslawitz, private communication.

2. Devora Omer, *The Teheran Operation: The Rescue of Jewish Children from the Nazis* (Washington, D.C.: B'nai B'rith Books, 1991), 265.

Chapter XXVIII
Lonek and Eliott

1. William B. Helmreich, *Against All Odds: Holocaust Survivors and the Successful Lives They Made in America* (New York: Simon & Schuster, 1992), 267–73.

2. Marianne Anderson, personal communication.

3. Dorit Bader Whiteman, "Holocaust Survivors and Escapees—Their Strengths," *Psychotherapy* 30, no. 3 (Fall 1993), 449.

4. Dorit Bader Whiteman, *The Uprooted—A Hitler Legacy: Voices of Those Who Escaped Before the "Final Solution"* (New York: Plenum, 1993), 380.

5. Ibid., 375–77.

6. Ibid., 377–78.

7. Ibid., 379.

8. Ibid., 399.

9. Ibid., 398.

10. Ibid., 397.

11. Ibid.